A MODERN BUDDHIST BIBLE

A
MODERN
BUDDHIST
BIBLE

Essential Readings

from East and West

Edited by Donald S. Lopez, Jr.

BEACON PRESS   BOSTON

Beacon Press
25 Beacon Street
Boston, Massachusetts 02108-2892
www.beacon.org

Beacon Press books
are published under the auspices of
the Unitarian Universalist Association of Congregations.

First Beacon Press edition published in 2002

Printed in the United States of America

06 05 04 03   8 7 6 5 4 3 2

This book is printed on acid-free paper that meets the uncoated paper
ANSI/NISO specifications for permanence as revised in 1992.

Composition by Wilsted & Taylor Publishing Services

Library of Congress Cataloging-in-Publication Data

A modern Buddhist bible : essential readings from East and West / edited by Donald S.
Lopez, Jr.
        p.   cm.
"Published originally in paperback edition by Penguin Books Ltd. in 2002."—CIP t.p.
verso.
    ISBN 0-8070-1243-2 (pbk. : alk. paper)
    1. Buddhism—Doctrines.   2. Religious life—Buddhism.   I. Lopez, Donald S.,
1952—

BQ4302 .M63 2002
294.3—dc21

                                                                2002012462

Contents

Introduction

By 7 a.m. on the morning of 26 August 1873, a crowd of some five thousand had gathered around a raised platform especially constructed for the occasion in the town of Panadure outside Colombo in Ceylon (Sri Lanka). The platform was divided in two. One side had a table covered in white cloth and adorned with evergreens. This was the side occupied by the Christian party and their spokesman. The other side of the platform was more richly decorated and filled by some two hundred Buddhist monks and their spokesman. A debate was to take place over the next two days, with sessions from 8 to 10 each morning and 3 to 5 each afternoon, each speaker being given one hour to speak in both the morning and afternoon sessions. A journalist described the scene:

Larger crowds may often be seen in very many places in Europe, but surely such a motley gathering as that which congregated on this occasion, can only be seen in the East. Imagine them all seated down and listening with wrapt [sic] attention to a yellow robed priest, holding forth from the platform filled with Budhist [sic] priests, clergymen, and Singhalese clad in their national costume, and your readers can form some idea – a very faint one indeed – of the heterogeneous mass that revelled in a display of Singhalese eloquence seldom heard in this country.[1]

The coastal areas of Ceylon had been conquered by the Portuguese in the early sixteenth century and Roman Catholic missions were soon established. The Portuguese were supplanted by the Dutch in 1636, who were in turn supplanted by the British, who brought the entire island under their control in 1815. Under the British, a number of

Protestant missions were established in the nineteenth century, seeking to convert the Buddhist populace to Christianity, and they achieved a certain degree of success. In 1862 a Buddhist monk named Gunananda had founded the Society for the Propagation of Buddhism and established his own printing press, publishing pamphlets attacking Christianity. A number of Wesleyan converts responded in both speeches and in print. And so in 1873 a public debate between Gunananda and a Christian representative, the Reverend David de Silva, was arranged.[2]

Each of the parties sought to demonstrate the fallacies of the other's sacred scriptures. The Reverend de Silva spoke first, making extensive references to the Pali scriptures that declare that there is no soul, that the person is only the aggregation of various impermanent constituents. According to Buddhism, then, human beings have no immortal soul and are 'on a par with the frog, pig, or any other member of the brute creation'.[3] Furthermore, if there is no soul there can be no punishment for sin and reward for virtue in the next life. Hence, 'no religion ever held out greater inducements to the unrighteous than Buddhism did'.[4]

The Buddhist monk Gunananda then rose to speak. He was described by the *Ceylon Times* (presumably partial to the Christian faction) as 'a well-made man of apparently forty-five or fifty years, rather short, very intellectual looking, with eyes expressive of great distrust, and a smile which may either mean profound satisfaction or supreme contempt.'[5] He began by stating that Reverend de Silva's knowledge of Pali was clearly deficient. It was therefore not surprising that he had misunderstood the Buddha's teachings on the nature of the person. He explained that in fact, according to the Buddhist doctrine of rebirth, the person reborn was neither precisely the same as nor different from the person who had previously died. He then turned to the shortcomings of Christianity, noting that in Genesis God regrets having created man and in Exodus instructs the Hebrews to mark their doors with blood so that he will know which houses to pass over as he kills the firstborn of the Egyptians. He concluded that neither of these appears to be the deed of an omniscient god.

And so the debate continued on into the afternoon and into the following day, with Gunananda being declared the winner by the acclamation of the multitude. This was not the first time that Buddhists and Christians had debated the primacy of their respective faiths. In 1550 the Jesuit missionary Francis Xavier had discussed the dharma with a Zen abbot in Japan. Around 1600 Matteo Ricci was denouncing Buddhism, in Chinese, to Buddhist monks in China. And in 1717 another Jesuit, Ippolito Desideri – living in the great monastery of Sera, outside Lhasa, in Tibet – was debating with monks the doctrine of rebirth and whether there can be creation without God. However, these three Jesuits were missionaries whose missions would ultimately fail; these lands and the souls who inhabited them would not be conquered and converted by Europe and its church. But Ceylon in the nineteenth century was a British colony, and Gunananda's denunciation of Christianity had strong, and far-reaching, ramifications. Regardless of what the intentions of the participants had been, the debate at Panadure marked the beginning of modern Buddhism.

What is this form of Buddhism, and in what sense is it modern? The relation between classical Buddhism and what I refer to as modern Buddhism is more than a matter of simple chronology or a standard periodization into the primitive, classical, medieval, premodern and modern. Certainly, modern Buddhism shares many of the characteristics of other projects of modernity, including the identification of the present as a standpoint from which to reflect upon previous periods in history and to identify their deficiencies in relation to the present. Modern Buddhism rejects many of the ritual and magical elements of previous forms of Buddhism, it stresses equality over hierarchy, the universal over the local, and often exalts the individual above the community. Yet, as will be clear in what follows, modern Buddhism does not see itself as the culmination of a long process of evolution, but rather as a return to the origin, to the Buddhism of the Buddha himself. There is certainly criticism of the past, but that critique is directed not at the most distant Buddhism, but at the most recent. Modern Buddhism seeks to distance itself most from those forms of Buddhism that immediately precede it, that are even contemporary with it. It is ancient Buddhism, and especially the enlightenment of the Buddha 2,500 years ago, that is seen as most modern, as most compatible with the ideals of the European Enlightenment that occurred so many centuries later, ideals embodied in such concepts as reason, empiricism, science, universalism, individualism, tolerance, freedom and the rejection of religious orthodoxy. Indeed, for modern Buddhists, the Buddha knew long ago what Europe would only discover much later. Yet what we regard as Buddhism today, especially the common portrayal of the Buddhism of the Buddha, is in fact a creation of modern Buddhism. Its widespread acceptance, both in the West and in much of Asia, is testimony to the influence of the thinkers whose words are collected here.

These considerations seem to preclude such mundane matters as identifying the precise dates at which periods begin and end. For the purposes of this anthology, however, modern Buddhism comprises the period from 1873 to 1980. The former is the date of the famous debate in Ceylon between Gunananda and Reverend de Silva. The latter date is more arbitrary, chosen in large part to provide a vague line of demarcation between the modern and the contemporary. It will be clear that the concerns of modern Buddhism, although developing more than a century ago, extend to the present. Yet, without the advantage of a certain hindsight (itself a characteristic of modernity), it is often difficult to judge the ultimate influence of figures who have appeared most recently. Therefore, in an effort to limit the scope of this book, I have reluctantly decided to exclude those authors whose rise to stature in contemporary Buddhism has occurred after 1980.

Like all religions, Buddhism has evolved over the centuries, and that evolution has moved at a rapid pace and in myriad directions in the last two centuries, during which traditional Buddhist societies encountered modernity (often through the route of colonialism). During the same period European and American scholars began to translate Buddhist texts into Western languages, thus making Buddhism available to a large reading public. Interest in Buddhism increased even further in the second half of the last century, when, as a result of the political upheaval caused by the Vietnam War and the Chinese invasion of Tibet, large Buddhist populations (including Buddhist monks) emigrated to the West.

The Buddhism encountered today, both in Asia and the West, is very much the product of this historical evolution. The starting point of that evolution would seem to be with the founder of Buddhism, the

Buddha himself, a yogin who wandered with his followers through northern India more than two millennia ago. Yet it is difficult to describe his original teachings, for none of the words traditionally attributed to the Buddha were written down until some four centuries after his death. Over the centuries Buddhists have sought to represent his original teachings and true intentions in an effort to secure the acceptance of a wide variety of developments in Buddhist thought and practice. During the past two centuries, Buddhist thinkers from across Asia and the West began to describe a Buddhism that transcends the concerns of locale and sect. This version of Buddhism, what I refer to as modern Buddhism, although hardly monolithic, has a number of characteristics (discussed below) that have been widely accepted around the world.

Despite the importance of the thinkers, both Asian and Western, who have created and developed modern Buddhism, their writings have not heretofore been gathered into a single volume. Some of the major figures in the evolution of modern Buddhism are not well known in the West, or have been forgotten. The works of others, although widely read, have not been presented in the context of the evolution of modern Buddhism. This book is the first to present some of the major works of modern Buddhism in a single anthology.

Several features of the debate in Ceylon bear identification as we begin to sketch the contours of modern Buddhism. First, Gunananda was clearly an educated monk, who not only knew his own scriptures but had studied the Bible as well. The leaders of the various modern Buddhist movements in Asia would be drawn from the small minority of learned monks, and not from the vast majority who chanted scriptures, performed rituals for the dead and maintained monastic properties. Second, the Buddhism that was portrayed in the debate, and in modern Buddhism more generally, tended to be that of technical doctrine and philosophy, rather than that of daily practice. Buddhism was portrayed as an ancient and profound philosophical system, fully the equal of anything that had developed in the Christian West. Indeed, Buddhism came to be portrayed – whether that portrayal was made in Sinhalese, Chinese or Japanese – as a world religion, fully the equal of Christianity in antiquity, geographical expanse, membership and philosophical profundity, with its own founder, sacred scriptures and fixed body of doctrine.

But before considering the characteristics of modern Buddhism in more detail, it is important not to lose sight of the more direct historical effects of the 1873 debate in Ceylon. Five years later an embellished account of the debate, entitled *Buddhism and Christianity Face to Face*, was published in Boston by James M. Peebles. It was read by Colonel Henry Steel Olcott, a journalist and veteran of the American Civil War. In New York in 1875, Olcott and Madame Helena Petrovna Blavatsky, a Russian émigré, had founded the Theosophical Society, whose goals were 'to diffuse among men a knowledge of the laws inherent in the universe; to promulgate the knowledge of the essential unity of all that is, and to determine that this unity is fundamental in nature; to form an active brotherhood among men; to study ancient and modern religion, science, and philosophy; and to investigate the powers innate in man.' The Theosophical Society arose as one of several responses to Darwin's theory of evolution during the late nineteenth century. Rather than seeking a refuge from science in religion, Blavatsky and Olcott were attempting to found a scientific religion, one that accepted the new discoveries in geology and archaeology while proclaiming an ancient and esoteric system of spiritual evolution more sophisticated than the physical evolution described by Darwin.

Madame Blavatsky claimed to have spent seven years in Tibet as an initiate of a secret order of enlightened masters called the Brotherhood of the White Lodge, who watch over and guide the evolution of humanity, preserving the ancient truths. These masters, whom she called 'mahatmas' ('great souls'), lived in Tibet but were not themselves Tibetan. In fact, the very presence of the mahatmas in Tibet was unknown to ordinary Tibetans. These masters had once lived throughout the world but had congregated in Tibet to escape the onslaught of civilization. The mahatmas had instructed her in the ancient truths of the mystic traditions, or Theosophy, which she also referred to as 'Esoteric Buddhism', of which the Buddhism being practised in Asia, including Tibet, was a corruption.

Throughout her career, she (and later, other members of the society) claimed to be in esoteric communication with the mahatmas, sometimes through dreams and visions, but most commonly through letters that either materialized in a cabinet in Madame Blavatsky's room or that she transcribed through automatic writing. The mahatmas' literary output was prodigious, conveying instructions on the most mundane matters of the functions of the Theosophical Society, as well as providing the content of the canonical texts of the society, such as A. P. Sinnett's *Esoteric Buddhism* (1885) and Madame Blavatsky's *The Secret Doctrine* (1888). Despite its unlikely beginnings, the Theosophical Society would play a profound role in the formation of modern Buddhism.

By 1878 Blavatsky and Olcott had shifted the emphasis of the society away from the investigation of psychic phenomena towards a broader promotion of a universal brotherhood of humanity, claiming affinities between Theosophy and the wisdom of the East, specifically Hinduism and Buddhism. Inspired by Olcott's reading of the account of Gunananda's defence of the dharma, they were determined to join the Buddhists of Ceylon in their battle against Christian missionaries. Thus they sailed to India, arriving in Bombay in 1879, where they proclaimed themselves to be Hindus. The following year they proceeded to Ceylon, where they both took the vows of lay Buddhists. Blavatsky's interest in Buddhism remained peripheral to her Theosophy. Olcott, however, enthusiastically embraced his new faith, being careful to note that he was a 'regular Buddhist' rather than a 'debased modern' Buddhist, and decried what he regarded as the ignorance of the Sinhalese about their own religion. As one of the founding figures of modern Buddhism, he identified his Buddhism with that of the Buddha himself: 'Our Buddhism was that of the Master-Adept Gautama Buddha, which was identically the Wisdom Religion of the Aryan Upanishads, and the soul of the ancient world-faiths. Our Buddhism was, in a word, a philosophy, not a creed.'[6]

Olcott took it as his task to restore 'true' Buddhism to Ceylon and to counter the efforts of the Christian missionaries on the island. In order to accomplish this aim, he adopted many of their techniques, founding the Buddhist Theosophical Society to disseminate Buddhist knowledge (and later assisted in the founding of the Young Men's Buddhist Association) and publishing in 1881 *The Buddhist Catechism*, modelled on works used by the Christian missionaries. Olcott shared the view of many enthusiasts in Victorian Europe and America, who saw the Buddha as the greatest philosopher of India's Aryan past and regarded his teachings as a complete philosophical and psychological system, based on reason and restraint, as opposed to ritual, superstition and sacerdotalism, demonstrating how the individual could live a moral life without the trappings of institutional religion. This Buddhism was to be found in texts, rather than in the lives of modern Buddhists of Ceylon, who, in Olcott's view, had deviated from the original teachings.

This would not be his only contribution to modern Buddhism. In 1885 the British government agreed to Olcott's demand that Wesak, the day conveniently marking the Buddha's birth, enlightenment and passage into nirvana, be observed as a national holiday in Ceylon. To mark the occasion, the Buddhist flag (which Olcott had helped to design) was unfurled. The person chosen to raise the flag was Gunananda, who twelve years before had participated in the debate that brought Olcott to Ceylon. Raising a Buddhist flag over Ceylon had obvious symbolic meanings for the anti-colonial movement. However, Olcott hoped it might also serve as a symbol under which all Buddhists could unite, like the cross in Christianity. In 1885 he set out on the grander mission of healing the schism he perceived between 'the Northern and Southern Churches' – that is, between the Buddhists of Ceylon and Burma ('Southern') and those of China and Japan ('Northern').

Olcott was referring to the division of the Buddhist world into what is known as the Theravada and the Mahayana. After the death of the Buddha, a number of sects developed in India, distinguished formally by the particular rendition of the monastic code they followed. One of the sects that was established in Ceylon, the Sthaviravada ('Tradition of the Elders' in the Sanskrit language), evolved into the Theravada ('Tradition of the Elders' in the Pali language), eventually becoming the orthodox form of Buddhism throughout Southeast Asia many centuries later. In India, some four centuries after the Buddha's death, a movement arose that came to be known as the Mahayana ('Great Vehicle'), which offered a different conception of the Buddha and of the path to enlightenment. In the mainstream (that is, non-Mahayana) traditions of India, the Buddha had passed into nirvana upon his death, never to return, although his relics remained as potent sources of blessing. In the Mahayana, the Buddha who appeared on earth was but a physical manifestation of an eternally enlightened being, one of thousands who populated the universe to deliver all beings from suffering. According to some schools of the Mahayana, all beings were destined to follow the path of the bodhisattva and become a buddha. In the mainstream schools, the traditional goal was to become an arhat, one who works to destroy the bonds of birth and death in order to pass into nirvana at death. The arhat was disparaged in much Mahayana literature for his limited aspiration and deficient compassion, and labelled as a follower of the Hinayana ('Vile Vehicle' or 'Base Vehicle'; often euphemized in English as 'Lesser Vehicle').

In descriptions of Buddhism from Olcott's day (and long after) one sometimes encounters the term 'Southern Buddhism' to describe the Buddhism of Ceylon, Thailand, Cambodia, Burma, Laos and parts of Vietnam, and the term 'Northern Buddhism', used in reference to China, Japan, Korea, Tibet and Mongolia. It was often said that Southern Buddhism is Theravada and Northern Buddhism is Mahayana. This is not historically accurate. Theravada has been the dominant school of Buddhism in most of Southeast Asia since the thirteenth century, with the establishment of the monarchies in Thailand, Burma, Cambodia and Laos. Prior to that period, however, many other strands of Buddhism were also widely present, including other mainstream sects, in addition to Mahayana and tantric groups. The great monument at Borobudur in Java reflects Mahayana doctrine and there are reports of Indian monks travelling to Sumatra to study with Mahayana and tantric masters there. Buddhist Bengal exerted a strong influence from the ninth to thirteenth centuries, and Sanskrit Mahayana and tantric texts were donated to Burmese monasteries as late as the fifteenth century. It was only after the demise of Buddhism in India that the Southeast Asian societies looked especially to Ceylon for their Buddhism, where the Theravada had become the orthodoxy.

Just as Southeast Asian Buddhism was not always Theravada, so 'Northern Buddhism' was not always Mahayana. The monastic codes practised in China, Japan, Korea and Tibet all were derived from the Indian mainstream orders. Furthermore, several of these orders flourished in Central Asia (including parts of modern-day Iran and Afghanistan), whence Buddhism was first introduced into China via the Silk Route. Recent scholarship has also suggested that the lines of doctrine and practice long thought to divide Theravada and Mahayana are not as sharply drawn as once imagined. Rather than being a popular (and largely lay) revolution against the Theravada, the Mahayana is seen as a variation on mainstream practices, divided largely over which texts are accepted as the word of the Buddha. As a seventh-century Chinese pilgrim observed about India, 'those who worship bodhisattvas and read Mahayana sutras are called the Mahayana, while those who do not do this are called the Hinayana'.

Yet in the five hundred years since the demise of Buddhism in India, contact between Theravada monks and Mahayana monks had been limited, and to the extent that each had any knowledge about the other, it tended to fall into stereotypes presented in their texts. The Theravadins perceived the followers of the Mahayana as worshippers of non-Buddhist deities who kept inauthentic monastic vows and revered inauthentic texts. Those from Mahayana traditions regarded the Theravadins as practitioners of the Hinayana who sought enlightenment only for themselves and who lacked access to the complete (and more advanced) teachings of the Buddha.

Olcott believed that a great rift had occurred in Buddhism 2,300 years earlier and that if he could simply persuade representatives of the Buddhist nations to agree to his list of 'fourteen items of belief' (he also referred to them as 'Fundamental Buddhistic Beliefs'), then it might be possible to create a 'United Buddhist World'. Olcott thus travelled to Burma and Japan, where he negotiated with Buddhist leaders until he could find a formulation to which they could assent. He also implored them to send missionaries to spread the dharma. His fourteen principles were sufficiently bland as to be soon forgotten even by those who had agreed to them. But Olcott was again shown to be prescient, for many others would later attempt not only to reduce the essence of Buddhism to a single book, as Olcott had done in his *Buddhist Catechism*, but to reduce it further to a series of propositions, as he had also attempted to do. Olcott was also the first to try to unite the various Asian forms of Buddhism into a single organization, an effort that bore fruit long after his death when the first world Buddhist organization, the World Fellowship of Buddhists, was founded in 1950.

In the end, however, Olcott's expression of his beliefs led to another schism. He incurred the wrath of Sinhalese Buddhist leaders when he mocked their belief in the authenticity of the precious tooth relic of the Buddha at Kandy by stating that it was in fact a piece of deer's horn. Shortly afterwards the monk who had certified the authenticity of Olcott's catechism found seventeen answers that were 'opposed to orthodox views of the Southern Church' and withdrew his certification. (Certification was restored after Olcott made revisions to a subsequent edition of the catechism, although he refused to endorse the traditional view that the Buddha was eighteen feet tall.) Even here, Olcott presages a common characteristic of modern Buddhism, which tends to see Buddhism as above all a system of rational and ethical philosophy, divorced from the daily practices of the vast majority of Buddhists, such as the worship of relics, which are dismissed as superstitious.

Olcott left one further legacy. Authority in Buddhism is often a matter of lineage, traced backwards in time from student to teacher, ideally ending with the Buddha himself. If one were to imagine a lineage of modern Buddhism traced forwards in time, one might begin with Gunananda (who clearly saw himself as representing the original teachings of the Buddha) to Colonel Olcott, to a young Sinhalese named David Hewaviratne, better known as Anagarika Dharmapala (1864–1933).

Hewaviratne was born into the small English-speaking middle class of Colombo. His family was Buddhist; at the age of nine he sat with his father in the audience of the Panadure debate, cheering for Gunananda. But like many middle-class children, he was educated in Catholic and Anglican schools. He met Blavatsky and Olcott during their first visit to Ceylon in 1880 and was initiated into the Theosophical Society four years later. In 1881 he changed his name to Anagarika Dharmapala ('Homeless Protector of the Dharma') and, although remaining a layman until late in life, wore the robes of a monk. In 1884, when Blavatsky departed for the Theosophical Society's headquarters in Adyar, India, after a subsequent visit to Ceylon, Dharmapala accompanied her. Upon his return to Ceylon, he became Colonel Olcott's closest associate, accompanying him on a trip to Japan in 1889. In 1898 he worked with Olcott to found the short-lived Dravidian Buddhist Society, dedicated to converting (or, according to Dharmapala, 'returning') the untouchables of south India to Buddhism. Clearly more political than Olcott in both Ceylon and India, he declared that 'India belongs to the Buddhas'.

In 1891, inspired by Edwin Arnold's account of the sad state of the site of the Buddha's enlightenment and by his own trip to the site that year, he founded the Maha Bodhi Society, whose aim was to wrest Bodh Gaya from Hindu control and make it a place of pilgrimage for Buddhists from around the world. Dharmapala achieved international fame after his bravura performance at the World's Parliament of Religions, held in conjunction with the Columbian Exposition in Chicago in 1893. His eloquent English and ability to quote from the Bible captivated the audience as he argued that Buddhism was clearly the equal, if not the superior, of Christianity in both antiquity and profundity, noting, for example, its compatibility with science. While in Chicago, he met not only the other Buddhist delegates to the parliament, such as the Japanese Zen priest Shaku Sōen, but American enthusiasts of Buddhism, including Paul Carus.

The lineage of modern Buddhism was passed to China, when Dharmapala stopped in Shanghai in 1893 on his journey back from the World's Parliament of Religions, where he met Yang Wen-hui (1837–1911). Yang was a civil engineer who had become interested in Buddhism after happening upon a copy of *The Awakening of Faith*, an important Mahayana treatise. He organized a lay society to disseminate the dharma by carving woodblocks for the printing of the Buddhist canon (a traditional form of merit-making). After serving at the Chinese embassy in London (where he met Max Müller, editor of the 'Sacred Books of the East' series, and his Japanese student Nanjo Bun'yu), he resigned from his government position to devote all of his energies to the publication of Buddhist texts.

Accompanying Dharmapala to Shanghai was the famous Baptist missionary Reverend Timothy Richard, who had also attended the parliament in Chicago. After an unsuccessful attempt by Dharmapala to enlist Chinese monks into the Maha Bodhi Society, Reverend Richard arranged for him to meet Yang Wen-hui. Yang did not think it possible for Chinese monks to go to India to assist in the cause of restoring Buddhism in India, but he suggested that Indians be sent to China to study the Buddhist canon. Here, we note another element of modern Buddhism. Dharmapala felt that the Buddhism of Ceylon was the most pure and authentic version of the Buddha's teachings and would have rejected as spurious most of the texts that Yang had been publishing. Yang, on the other hand, felt that the Buddhism of China was the most complete and authentic, such that the only hope of restoring Buddhism in India lay in returning the Chinese canon of translated Indian texts (including many Mahayana sutras) to the land of their birth. The ecumenical spirit found in much of modern Buddhism does not preclude the valuation of one's own form of Buddhism as supreme.

Yang and Dharmapala seem to have begun a correspondence that lasted over the next fifteen years, in which they agreed on the importance of spreading Buddhism to the West. Towards that end, Yang collaborated with Reverend Richard in an English translation of *The Awakening of Faith*, and in 1908 established a school to train Buddhist monks to serve as foreign missionaries, with Yang himself serving on the faculty, perhaps the first time in the history of Chinese Buddhism that monks had received instruction from a layman. Yang's contact with figures such as Müller and Dharmapala had convinced him that Buddhism was a religion compatible with the modern scientific world.

The situation faced by Buddhist monks in China was different from that in Ceylon. The challenge came not so much from Christian missionaries, although they were also a strong presence in China, but from a growing community of intellectuals who saw Buddhism as a form of primitive superstition impeding China's entry into the modern world. Buddhism had periodically been regarded with suspicion by the state over the course of Chinese history, and such suspicions were intensified in the early decades of the twentieth century (especially after the Republican revolution of 1911) when Buddhism was denounced both by Christian missionaries and by Chinese students returning from abroad imbued with the ideas of Dewey, Russell and Marx. In 1898 the emperor had issued an edict ordering many Buddhist temples (and their often substantial land holdings) to be converted into secular schools. Although the order was rescinded in 1905, a number of Buddhist schools and academies for the training of monks were founded at monasteries in an effort to prevent the seizure of the property and the establishment of secular schools. The monastic schools set out to train monks in the Buddhist classics, who would in turn go out in public and teach to the laity (as Christian missionaries did). Yang's academy was one such school. Although most were short-lived, they trained many of the future leaders of modern Buddhism in China, who sought to defend the dharma through founding Buddhist organizations, publishing Buddhist periodicals and leading lay movements to support the monastic community. One of the students at Yang's school was the monk T'ai Hsu, later to become one of the most famous Chinese Buddhists of the twentieth century. New organizations included the Buddhist Pure Karma Society, founded in 1925 in Shanghai, which ran an orphanage and a free outpatient clinic, sponsored public lectures on Buddhist texts, published the *Pure Karma Monthly* and operated radio station XMHB, 'The Voice of the Buddha'. The Chinese Metaphysical Society was founded in 1919 in Nanjing. Originally intended for laymen, monks were later allowed to attend, on the condition that they not meditate, recite the Buddha's name, or perform services for the dead. Here Buddhism was presented as a philosophy rather than a religion, and the emphasis was placed not on the recitation of the scriptures (sutras) but on the study of the scholastic treatises, especially those of the Fa-hsiang school, regarded as a form of Buddhist Idealism. For many who participated in these groups, the support and study of Buddhism served as a means of maintaining their Chinese identity during a period of sometimes chaotic social and political change.[7]

An important characteristic of modern Buddhism, especially in contrast to some early forms, has been the active and visible role of women. Women have contributed to modern Buddhism in a number of domains, but no issue has been more important, perhaps, than the question of the ordination of women as nuns. The Buddha is reported to have asserted that women are capable of following the path to enlightenment, but had only grudgingly permitted the founding of an order of nuns. He is said to have established an additional set of rules for nuns (including the rule that the most senior nun must always defer to the most junior monk) and to have predicted that as a consequence of his allowing women to enter the order, his teaching would only remain in the world for five hundred years. If he had not admitted women, he predicted, it would have lasted for one thousand years. Yet an order of fully ordained nuns was established and it eventually spread to Sri Lanka, Burma, China, Vietnam, Korea and Japan. However, it was difficult for this order to survive periods of social upheaval; the rules of discipline required that ten fully ordained nuns be present to confer ordination on a new nun, after which she was required to have a second ordination ceremony at which ten monks must be present. The order of nuns died out in Sri Lanka around the end of the tenth century. As a result of a protracted war with a king from southern India, Buddhist institutions were devastated to the point that there was no longer the requisite number of monks to provide for the ordination of new monks. The Sri Lankan king brought monks from Burma to revive the order of monks, but he did not make similar efforts for the order of nuns. Thus, although the order of nuns survives in China, Korea and Vietnam, it has died out in the Theravada countries of Sri Lanka and Southeast Asia.

In tracing the place of women in the lineage of modern Buddhism, Dharmapala again played a role, albeit indirectly. As mentioned above, in 1891 he had founded the Maha Bodhi Society, with the aim of uniting Buddhists from around the world and restoring Bodh Gaya (then under Hindu control) as a sacred centre and place of pilgrimage for all Buddhists. Dharmapala did not live to see this latter goal achieved; Bodh Gaya would not be returned to Buddhists until after India gained its independence from Britain in 1947. But in the decades that followed, Dharmapala's dream was realized, and Bodh Gaya became again a meeting place for Buddhists from across Asia, a place where a Buddhist woman from Thailand could meet a Chinese nun from Taiwan.

Voramai Kabilsingh was born near Bangkok, Siam (Thailand), in 1908, the youngest of six children. She was educated at a Catholic school and later worked as a teacher in a girls' school. She married a politician in 1942 and gave birth to a daughter in 1944. After undergoing surgery in 1955, Kabilsingh developed a strong interest in Buddhism and the practice of meditation, starting a monthly Buddhist magazine that same year. In 1956 she received the eight precepts of a Buddhist layperson, shaved her head and began to wear robes that were light yellow in colour. The order of nuns had never been established in Thailand, and the only Buddhist vocation for women has been that of the *mae ji*, women who shave their heads and wear white robes and keep some of the vows of a novice, although they are not ordained and have no official status in the Buddhist community. Typically coming from rural backgrounds and with little formal education, *mae ji*, in many cases widows and women without family support, do not occupy a high status in Thai society. They often live in temple compounds, where they receive food in exchange for cooking and cleaning duties, while others living elsewhere have to beg for their food.

Kabilsingh did not fall into this category and hence created a new one for herself, wearing robes that were neither the white colour of the *mae ji* or the dark ochre of the monks. The local Buddhist authorities lodged a protest against her, claiming that a woman wearing a yellow robe defiled the monastic order. However, Kabilsingh was exonerated because the shade of yellow that she wore was not permitted for monks. In 1957 she purchased land and constructed the first Thai Buddhist temple for women. She also founded an orphanage and a school. Because the order of nuns in the Theravada tradition had become extinct many centuries before, she was told that it was impossible for her to receive full ordination. Undaunted, she travelled to India and to Bodh Gaya, the site of Buddha's enlightenment, and prayed to the Buddha himself for ordination.

Bodh Gaya is a place of pilgrimage for Buddhists from around the world, and while she was there Kabilsingh met a Chinese Buddhist nun. The lineage of fully ordained Buddhist nuns had been introduced to China in the fifth century BCE, by a delegation of nuns from Sri Lanka, in fact. Since then, the order of nuns had died out in Sri Lanka but had continued in China, thriving also in Taiwan after the Communist revolution. But because Chinese nuns were adherents of the Mahayana, the Theravada monks of Thailand did not consider the Chinese ordination lineage of nuns to be authentic.

In 1971 Kabilsingh and her daughter (who had researched the origins of the Chinese lineage during her graduate study in Canada) travelled to Taiwan, where she received full ordination as a Buddhist nun, perhaps the first Thai woman in history to do so. Upon her return to Thailand, she continued the traditional merit-making deeds of a Buddhist laywoman, such as presenting offerings of food and robes to monks and having Buddha images made for temples. She also engaged in more modern charitable activities, such as providing food, clothing and books to impoverished schoolchildren. In addition, she did things that Thai Buddhist women had not done in the past, performing some of the traditional roles of a monk, such as teaching the dharma and giving instruction in meditation. Despite her fame, she has not been accepted as a member of the Thai order, many of whose members consider her simply a *mae ji*.[8]

In 1868 in Japan, the shogun was deposed and the emperor restored to power. One of the first acts of his new Meiji government was to establish Shinto as the state religion, with the emperor as its head priest. Prior to this time, Buddhism had effectively become the state religion of Japan with each household required by law to be registered at a nearby Buddhist temple. Shinto and Buddhist deities had been worshipped together, but now Buddhist images had to be removed from Shinto shrines and Buddhist monks were prohibited from performing rituals there. The new policies represented not only the creation of state Shinto but a suppression of Buddhism with such slogans as 'Exterminate the buddhas and destroy Shakyamuni [the Buddha]'. Buddhism was regarded as a foreign religion and hence not purely Japanese, as Shinto was considered to be. Over four thousand Buddhist temples were eliminated and thousands of monks were returned to lay life; many were drafted into the imperial army. In some parts of Japan the new policies sparked riots that had to be suppressed by the authorities.

In the face of these various policies directed against Buddhism, Buddhist leaders undertook measures to demonstrate their importance to the Japanese nation. In 1896 representatives of a number of sects joined together (for the first time in the history of Japanese Buddhism) to form the Alliance of United Sects for Ethical Standards, proclaiming support for the emperor and calling for the expulsion of the truly foreign religion in Japan, Christianity. Such acts met with the approval of the government, and Buddhist priests were allowed to serve in a newly established system of teaching academies for the promulgation of patriotic principles. With the identification of Shinto and the state, priests certified to teach in these academies (located at Buddhist temples and Shinto shrines) were expected to wear Shinto robes and recite Shinto prayers. Buddhist priests who did not receive certification to teach were prohibited from giving public teachings, performing rites or residing at Buddhist temples. The policy to establish teaching academies was soon abandoned, but the reforms of Buddhism continued.

A further assault on Buddhism took place in 1872, when the Meiji government removed any special status from monkhood. Henceforth, monks had to register in the household registry system and were subject to secular education, taxation and military conscription. Most controversially, the government declared that 'from now on Buddhist clerics will be free to eat meat, marry, grow their hair, and so on'. The new regulations, and especially the regulation permitting marriage, were met with alarm by the hierarchs of many of the Buddhist sects of Japan.[9] They feared that rescinding the law against clerical marriage would destroy the distinction between monk and layperson, bringing chaos to the state. For centuries Buddhist leaders in Japan had represented the dharma as having the power to protect the Japanese nation, a power that derived from the monks' strict observance of their vows, especially the vow of celibacy. The maintenance of the monastic code therefore provided what they regarded as Buddhism's greatest service, and hence its closest link, to the state. The Meiji government, however, sought to remove the marks that distinguished Buddhist monks from other subjects of the emperor, the most obvious of which were the shaved head, the vegetarian diet and celibacy. Indeed, the new law had been requested by a monk of the Zen sect who wished to put an end to the government's suppression of Buddhism by demonstrating the willingness of Buddhist priests to serve the nation. In response to protests from Buddhist leaders, the government subsequently issued an addendum to the law, stating that although meat eating and marriage were no longer criminal offences, the individual sects were free to regulate these activities as they saw fit. Most sects subsequently issued regulations either condemning or prohibiting marriage for its monks.

None the less, it became increasingly common for monks to marry, and today less than one per cent of monks in Japan observe the code of monastic discipline of a fully ordained monk.

In the last decades of the nineteenth century, Buddhist intellectuals strove to demonstrate the relevance of Buddhism to the interests of the Japanese nation by promoting a new Buddhism that was fully consistent with Japan's attempts to modernize and expand its realm. Buddhism had been attacked in the early years of the Meiji as a foreign and anachronistic institution, riddled with corruption, a parasite on society and the purveyor of superstition, standing in the way of progress and Japan's entry into the modern world. This New Buddhism was represented as both purely Japanese and purely Buddhist, more Buddhist, in fact, than the other forms of Buddhism in Asia. It was also committed to social welfare, urging education for all, and the foundation of hospitals and charities. New Buddhism was fully consistent with modern science. And it supported the expansion of the Japanese empire. Indeed, Buddhist leaders were united in their call to restore true Buddhism (that they believed to exist only in Japan) throughout the rest of Asia, beginning with the Sino-Japanese War of 1894–5 and continuing until the defeat of Japan by the Allies in 1945.[10]

One of the leading figures of the New Buddhism was Shaku Sōen (1859–1919). Ordained as a novice of the Rinzai Zen sect at the age of twelve, he studied under the Rinzai master Imakita Kōsen (1816–92), who had served as one of the government-certified teachers during the 1870s. Shaku Sōen trained under Imakita at the famous Engakuji monastery in Kamakura, receiving 'dharma transmission', and hence authority to teach, at the age of twenty-four. Seeking to combine both Buddhist training and Western-style education, he attended Keiō University, and then travelled to Ceylon to study Pali and live as a Theravada monk. Upon his return, he was chosen by a conference of abbots to be one of the four editors of a book entitled *The Essentials of Buddhism – All Sects*. Like many of the leading figures of modern Buddhism, he was devoted to teaching meditation to laypeople, providing instruction both in Tokyo and at his monastery. He was selected to be one of the Japanese representatives to the World's Parliament of Religions in 1893, his address being translated into English by one of his lay disciples, D. T. Suzuki. In his report on the parliament, he described the work of the Japanese delegation:

We invited the attention of the participants, both foreign and Japanese, to the following points at least: that the Japanese are people with abundantly loyal and patriotic spirits; that Buddhism has exercised great influence on Japanese spirituality, and had had influence on successive emperors too; that Buddhism is a universal religion and it closely corresponds to what science and philosophy say today; that we cleared off the prejudice that Mahayana Buddhism was not the true teaching of the Buddha; that Mr Straw, a wealthy merchant in New York, had a conversion ceremony carried on at the congress hall in which he became a Buddhist; that a leading Japanese staying in the United States arranged a Buddhist lecture meeting twice for us in the Exposition building, and so on.[11]

Sōen served as a Buddhist chaplain in Manchuria during the Russo-Japanese War of 1904–5. He had become sufficiently well known by that time that Leo Tolstoy sought to enlist his support in condemning the war between their two nations, a request that Sōen refused.

Sōen had, in a way, entered the lineage of modern Buddhism some years before, when he met Dharmapala during his studies in Ceylon. But Sōen's presence in Chicago was an important moment in the history of modern Buddhism, not so much for his address, but for his meeting with Paul Carus, a German immigrant living in Illinois and the proponent of the Religion of Science, something which Carus would see most perfectly embodied in Buddhism. Sōen later arranged for D. T. Suzuki to stay with Carus in La Salle, Illinois, a period that was to prove important for Suzuki's representation of Zen, and hence for modern Buddhism.[12] According to legend, Zen began when the Buddha silently held up a flower. Only one monk in the audience smiled in recognition, receiving from the Buddha a 'mind-to-mind transmission', allowing him to see into his true nature and become enlightened. This teaching is said to have been passed from teacher to student, from India to China (where it was called Chan, meaning 'meditation') to Japan, where it was called Zen (the Japanese pronunciation of the Chinese character Chan). Over the course of his long life after leaving La Salle, Suzuki wrote many words about this tradition that did not rely on words. His books came to play a profound role in the propagation of Zen in the West, especially in intellectual and artistic circles. Indeed, many of the extracts presented in this book are by writers who were inspired by Suzuki. The place of the Beat writers, for example, in the lineage of modern Buddhism, can be traced directly to Suzuki, the disciple of Shaku Sōen.

The practice of Zen meditation in the West arrived via different routes. In the first decades of the twentieth century, a Zen priest named Harada Daiun (1871–1961) began giving instruction in Zen meditation to both priests and laypeople in Japan. His meditation retreats became famous for their rigour and for Harada's emphasis on kensho, an experience of enlightenment. Although many in the Zen establishment considered the achievement of kensho to be a rare event, Harada taught that it was within the reach of everyone who received the proper instruction, whether they be ordained priests or ordinary laypeople. Like many New Buddhists, Harada was a strong defender of Japanese imperialism and remained on the far right wing of the Japanese political spectrum after 1945. His successor was Yasutani Hakuun (1885–1973), a Zen priest who worked as a schoolteacher before beginning to practise under Harada in 1925. Harada granted him permission to teach in 1943, and after the war he started a meditation group for laypeople on the northern island of Hokkaido. Despite being a priest of the Soto sect of Zen, he became increasingly critical of the Soto establishment and in 1954 he declared his independence from the sect and founded the Sanbokyodan ('Three Treasures Association'). Yasutani criticized and dispensed with those elements of traditional Zen monastic life that he deemed superfluous, especially the wearing of monastic robes, the performance of liturgies and ceremonial rites, and the study of Buddhist scriptures. His emphasis on a streamlined practice and rapid attainment of kensho was ideally suited to laypeople, and especially to foreigners in Japan who had become interested in Zen through the writings of D. T. Suzuki, but whose knowledge of Japanese was insufficient to allow them to enrol in the traditional Zen training monasteries. Two American disciples of Yasutani, Philip Kapleau (1912–) and Robert Aitken (1917–), would become among the first American Zen masters, and Japanese disciples of Yasutani, such as Maezumi Roshi and Eido

Roshi, would become prominent Zen teachers. In this way, a relatively marginal Zen teacher in Japan established what would become mainstream Zen practice in America.[13]

In the Theravada nations of Sri Lanka and Southeast Asia there has been a long tradition of dividing monastic practice into two categories: the vocation of texts and the vocation of meditation. In commentaries dating from as early as the fifth century, a preference was expressed for the former. Strong and able monks were expected to devote themselves to study, with meditation regarded as the vocation of those who were somehow less able, especially those who became monks late in life. It was also widely believed that after the first generations of disciples of the Buddha, it was impossible to achieve nirvana in the human realm. This is not to suggest that meditation was not practised; it remained the vocation of small groups called 'forest monks' who lived in remote areas, but it was not the focus of the majority of monks and monasteries.

A revival of meditation practice began in Burma in the late nineteenth century. Like Sri Lanka, Burma was formerly a British colony and had been under British control since 1885. Without its traditional royal patronage, the monastic community lost much of its state support, yet Buddhism became strongly associated with Burmese national identity, with leadership provided by both monks and laymen during and after the struggle for independence, achieved in 1948. One of the key figures in the resurgence of meditation practice was Mahasi Sayadaw (1904–82). He became a novice monk at the age of twelve, deciding not to return to lay life when he became an adult (as was commonly done in Burma) but to become a fully ordained monk, taking his vows at the age of nineteen. After completing advanced scriptural studies in Mandalay, he returned to a monastery in the countryside to teach. Shortly afterwards he met the famous monk Mingun Jetavan Sayadaw, who was teaching a form of meditation known as vipassana.

Buddhist meditation is traditionally divided into two forms. The first is called samatha, or serenity meditation, and is intended to lead to a deep level of concentration, in which one is able to focus the mind one-pointedly on an object, without distraction. Serenity is generally presented as a prerequisite for the second form of meditation, vipassana or insight meditation. Here, the concentrated mind is used to analyse the constituents of experience in an effort to discover their true nature. Insight into this nature is a form of wisdom which, when deepened, results in enlightenment and liberation from future rebirth. Mingun Sayadaw was teaching a form of meditation that he had learned from a forest monk, based on teachings ascribed to the Buddha in a text called the *Discourse on the Establishment of Mindfulness* (*Satipatthana Sutta*).

According to the technique that Mahasi Sayadaw learned from his teacher, the formal practice of serenity is dispensed with, and one begins immediately with the development of insight by focusing attention on the rising and falling of the abdomen that occurs with each inhalation and exhalation of the breath. In 1941 Mahasi began teaching this technique to both monks and laypeople in his native village, located in a region that did not suffer greatly during the Japanese invasion and occupation of Burma. In 1947 a wealthy lay disciple of Mahasi donated land for a meditation centre in Rangoon. By this time Mahasi Sayadaw's fame was such that the prime minister of the newly independent Burma, U Nu, invited him to be the resident teacher at this new meditation centre in the capital. Over the next decade, Mahasi established similar centres throughout Burma and in Thailand and Ceylon, providing meditation instruction (in what came to be known as 'the Burmese method', also taught, with some variations, by the Burmese lay teacher U Ba Khin) to hundreds of thousands of Buddhist monks and laypeople in the Theravada countries, and later in Europe and America. 'Insight meditation' would (together with Zen meditation) become a primary practice of modern Buddhism, and Mahasi Sayadaw is honoured in the lineage of modern Buddhism as the teacher who brought it to the world.

Modern Buddhism did not come to Tibet. There were no movements to ordain women, no publication of Buddhist magazines, no formation of lay Buddhist societies, no establishment of orphanages, no liberal critique of Buddhism as contrary to scientific progress, no Tibetan delegates to the World's Parliament of Religions, no efforts by Tibetans to found (or join) world Buddhist organizations. Tibet remained relatively isolated from the forces of modern Buddhism, in part because it never became a European colony. Christian missionaries never became a significant presence, Buddhist monks were not educated in European languages, European educational institutions were not established, the printing press was not introduced. Indeed, because of its relative isolation, many, both in Asia and the West, considered Tibet to be a pure abode of Buddhism, unspoiled by the forces of modernity. There was, however, one Tibetan who might be considered a modern Buddhist. He was the monk Gendun Chopel (Dge 'dun chos 'phel, 1903–51), who spent the years 1934–46 travelling in India and Ceylon, where he encountered many of the constituents of modern Buddhism, writing about them in his travel journals. There one finds scathing criticisms of the avaricious European colonial powers, speculations on the compatibility of Buddhism and science, and even an assessment of Madame Blavatsky. In describing the pilgrimage site of Bodh Gaya in 1939, he writes:

Then, because of the troubled times, the place [Bodh Gaya] fell into the hands of heretical [i.e. Hindu] yogins. They did many unseemly things such as building a non-Buddhist temple in the midst of the stupas, erecting a statue of Shiva in the temple, and performing blood sacrifices. The novice Dharmapala was not able to bear this. He died as a result of his great efforts to bring lawsuits in order that the Buddhists could once again gain possession [of Bodh Gaya]. Still, despite his efforts in the past and the passage of laws, his noble vision has not yet come to fruition. Therefore, Buddhists from all of our governments must unite and make all possible effort so that this special place of blessings, which is like the heart inside us, will come into the hands of the Buddhists who are its rightful owners.[14]

Here Gendun Chopel belatedly adds a Tibetan voice in support of the goals of Dharmapala's Maha Bodhi Society, founded almost fifty years earlier. Adopting the stance of a modern Buddhist, he calls on Tibetans to join with Buddhists from around the world in the crusade to return the most sacred Buddhist site to Buddhist control. But he was an exception among Tibetans. He was imprisoned by the Tibetan government shortly after returning to Tibet in 1946 and died in 1951. Tibet was invaded by China in 1950, and after a decade of increasing tensions, the young Dalai Lama escaped to India during a popular uprising against the Chinese army in Lhasa. Since then, he has become an eloquent spokesman for many of the concerns of modern Buddhism, including the compatibility of Buddhism and science, the rights of women, concern for the environment, and the role of Buddhism in the promotion of world peace.

It is clear from this desultory series of vignettes of modern Buddhist figures from Sri Lanka, China, Thailand, Japan, Burma and Tibet that each of these nations has its own history and its own Buddhism, suggesting that it may be a mistake to speak of something called 'modern Buddhism', at least in the singular. At the same time, there are a remarkable number of links and connections among the figures whose words appear in this anthology. And although it may be misleading to speak of a single form of modern Buddhism in the traditionally Buddhist nations of Asia, the various trends that began at disparate locations throughout the continent of Asia over the past 150 years have made their way, through a variety of conduits, to Europe and America, where they have been combined, sometimes uneasily, and condensed not into a particular variety of Buddhism, such as Burmese Buddhism or Korean Buddhism, but rather something simply called Buddhism. This Buddhism has a number of characteristics, many of which originated not with the Buddha but with Buddhist reformers of the nineteenth century who were themselves responding to the colonial situation.

In 1909, before she found magic and mystery in Tibet, Alexandra David-Neel published a book in Paris entitled *Le modernisme Bouddhist et le Bouddhisme du Bouddha*. She was not contrasting Buddhist modernism and the Buddhism of the Buddha but rather equating them. Like all Buddhist reform movements over the centuries, modern Buddhism has been represented as a return to the teachings of the Buddha, or better, to his ineffable experience beneath the Bodhi tree on that night of the full moon in May. Implicit in this most traditional of claims, however, was a criticism of traditional Buddhism, of the Buddhism of Asia in 1909. The call to return to original Buddhism allowed modern Buddhists like David-Neel to concede many of the charges made by its critics, whether they were Orientalists, colonial officials, Christian missionaries, or Asian secularists, who found contemporary Buddhists to be benighted idolaters, crushed by centuries of superstition, exploited by an effete and corrupt monastic order. Such charges were made with a remarkable consistency in European accounts of societies as different as Ceylon, Tibet, China, and Japan. Rather than seeking to defend the Buddhism that they knew, many of the leading figures of modern Buddhism sought to accept the claim that Buddhism had suffered an inevitable decline since the master passed into nirvana. The time was ripe to remove the encrustations of the past centuries and return to the essence of Buddhism.

This Buddhism is above all a religion of reason dedicated to bringing an end to suffering. Suffering was often interpreted by modern Buddhists to mean not the sufferings of birth, ageing, sickness and death, but the sufferings caused by poverty and social injustice. The Buddha's ambiguous statements on caste (he did not reject the caste system but regarded caste as irrelevant to success on the path) were selectively read by Victorian readers, both in Europe and in South Asia, to portray him as a crusader against inequality and a social hierarchy based on birth rather than merit. One of the constituents of modern Buddhism is, therefore, the promotion of the social good, whether it be in the form of rebellion against political oppression (especially by colonial powers), of projects on behalf of the poor, or in the more general claim that Buddhism is the religion most compatible with the technological and economic benefits that result from modernization.

Efforts on behalf of the poor were often made in direct response to the criticisms levelled at Buddhist monks by Christian missionaries. With some important exceptions, Buddhist monks had not traditionally been concerned with the needs of laypeople in this life. Their talents (the performance of rituals, the chanting of scriptures) were better directed towards the needs of the future life. Monks were not meant to provide charity to laypeople, their vocation instead was to receive charity from them, serving as a pure 'field of merit' for their donations, thereby causing the donors to accumulate the good karma that would result in a happy rebirth for them and their departed loved ones. These were deemed more important concerns than the vicissitudes of this life, which were caused by not having accumulated such good karma in the past. As a result, and again with some exceptions, Buddhist charitable organizations have been founded by reformist monks or by laypeople, a trend that continues today in 'Engaged Buddhism'.

The Buddhism of the Buddha was also said to be free from the veneration of images. To the extent that reverence was offered to an image of the Buddha, it was a simple expression of thanksgiving for his teachings, given in full recognition that the Buddha had long ago entered into nirvana. This modern portrayal of Buddhist icons was also at odds with traditional practice. In the first centuries of its introduction into China, Buddhism was known as 'the religion of images', suggesting the central importance that images of the Buddha have held, and continue to hold, throughout Buddhist Asia. Although there is no historical evidence of images of the Buddha being made until centuries after his death, there are a number of images whose sanctity derives from the belief that the Buddha posed for the artists who created them, and these are among the most venerated images in Asia, serving as important actors in the histories of those kings and emperors who possessed them. Relics of the Buddha are believed to be infused with his living presence and thus capable of bestowing all manner of blessings upon those who venerate them. That modern Buddhists (especially in the West) either ignored this most pervasive of Buddhist practices or dismissed it as superstition again demonstrates the importance of the colonial legacy of Christian missionaries (who consistently labelled Buddhists as idolaters) in the formation of modern Buddhism.

The domain in which modern Buddhists most consistently proclaimed the superiority of their religion over Christianity was that of science. The compatibility of Buddhism and science has been asserted by such disparate figures as Dharmapala in Ceylon, T'ai Hsu in China, Shaku Sōen in Japan, and more recently by the Dalai Lama. The focus is again on the Buddha himself, who is seen as denying the existence of a creator deity, rejecting a world view in which the universe is controlled by the sacraments of priests, and setting forth instead a rational approach in which the universe operates through the mechanisms of causation. These and other factors make Buddhism, more than any other religion, compatible with modern science and hence able to thrive in the modern age. Elements of traditional cosmology that did not accord with science (such as a flat earth) were generally dismissed as cultural accretions that were incidental to the Buddha's original teaching.

Despite general agreement that the Buddha had long ago anticipated the discoveries of modern science, modern Buddhists were not unanimous in their views of science. Some saw Buddhism, with its denial of a creator deity and emphasis on causation, to anticipate theories of a mechanistic universe. Others predicted that the East would receive technology from the West and the West would receive spiritual peace from the East, because the West excelled in investigating the external world of matter while the East excelled in investigating the inner world of consciousness. One finds here yet another characteristic of modern Buddhism. It had become a commonplace of European colonial discourse that the West was more advanced than the East because Europeans were extroverted, active and curious about the external world, while Asians were introverted, passive and obsessed with the mystical. It was therefore the task of Europeans to bring Asians into the modern world. In modern Buddhism this apparent shortcoming is transformed into a virtue, with Asia, and especially Buddhists, endowed with a peace, a contentment and an insight that the acquisitive and distracted Western mind sorely needs.

Prior to the development of modern Buddhism, the many forms of Buddhism in Asia had developed regionally, with contacts among various traditions occurring across local borders. The lineage of monastic ordination in the Theravada had been established in Burma by monks from Sri Lanka, spreading from Burma to Thailand. When that lineage became threatened in Sri Lanka as a result of wars, a delegation of monks was invited from Burma around 1070 and later from Siam in 1753 to ordain Sinhalese monks, thereby reviving the lineage in the nation from whence it had come. In the early centuries of Japanese Buddhism, monks would often make the perilous sea voyage to China to retrieve texts and teachings. Tibetans invited Indian Buddhist masters to Tibet and Indian masters would sail to Sumatra to study. Yet, as each national tradition developed, the importance placed on such contacts diminished, and each type of Buddhism developed its own character and its own sense of being the repository of the true teaching. Monks from Sri

Lanka regarded monks from East Asia as inauthentic because they did not hold the Theravada ordination. Monks from East Asia or Tibet regarded the Theravada monks as lacking the full dispensation of the Buddha's teachings found in the Mahayana sutras, texts that Theravada monks considered spurious. Yet such characterizations were largely rhetorical, since travel over long distances was difficult and India, the common place of pilgrimage for all Buddhists, had long since lost its own Buddhist tradition.

All of this changed with the advent of modern Buddhism and the modern age, with greater opportunities for foreign travel. As we have seen, Dharmapala's vision was to develop a world Buddhist mission, one which would restore the great pilgrimage places of India to Buddhist control. But this immediately raised the question of what was meant by 'Buddhism'. Dharmapala regarded the Theravada, especially as it was practised in Ceylon, to be the true Buddhism, the Buddhism of the Buddha, a view supported by many of the scholars of the day. Hence, there is a tendency in some branches of modern Buddhism to represent the Theravada, despite its considerable regional variations in Sri Lanka, Thailand, Burma and Cambodia, as a monolith and as the purest form of Buddhism. Consequently, foreign monks from East Asia who visited Ceylon were often encouraged to take a second ordination there, to return them to the original monastic order. At the same time, modern Buddhists from China and Japan were intent on demonstrating that the Mahayana or, as it was often referred to at that time, 'Northern Buddhism', was the word of the Buddha. D. T. Suzuki's first book in English, *Outlines of Mahayana Buddhism* (1907), was essentially an apology for the Mahayana. His teacher, Shaku Sōen, as we have seen, had defended its authenticity at the World's Parliament of Religions.

But the question of the authenticity of the Mahayana and the historical primacy of the Theravada was not to be resolved by the modern Buddhists. Instead, many sought to identify something that had not existed before, a Buddhism that was free of sectarian concerns and historical developments. There was a sense among many that the various forms of Buddhism in Asia had been polluted by all manner of cultural influences, making them more and more distant from the original teachings of the Buddha. This was not a new idea. Indeed, from early on in India there was the doctrine of the 'decline of the dharma', that in the centuries that followed the death of the Buddha it would become harder and harder to maintain the precepts and follow the path that the Buddha had set forth. In the Pure Land schools of Japanese Buddhism, it was deemed impossible to follow the path of the great saints of the past during the present degenerate age; the only recourse was to accept the grace of the buddha Amitabha and be delivered upon death into his pure land. In much of the Theravada world, it was held that it was no longer possible to attain nirvana. Instead, one should accumulate merit in order to be reborn as a disciple of the next buddha, Maitreya, in the far future.

What was different about modern Buddhism was the conviction that centuries of cultural and clerical ossification could be stripped from the teachings of the Buddha to reveal a Buddhism that was neither Theravada or Mahayana, neither monastic or lay, neither Sinhalese, Japanese, Chinese or Thai. This was a form of Buddhism whose essential teachings could be encompassed within the pages of a single book. Hence, for the first time in the history of Buddhism, we find in modern Buddhism the tendency to summarize Buddhism in one volume. And it is noteworthy that the first attempts to do so were made not by Buddhist monks in Asia, but by Americans. In 1881, when Colonel Olcott published the first edition of *The Buddhist Catechism*, it was immediately translated into Sinhala by Dharmapala. In the preface to the thirty-sixth edition he wrote: 'It has always seemed incongruous that an American making no claims at all to scholarship, should be looked to by the Sinhalese nation to help them teach the Dharma to their children, and as I believe I have said in an earlier edition, I only consented to write the *Buddhist Catechism* after I found that no Bhikkhu [monk] would undertake it.'[15] That no such monk was forthcoming suggests more about Olcott's assumptions about Buddhism than it does about any deficiencies in the Sinhalese clergy. In 1894 Paul Carus published *The Gospel of the Buddha According to Old Records*, a work that D. T. Suzuki, on the instructions of Shaku Sōen, translated into Japanese for use in Buddhist seminaries in Japan. In 1938 Dwight Goddard published *A Buddhist Bible*, in which he included texts of his own composition. Thus, when Christmas Humphreys, who had founded the Buddhist Society in London in 1924 (originally as a branch of the Theosophical Society), published the third edition of his *Buddhism* (1962), he would explain that his 'interest is in world Buddhism as distinct from any of its various Schools', believing 'that only in a combination of all Schools can the full grandeur of Buddhist thought be found'.[16] Such a 'world Buddhism', transcending all regional designation and sectarian affiliation, had not existed prior to the advent of modern Buddhism. The contact of the various forms of Buddhism in Asia during the nineteenth century required the quest to separate what was essential from what was merely cultural, to create something simply called Buddhism.

It was only in this sense that Buddhism could be regarded as a universal religion. As such, many of the distinctions of other forms of Buddhism faded. For example, whereas it was traditionally held that Buddhism could not exist without the presence of an ordained clergy, many of the leaders of modern Buddhism were laypeople and many of the monks who became leaders of modern Buddhism did not always enjoy the respect, and sometimes not even the cognizance, of the monastic establishment. Indeed, one of the characteristics of modern Buddhism is that teachers who were marginal figures in their own cultures became central on the international scene. Freed from the sexism that has traditionally pervaded the Buddhist monastic orders, women played key roles in the development of modern Buddhism. But modern Buddhism did not dispense with monastic concerns. Instead, it blurred the boundary between the monk and the layperson, with laypeople taking on the vocations of the traditionally elite monks: the study and interpretation of scriptures and the practice of meditation. Each of these factors contributes to a sense of modern Buddhism as shifting emphasis away from the corporate community (especially the community of monks) to the individual, who was able to define for him- or herself a new identity that had not existed before, sometimes even designing new robes that marked a status between the categories of monk and layperson.

The essential practice of modern Buddhism was meditation. In keeping with the quest to return to the origin, modern Buddhists looked back to the central image of the tradition, the Buddha seated in silent meditation beneath a tree, contemplating the ultimate nature of the universe. This silent practice allowed modern Buddhism generally to dismiss the rituals of consecration, purification, expiation and exorcism so common throughout Asia as extraneous elements that had crept into the tradition in response to the needs of those unable to follow the higher path. Silent meditation allowed modern Buddhism once again to transcend local expressions, which required form and language. At the same time, its very silence provided a medium for moving beyond sectarian concerns of institutional and doctrinal formulations by making Buddhism, above all, an experience. Although found in much of modern Buddhism, this view was put forth most strongly in the case of Zen, moving it outside the larger categories of Buddhism and even religion into a universal sensibility of the sacred in the secular.

The strong emphasis on meditation as the central form of Buddhist practice marked one of the most extreme departures of modern Buddhism from previous forms. The practice of meditation had been throughout Buddhist history the domain of monks, and even here meditation was merely one of many vocations within the monastic institution. In China it is estimated that 80 per cent of Buddhist monks resided not in the large training monasteries but in hereditary temples where they earned their livelihood by performing funeral rites and memorial services, and rarely practised meditation. In modern Japan the great majority of Zen priests are the sons of Zen priests and administer the family temple, again devoting much of their energies to services for the dead. They would have received instruction in meditation (as well as other ritual forms) during a stay of one month to three years at a Zen training monastery, usually when they were in their early twenties. During their stay they would receive 'dharma transmission' and hence permission to serve as the head priest of a Zen temple. In Sri Lanka monks who are scholars have traditionally been regarded more highly than meditators. In modern Buddhism, however, meditation is a practice recommended for all, with the goal of enlightenment moved from the distant future to the immediate present.

What, then, is modern Buddhism? The question of the extent to which it is authentically Buddhist is difficult to answer, without first defining what authentic Buddhism might be, a question that has occupied so many modern Buddhists. It seems clear that much of what we regard as Buddhism today is, in fact, modern Buddhism. And modern Buddhism seems to have begun, at least in part, as a response to the threat of modernity, as perceived by certain Asian Buddhists, especially those who had encountered colonialism. Yet these modern Buddhists were very much products of modernity, with the rise of the middle class, the power of the printing press, the ease of international travel. Many of these leaders were deeply involved in independence movements and identified Buddhism with the interests of the state; one thinks of Dharmapala in Ceylon, T'ai hsu in China, Shaku Sōen in Japan, Ledi Sayadaw in Burma and, more recently, the Dalai Lama in exile from Tibet. Yet together they have forged an international Buddhism that transcends cultural and national boundaries, creating in the following generation a cosmopolitan network of intellectuals, writing most often in English.

It is perhaps best to consider modern Buddhism not as a universal religion beyond sectarian borders, but as itself a Buddhist sect. There is Thai Buddhism, there is Tibetan Buddhism, there is Korean Buddhism, and there is Modern Buddhism. Unlike previous forms of national Buddhism, this new Buddhism does not stand in a relation of mutual exclusion to these other forms. One may be a Chinese Buddhist and also be a modern Buddhist. Yet one may also be a Chinese Buddhist without being a modern Buddhist. Like other Buddhist sects, modern Buddhism has its own lineage, its own doctrines, its own practices, some of which have been outlined above. And like other Buddhist sects, modern Buddhism has its own canon of sacred scriptures, many of which appear in the pages that follow.

This book presents selections from the works of thirty-one figures – monks and laymen, nuns and laywomen, poets and missionaries, meditation masters and social revolutionaries – who have figured in the formation of modern Buddhism. Each extract is preceded by a short introduction, providing a biographical sketch of the author in question and brief comment on the reading. What is remarkable about the lives of these figures is the degree of their interconnection. There is not a single author included here who was not acquainted with at least one other, thus creating the lineage so essential to modern Buddhism. In order to emphasize the development of this lineage, the authors are presented chronologically, in order of the year of their birth. The passages from their works are presented as they appear in the editions from which they are drawn, preserving the variant spellings, transliteration and punctuation (or lack of it). A few misprints have been silently emended, and some elements of presentation (such as footnote markers) made consistent.

This anthology is very much a preliminary work. The lives and works of the authors included here deserve much more comment and analysis than I have been able to provide. And many other figures might have been included. For example, none of the major scholars in the development of the academic discipline of Buddhist Studies are discussed, despite their great importance in the formation of popular conceptions of Buddhism. And many of the more recent leaders of modern Buddhism deserve study. The present work seeks more modestly to offer a small sample of the remarkable group of men and women whose works and lives – some peripherally, some directly – have created a form of Buddhism that is both so new, and so familiar.

NOTES

1. *A Full Account of the Buddhist Controversy, held at Pantura, in August, 1873. By the 'Ceylon Times' Special Reporter: with the Addresses Revised and Amplified by the Speakers* (Colombo: Ceylon Times Office, 1873), p. 2.
2. For a detailed study of the debate, its antecedents and aftermath, see R. F. Young and G. P. V. Somaratna, *Vain Debates: The Buddhist–Christian Controversies of Nineteenth-Century Ceylon* (Vienna: de Nobili Research Library, 1996).
3. *A Full Account of the Buddhist Controversy, held at Pantura, in August, 1873,* pp. 10–11.
4. Ibid., p. 13.
5. Ibid., pp. 2–3.
6. Cited in Stephen Prothero, *The White Buddhist: The Asian Odyssey of Henry Steel Olcott* (Bloomington: Indiana University Press, 1996), p. 96.
7. This description of Chinese Buddhism is drawn from what remains the

standard work on the subject: Holmes Welch, *The Buddhist Revival in China* (Cambridge, Mass.: Harvard University Press, 1968).

8. The biography of the Venerable Voramai Kabilsingh was drawn from Chatsumarn Kabilsingh, 'Voramai Kabilsingh' in *Spring Wind: Buddhist Cultural Forum*, vol. 6, nos. 1—3: pp. 202—9.

9. On the debates over clerical marriage, see Richard Jaffe, *Neither Monk Nor Layman: Clerical Marriage in Modern Japanese Buddhism* (Princeton, NJ: Princeton University Press, 2001).

10. On Meiji policies regarding Buddhism and Buddhist responses, see Richard Jaffe, *Neither Monk Nor Layman: Clerical Marriage in Modern Japanese Buddhism* (Princeton, NJ: Princeton University Press, 2001); James Edward Ketelaar, *Of Heretics and Martyrs in Meiji Japan* (Princeton, NJ: Princeton University Press, 1990); and Brian Victoria, *Zen at War* (New York: Weatherhill, 1997).

11. Shokin Furuta, 'Shaku Sōen: The Footsteps of a Modern Japanese Zen Master' in *The Modernization of Japan*, a Special Edition in the Philosophical Studies of Japan series, vol. 7 (Tokyo: Japan Society for the Promotion of Science, 1967), p. 76. The biography of Sōen presented here is drawn largely from this source.

12. See Robert Sharf, 'The Zen of Japanese Nationalism' in Donald S. Lopez, Jr (ed.), *Curators of the Buddha: The Study of Buddhism Under Colonialism* (Chicago: University of Chicago Press, 1995), pp. 107—60.

13. On Yasutani and his influence, see Robert Sharf, 'Sanbokyodan: Zen and Way of the New Religions,' *Japanese Journal of Religious Studies* 22, 3—4 (Autumn 1995): pp. 417—58.

14. Dge 'dun chos 'phel, *Rgya gar gyi gnas chen khag la bgrod pa'i lam yig* (*Guide to the Holy Places of India*) in Hor khang bsod nams dpal 'bar (ed.), *Dge 'dun chos 'phel gyi gsung rtsom*, vol. 2 (Gang can rig mdzod 12; Lhasa: Bod ljongs bod yig dpe rnying dpe skrun khang, 1990), p. 319.

15. Henry S. Olcott, *The Buddhist Catechism*, 44th edition (Adyar, India: Theosophical Publishing House, 1947), p. xii. It is important to note that Gunananda, who had fallen out with Olcott over matters both financial and ideological, wrote his own 'catechism' in 1887 (see Young and Somaratna, pp. 206—9). Gunananda particularly objected to Olcott's condemnation of traditional forms of Buddhist devotion. In 1888 he denounced Theosophy as a heresy and a threat to Buddhism (see Young and Somaratna, p. 212).

16. Christmas Humphreys, *Buddhism*, 3rd edition (London: Penguin, 1962), p. i.

Madame Blavatsky

Helena Petrovna Blavatsky (1831–91) was a founder and the most famous figure of the Theosophical Society. She was born in the Ukraine to an aristocratic family, the daughter of a military officer and a well-known novelist. She was largely self-educated. After a failed marriage, she arrived eventually in New York in 1873. Two years later she and Henry Steel Olcott founded the Theosophical Society, an organization which played a prominent role in the introduction of Asian religions to Europe and America.

Madame Blavatsky claimed to have fought with Garibaldi in Italy and to have spent seven years in Tibet studying with masters whom she called 'mahatmas', preservers of an ancient wisdom that provided the foundation for all mystical traditions. She remained in telepathic communication with these masters throughout her life. After attempts at alliances with various Asian teachers in India, Madame Blavatsky concluded that the modern manifestations of Hinduism and Buddhism had drifted far from their original essence; she devoted much of her voluminous writings to expounding the true teaching, which she sometimes referred to as 'Esoteric Buddhism'.

Her magnum opus is *The Secret Doctrine* (1888). There, claiming to be commenting upon the ancient *Book of Dzyan*, written in the secret language of Senzar, she describes a system of seven rounds, seven root races and seven sub-races. According to her description, the Earth has passed through three rounds during which it has evolved from a spiritual form to its current material form. We are currently in the fourth round. Over the final three rounds it will slowly return to its spiritual form. The universe is populated by individual souls, or monads, themselves ultimately identical with the universal 'over-soul'. These monads are reincarnated according to the law of karma.

This theory of spiritual evolution was presented more poetically in a subsequent work, entitled *The Voice of the Silence* (1889). Madame Blavatsky presented it as a translation of a work, also written in the Senzar language, that she had studied in Tibet under the mahatmas. Despite persistent attempts by her followers, the original text has not been discovered and a language called Senzar has not been identified. None the less, *The Voice of the Silence* has been considered as a Buddhist text by such prominent figures as D. T. Suzuki and Christmas Humphreys, who included a selection from it in his 1960 anthology, *The Wisdom of Buddhism*. The passage below gives a good sense of the style and content of Madame Blavatsky's work, the verses being presented as her translation from the Senzar, augmented with her own notes, which reveal both her wide reading and her idiosyncratic vision.

Before thou standest on the threshold of the Path; before thou crossest the foremost Gate, thou hast to merge the two into the One and sacrifice the personal to SELF impersonal, and thus destroy the 'path' between the two – *Antaskarana*.★

Thou hast to be prepared to answer Dharma, the stern law, whose voice will ask thee at thy first, at thy initial step:

'Hast thou complied with all the rules, O thou of lofty hopes?'

'Hast thou attuned thy heart and mind to the great mind and heart of all mankind? For as the sacred River's roaring voice whereby all Nature-sounds are echoed back,† so must the heart of him "who in

★ *Antaskarana* is the lower *Manus*, the Path of communication of communion between the personality and the higher *Manus* or human soul. At death it is destroyed as a Path or medium of communication, and its remains survive in a form as the *Kamarupa* – the 'shell.'
† The Northern Buddhists, and all Chinamen, in fact, find in the deep roar of some of the great and sacred rivers the key-note of Nature. Hence the simile. It is a well-known fact in Physical Science, as well as in Occultism, that the aggregate sound of Nature – such as heard in the roar of great rivers, the noise produced by the waving tops of trees in large forests, or that of a city heard at a distance – is a definite single tone of quite an appreciable pitch. This is shown by physicists and musicians. Thus Prof. Rice (*Chinese Music*) shows that the Chinese recognized the fact thousands of years ago by saying that

the stream would enter," thrill in response to every sigh and thought of all that lives and breathes.'

Disciples may be likened to the strings of the soul-echoing *Vina*; mankind, unto its sounding board; the hand that sweeps it to the tuneful breath of the GREAT WORLD-SOUL. The string that fails to answer 'neath the Master's touch in dulcet harmony with all the others, breaks – and is cast away. So the collective minds of *Lanoo-Sravakas*. They have to be attuned to the Upadya's mind – one with the Over-Soul – or, break away.

Thus do the 'Brothers of the Shadow' – the murderer of their Souls, the dread Dad-Dugpa clan.*

Hast thou attuned thy being to Humanity's great pain, O candidate for light?

Thou hast? . . . Thou mayest enter. Yet, ere thou settest foot upon the dreary Path of sorrow, 'tis well thou should'st first learn the pitfalls on thy way.

Armed with the key of Charity, of love and tender mercy, thou art secure before the gate of Dâna, the gate that standeth at the entrance of the PATH.

Behold, O happy Pilgrim! The portal that faceth thee is high and wide, seems easy of access. The road that leads therethrough is straight and smooth and green. 'Tis like a sunny glade in the dark forest depths,

---

'the waters of the Hoang-ho rushing by, intoned the *kung*' called 'the great tone' in Chinese music; and he shows this tone corresponding with the F, 'considered by modern physicists to be the actual tonic of Nature.' Professor B. Silliman mentions it, too, in his *Principles of Physics*, saying that 'this tone is held to be the middle F of the piano; which may, therefore, be considered the key-note of Nature.'

* The *Bhons* or *Dugpas*, the sect of the 'Red Caps,' are regarded as the most versed in sorcery. They inhabit Western and little Tibet and Bhutan. They are all Tantrikas. It is quite ridiculous to find Orientalists who have visited the borderlands of Tibet, such as Schlagintweit and others, confusing the rites and disgusting practices of these with the religious beliefs of the Eastern Lamas, the 'Yellow Caps', and their *Narjols* or holy men. The following is an instance.

a spot on earth mirrored with Amitabha's paradise. There, nightingales of hope and birds of radiant plumage sing perched in green bowers, chanting success to fearless Pilgrims. They sing of Bôdhisattvas; virtues five, the fivefold source of Bodhi power, and of the seven steps in Knowledge.

Pass on! For thou hast brought the key; thou art secure.

And to the second gate the way is verdant too. But it is steep and winds up hill; yea, to its rocky top. Grey mists will over-hang its rough and stony height, and all be dark beyond. As on he goes, the song of hope soundeth more feeble in the pilgrim's heart. The thrill of doubt is now upon him; his step less steady grows.

Beware of this, O candidate! Beware of fear that spreadeth, like the black and soundless wings of midnight bat, between the moonlight of thy Soul and thy great goal that loometh in the distance far away.

Fear, O disciple, kills the will and stays all action. If lacking in the Shîla virtue, – the pilgrim trips, and Karmic pebbles bruise his feet along the rocky path.

Be of sure foot, O candidate. In Kshanti's* essence bathe thy Soul; for now though dost approach the portal of that name, the gate of fortitude and patience.

Close not thine eyes, nor lose thy sight of Dorje;† Mara's arrows ever smite the man who has not reached Virâga.‡

* Kshanti, 'patience', *vide supra* the enumeration of the golden keys.
† *Dorje* is the Sanskrit *Vajra*, a weapon or instrument in the hands of some gods (the Tibetan *Dragshed*, the *Devas* who protect men), and is regarded as having the same occult power of repelling evil influences by purifying the air as Ozone in chemistry. It is also a *Mudra*, a gesture and posture used in sitting for meditation. It is, in short, a symbol of power over invisible evil influences, whether as a posture or a talisman. The *Bhons* or *Dugpas*, however, having appropriated the symbol, misuse it for purposes of Black Magic. With the 'Yellow Caps', or *Gelugpas*, it is a symbol of power, as the Cross is with the Christians, while it is in no way more 'superstitious'. With the *Dugpas*, it is like the *double triangle reversed*, the sign of sorcery.
‡ *Virâga* is that feeling of absolute indifference to the objective universe, to pleasure and to pain. 'Disgust' does not express its meaning, yet it is akin to it.

Beware of trembling. 'Neath the breath of fear the key of Kshanti rusty grows: the rusty key refuseth to unlock.

The more thou dost advance, the more thy feet pitfalls will meet. The path that leadeth on, is lighted by one fire – the light of daring, burning in the heart. The more one dares, the more he shall obtain. The more he fears, the more that light shall pale – and that alone can guide. For as the lingering sunbeam, that on the top of some tall mountain shines, is followed by the black night when out it fades, so is heart-light. When out it goes, a dark and threatening shade will fall from thine own heart upon the path, and root thy feet in terror on the spot.

Beware, disciple, of that lethal shade. No light that shines from Spirit can dispel the darkness of the nether Soul, unless all selfish thought has fled therefrom, and that the pilgrim saith: 'I have renounced this passing frame; I have destroyed the cause: the shadows cast can, as effects, no longer be.'

H. P. Blavatsky, *The Voice of the Silence* (Pasadena, CA: Theosophical University Press, 1971), pp. 50–54.

Sir Edwin Arnold

Sir Edwin Arnold (1832–1904) was educated at Oxford. He served as principal of a government college in Pune, India, from 1856–61, during which time he studied Indian languages and published a translation from the Sanskrit. Upon his return to England, he became a writer for the *Daily Telegraph* and was appointed chief editor in 1873. It was during his time at the *Daily Telegraph* that he wrote his most famous work, *The Light of Asia*. After leaving his editorial position, he travelled widely in Asia, especially in Japan, and published popular accounts of his travels. He is not remembered as a great poet; *The Dictionary of National Biography* states: 'Somewhat insensitive to the finer kinds of metrical effect, he is as a poet over-sensuous, and at times allows his glowing imagery to vitiate his taste.'

Yet, anyone in England or America with an interest in Buddhism one hundred years ago would have read *The Light of Asia*, a work largely forgotten today. First published in 1879, it has gone through more than one hundred editions in English, and has been translated into many languages. Although arousing animosity in many pulpits, it was a favourite of Queen Victoria, who nominated its author to be poet laureate. Her nomination was opposed by Gladstone, and Arnold was knighted instead.

The Light of Asia is a poetic rendering of the life of the Buddha, in blank verse. Arnold used as his chief source a French translation of one of the more ornate Indian biographies of the Buddha, entitled the *Lalitavistara*. But Arnold added his own embellishments, as the extract below demonstrates. In the passage below, Prince Siddhartha has just returned from his final chariot ride into the city, having discovered, after years of a sheltered existence in an opulent palace, that all beings are subject to old age, sickness and death. In traditional accounts he seeks comfort that night in his harem, but as his beautiful courtesans fall asleep in all manner of indecorous poses, he finds that he is now disgusted by the female body and decides to renounce the world. This scene has provided Buddhist authors with an occasion to describe the female form in intimate detail, while condemning its deceptive nature.

Arnold uses the scene differently, presenting the purdah as an abode of only beauty; the courtesans are asleep, but they retain their grace. As the prince passes by, each woman is more beautiful than the last, culminating in his own wife, the Princess Yasodhara. She tells him of three ominous dreams, portending that something wondrous is about to occur, but that her husband shall leave her. The prince then confesses that he must set out to save the world for the sake of all beings, that he must extend his love and care from her, and from their unborn son, to the entire universe.

In most accounts of the life of the Buddha, the princess is also sleeping when Siddhartha creeps into her chamber. Fearing that should he rouse her from her sleep, he will lose his resolve to leave the palace and renounce the world, he does not awaken her. But Arnold uses the occasion of the departure for extended speeches by the loving couple, with the prince displaying his nobility by sacrificing his throne, his palace, 'and thine arms, sweet Queen!/ Harder to put aside than all the rest!' in order to save the world.

> Half risen from her soft nest at his side,
> The chuddah fallen to her waist, her brow
> Laid in both palms, the lovely Princess leaned
> With heaving bosom and fast falling tears.
> Thrice with her lips she touched Siddârtha's hand,
> And at the third kiss moaned: 'Awake, my Lord!
> Give me the comfort of thy speech!' Then he –
> 'What is with thee, O my life?' but still
> She moaned anew before the words would come:
> Then spake: 'Alas, my Prince! I sank to sleep
> Most happy, for the babe I bear of thee
> Quickened this eve, and at my heart there beat
> That double pulse of life and joy and love
> Whose happy music lulled me, but – aho! –

In slumber I beheld three sights of dread,
With thought whereof my heart is throbbing yet.
I saw a white bull with wide branching horns,
A lord of pastures; pacing through the streets,
Bearing upon his front a gem which shone
As if some star had dropped to glitter there,
Or like the kantha-stone the great Snake keeps
To make bright daylight underneath the earth.
Slow through the streets toward the gates he paced,
And none could stay him, though there came a voice,
From Indra's temple, "If ye stay him not,
The glory of the city goeth forth."
Yet none could stay him. Then I wept aloud,
And locked my arms about his neck, and strove,
And bade them bar the gates; but that ox-king
Bellowed, and, lightly tossing free his crest,
Broke from my clasp, and bursting through the bars,
Trampled the warders down and passed away.
The next strange dream was this: Four Presences
Splendid with shining eyes, so beautiful
They seemed the Regents of the Earth who dwell
On Mount Sumeru, lighting from the sky
With retinue of countless heavenly ones,
Swift swept unto our city, where I saw
The golden flag of Indra on the gate
Flutter and fall; and lo! there rose instead
A glorious banner, all the folds whereof
Rippled with flashing fire of rubies sewn
Thick on the silver threads, the rays wherefrom
Set forth new words and weighty sentences
Whose message made all living creatures glad;
And from the east the wind of sunrise blew
With tender waft, opening those jewelled scrolls
So that all flesh might read; and wondrous blooms –
Plucked in what clime I know not – fell in showers,
Coloured as none are coloured in our groves.'

Then spake the Prince: 'All this, my Lotus-flower!
Was good to see.'

    'Ay Lord,' the Princess said,
'Save that it ended with a voice of fear
Crying, "The time is nigh! the time is nigh!"
Thereat the third dream came; for when I sought
Thy side, sweet Lord! ah, on our bed there lay
An unpressed pillow and an empty robe –
Nothing of thee but those! – nothing of thee,
Who art my life and light, my king, my world!
And sleeping still I rose, and sleeping saw
Thy belt of pearls, tied here below my breasts,
Change to a stinging snake; my ankle-rings
Fall off, my golden bangles part and fall;
The jasmines in my hair wither to dusk;
While this our bridal-couch sank to the ground,
And something rent the crimson purdah down;
Then far away I heard the white bull low,
And far away the embroidered banner flap,
And once again that cry, "The time is come!"
But with that cry – which shakes my spirit still –
I woke! O Prince! what may such visions mean
Except I die, or – worse than any death –
Thou shouldst forsake me or be taken?'

    Sweet
As the last smile of sunset was the look
Siddârtha bent upon his weeping wife.
'Comfort thee, dear!' he said, 'if comfort lives
In changeless love; for though thy dreams may be
Shadows of things to come, and though the gods
Are shaken in their seats, and though the world
Stands nigh, perchance, to know some way of help,
Yet, whatsoever fall to thee and me,

Be sure I loved and love Yasôdhara.
Thou knowest how I muse these many moons,
Seeking to save the sad earth I have seen;
And when the time comes, that which will be will.
But if my soul yearns sore for souls unknown,
And if I grieve for griefs which are not mine,
Judge how my high-winged thoughts must hover here
O'er all these lives that share and sweeten mine –
So dear! and thine the dearest, gentlest, best,
And nearest. Ah, thou the mother of my babe!
Whose body mixed with mine for this fair hope,
When most my spirit wanders, ranging round
The lands and seas – as full of ruth for men
As the far-flying dove is full of ruth
For her twin nestlings – ever it has come
Home with glad wing and passionate plumes to thee,
Who art the sweetness of my kind best seen,
The utmost of their good, the tenderest
Of all their tenderness, mine most of all.
Therefore, whatever after this betide,
Bethink thee of that lordly bull which lowed,
That jewelled banner in thy dreams which waved
Its folds departing, and of this be sure,
Always I loved and always love thee well,
And what I sought for all sought most for thee.
But thou, take comfort; and, if sorrow falls,
Take comfort still in deeming there may be
A way of peace on earth by woes of ours;
And have with this embrace what faithful love
Can think of thanks or frame for benison –
Too little, seeing love's strong self is weak –
Yet kiss me on the mouth, and drink these words
From heart to heart therewith, that thou mayst know –
What others will not – that I loved thee most
Because I loved so well all living souls.
Now, Princess! rest, for I will rise and watch.'

Then in her tears she slept, but sleeping sighed –
As if that vision passed again – 'The time!
The time is come!' Whereat Siddârtha turned,
And, lo! the moon shone by the Crab! the stars
In that same silver order long foretold
Stood ranged to say: 'This is the night! – choose thou
The way of greatness or the way of good:
To reign a King of kings, or wander lone,
Crownless and homeless, that the world be helped.'
Moreover, with the whispers of the gloom
Came to his ears again that warning song,
As when the Devas spoke upon the wind:
And surely gods were round about the place
Watching our Lord who watched the shining stars.
'I will depart,' he spake; 'the hour is come!
Thy tender lips, dear sleeper, summon me
To that which saves the earth but sunders us;
And in the silence of yon sky I read
My fated message flashing. Unto this
came I, and unto this all nights and days
Have led me; for I will not have that crown
Which may be mine: I lay aside those realms
Which wait the gleaming of my naked sword:
My chariot shall not roll with bloody wheels
From victory to victory, till earth
Wears the red record of my name. I choose
To tread its path with patient, stainless feet,
Making its dust my bed, its loneliest wastes
My dwelling, and its meanest things my mates:
Clad in no prouder garb than outcasts wear,
Fed with no meats save what the charitable
Give of their will, sheltered by no more pomp
Than the dim cave lends or the jungle-bush.
This will I do because the woful cry
Of life and all flesh living cometh up

Into my ears, and all my soul is full
Of pity for the sickness of this world;
Which I will heal, if healing may be found
By uttermost renouncing and strong strife.
For which of all the great and lesser gods
Have power or pity? Who hath seen them – who?
What have they wrought to help their worshippers?
How hath it steaded man to pray, and pay
Tithes of the corn and oil, to chant the charms,
To slay the shrieking sacrifice, to rear
The stately fane, to feed the priests, and call
On Vishnu, Shiva, Surya, who save
None – not the worthiest – from the griefs that teach
Those litanies of flattery and fear
Ascending day by day, like wasted smoke?
Hath any of my brothers 'scaped thereby
The aches of life, the stings of love and loss,
The fiery fever and the ague-shake,
The slow, dull sinking into withered age,
The horrible dark death – and what beyond
Waits – till the whirling wheel comes up again,
And new generations for the new desires
Which have their end in the old mockeries?
Hath any of my tender sisters found
Fruit of the fast or harvest of the hymn,
Or brought one pang the less at bearing-time
For white curds offered and trim tulsi-leaves?
Nay; it may be some of the gods are good
And evil some, but all in action weak;
Both pitiful and pitiless, and both –
As men are – bound upon this wheel of change,
Knowing the former and after lives.
For so our scriptures truly seem to teach,
that – once, and wheresoe'er, and whence begun –
Life runs its rounds of living, climbing up
From mote, and gnat, and worm, reptile, and fish,

Bird and shagged beast, man, demon, Deva, God,
To clod and mote again; so are we kin
To all that is; and thus, if one might save
Man from his curse, the whole wide world should share
The lightened horror of his ignorance
Whose shadow is chill fear, and cruelty
Its bitter pastime. Yea, if one might save!
And means must be! There must be refuge! Men
Perished in winter-winds till one smote fire
From flint-stones coldly hiding what they held,
The red spark treasured from the kindling sun.
They gorged on flesh like wolves, till one sowed corn,
Which grew a weed, yet makes the life of man;
They mowed and babbled till some tongue struck speech,
And patient fingers framed the lettered sound.
What good gift have my brothers but it came
From search and strife and loving sacrifice?
If one, then, being great and fortunate,
Rich, dowered with health and ease, from birth designed
To rule – if he would rule – a King of kings;
If one, not tired with life's long day, but glad
I' the freshness of its morning, one not cloyed
With love's delicious feasts, but hungry still;
If one not worn and wrinkled, sadly sage,
But joyous in the glory and the grace
That mix with evils here, and free to choose
Earth's loveliest at his will: one even as I,
Who ache not, lack not, grieve not, save with griefs
Which are not mine, except as I am man; –
If such a one, having so much to give,
Gave all, laying it down for love of men.
And thenceforth spent himself to search for truth,
Wringing the secret of deliverance forth,
Whether it lurk in hells or hide in heavens,
Or hover, unrevealed, nigh unto all:
Surely at last, far off, sometime, somewhere,

The veil would lift for his deep-searching eyes,
The road would open for his painful feet,
That should be won for which he lost the world,
And Death might find him conqueror of death.
This will I do, who have a realm to lose,
Because I love my realm, because my heart
Beats with each throb of all the hearts that ache,
Known and unknown, these that are mine and those
Which shall be mine, a thousand million more
Saved by this sacrifice I offer now.
Oh, summoning stars! Oh, mournful earth!
For thee and thine I lay aside my youth,
My throne, my joys, my golden days, my nights,
My happy palace – and thine arms, sweet Queen!
Harder to put aside than all the rest!
Yet thee, too, I shall save, saving this earth;
My child, the hidden blossom of our loves,
Whom if I wait to bless my mind will fail.
Wife! child! father! and people! ye must share
A little while the anguish of this hour
That light may break and all flesh learn the Law.
Now am I fixed, and now I will depart,
Never to come again till what I seek
Be found – if fervent search and strife avail.'

Sir Edwin Arnold, 'Book the Fourth' of *The Light of Asia* (Philadelphia: David McKay Company, n.d.), pp. 72–83.

Henry Steel Olcott

Colonel Henry Steel Olcott (1832–1907) was born in New Jersey to a Presbyterian family, but developed an interest in spiritualism during his twenties. He served in the Union Army during the American Civil War and subsequently was appointed to the commission that investigated the assassination of Lincoln. Working as a journalist in New York, he travelled to Vermont in 1874 to investigate paranormal events occurring in a farmhouse. While there he met the Russian émigré and spiritualist Helena Petrovna Blavatsky. Together they founded the Theosophical Society in New York in 1875, an organization that was responsible for bringing the teachings of the Buddha, at least as interpreted by the society, to a large audience in Europe and America.

With the aim of establishing links with Asian teachers, Blavatsky and Olcott travelled to India, arriving in Bombay in 1879 and proceeding to Ceylon the year after. Although they both took the vows of lay Buddhists (presumably the first European and American to do so), Blavatsky's interest remained primarily in Theosophy. Olcott, however, took to Buddhism wholeheartedly, feeling that it contained no dogma that he was compelled to accept. Shocked at what he perceived as the ignorance of the Sinhalese about their own religion, Olcott took it as his task to bring 'true' Buddhism back to Ceylon, founding lay and monastic branches of the Buddhist Theosophical Society to disseminate Buddhist knowledge and publishing in 1881 *The Buddhist Catechism*. His fame in Ceylon only increased in the following year when, in an attempt to counter the efforts of Catholic missionaries, he began performing psychic healings in the name of the Buddha. However, his relations with Buddhist leaders often proved difficult. They were alarmed at his rejection of traditional devotional practices and feared that he was appropriating their Buddhism into a universalist Theosophy.

In 1885 Olcott embarked on the even more ambitious project of attempting to unite the 'Northern and Southern Churches' of Buddhism to create a 'United Buddhist World' by persuading Buddhist leaders to accept his 'fourteen items of belief' (see the Introduction). Although these fourteen principles were soon forgotten, Olcott had established what would come to be accepted by many modern Buddhists, that Buddhism is, above all, a philosophical system. *The Buddhist Catechism*, in which he also attempted to capture the essence of Buddhism, had immediate success. Printed in some forty editions in twenty languages, it is still in use in schools in Sri Lanka today. In the extract below, Olcott lays out many of the characteristics of Buddhism as it was regarded by enthusiasts at the end of the nineteenth century (and which have become tenets of modern Buddhism): that it accords with science; that karma is a system of cosmic justice; that Buddhism rejects idolatry; and that the Buddhism practised in Asia is a corruption of the Buddha's true teachings.

158. Q. *How would a Buddhist describe true merit?*

A. There is no great merit in any merely outward act; all depends upon the inward motive that provokes the deed.

159. Q. *Give an example.*

A. A rich man may expend lakhs of rupees in building dāgobas or vihāras, in erecting statues of Buddha, in festivals and processions, in feeding priests, in giving alms to the poor, or in planting trees, digging tanks, or constructing rest-houses by the roadside for travellers, and yet have comparatively little merit if it be done for display, and to make himself praised by men, or for any other selfish motives. But he who does the least of these things with a kind motive, as from love for his fellow-men, gains great merit. A good deed done with a bad motive benefits others, but not the doer, One who approves of a good deed when done by another shares in the merit, *if his sympathy is real, not pretended*. The same rule as to evil deeds.

170. Q. *If we were to try to represent the whole spirit of the Buddha's doctrine by one word, which word would we choose?*

A. Justice.

171. Q. *Why?*

A. Because it teaches that every man gets, under the operations of unerring KARMA, exactly that reward or punishment which he has deserved, no more and no less. No good deed or bad deed, however trifling, and however secretly committed, escapes the evenly balanced scales of Karma.

172. Q. *What is Karma?*

A. A causation operating on the moral, as well as on the physical and other planes. Buddhists say there is no miracle in human affairs: what a man sows that he must and will reap.

179. Q. *Did the Buddha hold to idol-worship?*

A. He did not; he opposed it. The worship of gods, demons, trees, etc., was condemned by the Buddha. External worship is a fetter that one has to break if he is to advance higher.

180. Q. *But do not Buddhists make reverence before the statue to the Buddha, his relics, and the monuments enshrining them?*

A. Yes, but not with the sentiment of the idolater.

181. Q. *What is the difference?*

A. Our Pagan brother not only takes his images as visible representations of the unseen God or gods, but the refined idolater, in worshipping, considers that the idol contains in its substance a portion of the all-pervading divinity.

182. Q. *What does the Buddhist think?*

A. The Buddhist reverences the Buddha's statue and the other things you have mentioned, only as mementos of the greatest, wisest, most benevolent and compassionate man in this world-period (Kalpa). All races and people preserve, treasure up, and value the relics and mementos of men and women who have been considered in any way great. The Buddha, to us, seems more to be revered and beloved than any one else, by every human being who knows sorrow.

183. Q. *Has the Buddha himself given us something definite upon this subject?*

A. Certainly. In the *Mahā Pari-Nirvāna Sutta* he says that emancipation is attainable only by leading the Holy life, according to the Noble Eight-fold Path, not by external worship (*āmisa pūjā*), nor by adoration of himself, or another, or of any image.

184. Q. *What was the Buddha's estimate of ceremonialism?*

A. From the beginning, he condemned the observance of ceremonies and other external practices, which only tend to increase our spiritual blindness and our clinging to mere lifeless forms.

185. Q. *What as to controversies?*

A. In numerous discourses he denounced this habit as most pernicious. He described penances for Bhikkhus who waste time and weaken their higher intuitions in wrangling over theories and metaphysical subtleties.

186. Q. *Are charms, incantations, the observances of lucky hours, and devil-dancing a part of Buddhism?*

A. They are positively repugnant to its fundamental principles. They are the surviving relics of fetishism and pantheistic and other foreign religions. In the *Brahmajāla Sutta* the Buddha has categorically described these and other superstitions as Pagan, mean and spurious.*

187. Q. *What striking contrasts are there between Buddhism and what may be properly called 'religions'?*

A. Among others, these: It teaches the highest goodness without a creating God; a continuity of life without adhering to the superstitious and selfish doctrine of an eternal, metaphysical soul-substance that goes out of the body; a happiness without an objective heaven; a method of salvation without a vicarious Saviour; redemption by oneself as the Redeemer, and without rites, prayers, penances, priests or intercessory saints; and a *summum bonum*, i.e. Nirvāna, attainable in this life and in this world by leading a pure, unselfish life of wisdom and compassion to all beings.

190. Q. *Does popular Buddhism contain nothing but what is true and in accord with science?*

A. Like every other religion that has existed many centuries, it certainly now contains untruth mingled with truth; even gold is found mixed with dross. The poetical imagination, the zeal, or the lingering superstition of Buddhist devotees have, in various ages and in various lands, caused the noble principles of the Buddha's moral doctrines to be coupled more or less with what might be removed to advantage.

224. Q. *What is the spiritual status of woman among Buddhists?*

A. According to our religion they are on a footing of perfect equality with men. 'Women,' says the Buddha, in the *Chūlavedalla*

---

* The mixing of these arts and practices with Buddhism is a sign of deterioration. Their facts and phenomena are real and capable of scientific explanation. They are embraced in the term 'magic', but when resorted to for selfish purposes, attract bad influences about one, and impede spiritual advancement. When employed for harmless and beneficent purposes, such as healing the sick, saving life, etc., the Buddha permitted their use.

Sutta, 'may attain the highest path of holiness – Arhatship, that is open to man.'

225. Q. *What does a modern critic say about the effect of Buddhism on woman?*

A. That 'it has done more for the happiness and enfranchisement of woman than any other creed' (Sir Lepel Griffin).

279. Q. *As regards the number of its followers, how does Buddhism at this date compare with the other chief religions?*

A. The followers of the Buddha Dharma out-number those of every other religious teacher.

280. Q. *What is the estimated number?*

A. About five hundred millions (5,000 lakhs, or 500 crores): this is five-thirteenths, or not quite half, of the estimated population of the globe.

281. Q. *Have many great battles been fought and many countries conquered, has much human blood been spilt to spread the Buddha Dharma?*

A. History does not record one of those cruelties and crimes as having been committed to propagate our religion. So far as we know, it has not caused the spilling of a drop of blood [. . .]

282. Q. *What then, is the secret of its wonderful spread?*

A. It can be nothing else than its intrinsic excellence: its self-evident basis of truth, its sublime moral teaching, and its sufficiency for all human needs.

312. Q. *Why is it that Buddhism, which was once the prevailing religion throughout India, is now almost extinct there?*

A. Buddhism was at first pure and noble, the very teaching of the Tathāgata; its Sangha were virtuous and observed the Precepts; it won all hearts and spread joy through many nations, as the morning light sends life through the flowers. But after some centuries, bad Bhikkhus got ordination (*Upasampadā*), the Sangha became rich, lazy, sensual, the Dharma was corrupted, and the Indian nations abandoned it.

313. Q. *Did anything happen about the ninth or tenth century AD to hasten its downfall?*

A. Yes.

314. Q. *Anything besides the decay of spirituality, the corruption of the Sangha, and the reaction of the populace from a higher ideal of man to unintelligent idolatry?*

A. Yes. It is said that the Musalmāns invaded, overran and conquered large areas of India, everywhere doing their utmost to stamp out our religion.

315. Q. *What cruel acts are they charged with doing?*

A. They burnt, pulled down or otherwise destroyed our vihāras, slaughtered our Bhikkhus, and consumed with fire our religious books.

316. Q. *Was our literature completely destroyed in India?*

A. No. Many Bhikkhus fled across the borders into Tibet and other safe places of refuge, carrying their books with them.

317. Q. *Have any traces of these books been recently discovered?*

A. Yes. Rai Bahādur Sarat Chandra Dās, CIE, a noted Bengali pandit, saw hundreds of them in the vihāra libraries of Tibet, brought copies of some of the most important back with him, and is now employed by the Government of India in editing and publishing them.

322. Q. *Are there signs that the Buddha Dharma is growing in favor in non-Buddhistic countries?*

A. There are. Translations of our more valuable books are appearing, many articles in reviews, magazines and newspapers are being published, and excellent original treatises by distinguished writers are coming from the press. Moreover, Buddhist and non-Buddhist lecturers are publicly discoursing on Buddhism to large audiences in Western countries. The Shin Shu sect of Japanese Buddhists have actually opened missions at Honolulu, San Francisco, Sacramento and other American places.

323. Q. *What two leading ideas of ours are chiefly taking hold upon the Western mind?*

A. Those of Karma and Re-incarnation. The rapidity of their acceptance is very surprising.

361. Q. *In what does our modern scientific belief support the theory of Karma, as taught in Buddhism?*

A. Modern scientists teach that every generation of men is the heir to the consequences of the virtues and the vices of the preceding generations not in the mass, as such, but in every individual case. Every one of us, according to Buddhism, gets a birth which represents the causes generated by him in an antecedent birth. This is the idea of Karma.

362. Q. *What says the Vāseṭṭha Sutta about the causation in Nature?*

A. It says: 'The world exists by cause; all things exist by cause; all beings are bound by cause.'

363. Q. *Does Buddhism teach the unchangeableness of the visible universe; our earth, the sun, the moon, the stars, the mineral, vegetable, animal and human kingdoms?*

A. No. It teaches that all are constantly changing, and all must disappear in course of time.

364. Q. *Never to reappear?*

A. Not so: the principle of evolution, guided by Karma, individual and collective, will evolve another universe with its contents, as our universe was evolved out of the Ākāsha.

365. Q. *Does Buddhism admit that man has in his nature any latent powers for the production of phenomena commonly called miracles?*

A. Yes; but they are natural, not supernatural. They may be developed by a certain system which is laid down in our sacred books, the *Visuddhi Mārga* for instance.

Henry S. Olcott, *The Buddhist Catechism*, 44th edition (Adyar, Madras: Theosophical Publishing House, 1947), pp. 37–8, 40–41, 43–5, 46, 55.

Paul Carus

Paul Carus (1852–1919) was born in Ilsenburg am Harz in Germany and educated at the University of Tübingen. He emigrated to America in 1884, settling in La Salle, Illinois, where he assumed the editorship of the Open Court Publishing Company and such journals as *The Open Court* and *The Monist*. He attended the World's Parliament of Religions in Chicago in 1893 and became friends with several of the Buddhist delegates, including Dharmapala of Ceylon and Shaku Sōen of Japan (see the Introduction). Carus was a proponent of what he called the 'Religion of Science', a faith believed to be purified of all superstition and irrationality, which, in harmony with science, would bring about solutions to all of the world's problems. He regarded the Buddha as a radical freethinker and 'the first prophet of the Religion of Science'.

In 1894 Carus published the fascinating *Gospel of Buddha According to Old Records*, an anthology of passages from Buddhist texts drawn from contemporary translations in English, French and German, making especial use of translations from the Pali by Thomas W. Rhys Davids, in addition to translations of the life of the Buddha from Chinese and Tibetan. The work was arranged like the Bible, with numbered chapters and verses, and a table at the end that listed parallel passages from the New Testament. *The Gospel of Buddha* was intended to point up the many agreements between Buddhism and Christianity, thereby bringing out 'that nobler Christianity which aspires to the cosmic religion of universal truth'. Carus was free in his manipulation of his sources, writing in the preface that he has rearranged, rendered freely and abbreviated selections to make them more accessible. In addition, he mentions how he has added several 'purely original additions' of his own creation. These include the opening passage of *The Gospel*, 'Rejoice at the glad tidings! Buddha, our Lord, has found the root of all evil. He has shown us the way of salvation.'

The Gospel would rank second only to Arnold's *The Light of Asia* in its influence. By 1915 it was in its thirteenth edition in English and had been translated into French, German, Dutch, Spanish, Chinese, Japanese and Urdu. Dharmapala advocated the text in Ceylon. Shaku Sōen had his disciple D. T. Suzuki translate it into Japanese, a translation that was eventually adopted for use at Tokyo Imperial University. Suzuki eventually came to study with Carus in La Salle, where he would spend eleven years performing a variety of services at the Open Court. Many of Suzuki's views on the compatibility of Buddhism and science and on the absence of ritual and the supernatural in Zen seem to stem from this period and from Carus.

Although remembered today for his *Gospel*, Carus wrote some seventy books and more than a thousand articles. His books include studies of Goethe, Schiller, Kant, Chinese thought, the foundations of mathematics and a history of the devil.

The preface is reproduced in full below. Here Carus makes clear his project to present Buddhism in its ideal form, free from the complications presented by the accretions of sects and history. His ultimate goal is to lead his readers to the Religion of Science, towards which both Buddhism and Christianity, when understood correctly, point the way. Carus's study of Buddhism inspired him to compose his own Buddhist texts, which he also included in *The Gospel*. Three of these are included below.

PREFACE

This booklet needs no preface for him who is familiar with the sacred books of Buddhism, which have been made accessible for the Western world by the indefatigable zeal and industry of scholars like Burnouf, Hodgson, Bigandet, Bühler, Foucaux, Senart, Weber, Fausböll, Alexander Csoma, Wassiljew, Rhys Davids, F. Max Müller, Childers, Oldenberg, Schiefner, Eitel, Beal, and Spence Hardy. To those not familiar with the subject it may be stated that the bulk of its contents is derived from the old Buddhist canon. Many passages, and indeed the most important ones, are literally copied from the translations of the original texts. Some are rendered rather freely in order to make them intelligible to the present generation. Others have been rearranged; still others are abbreviated. Besides the three introductory and the three concluding chapters there are only a few purely original additions, which, however, are neither mere literary embellishments nor deviations from Buddhist doctrines. They contain nothing but ideas for which prototypes can be found somewhere among the traditions of Buddhism, and have been added as elucidations of its main principles. For those who want to trace the Buddhism of this book back to its fountainhead a table of references has been added, which indicates as briefly as possible the main sources of the various chapters and points out the parallelisms with Western thought, especially in the Christian Gospels.

Buddhism, like Christianity, is split up into innumerable sects, and these sects not unfrequently cling to their sectarian tenets as being the main and most indispensable features of their religion. The present book follows none of the sectarian doctrines, but takes an ideal position upon which all true Buddhists may stand as upon a common ground. Thus the arrangement into harmonious and systematic form of this Gospel of Buddha, as a whole, is the main original feature of the book. Considering the bulk of its various details, however, it must be regarded as a mere compilation, and the aim of the compiler has been to treat his material about in the same way as he thinks that the author of the Fourth Gospel of the New Testament used the accounts of the life of Jesus of Nazareth. He has ventured to present the data of Buddha's life in the light of their religio-philosophical importance; he has cut out most of their apocryphal adornments, especially those in which the Northern traditions abound, yet he did not deem it wise to shrink from preserving the marvellous that appears in the old records, whenever its moral seemed to justify its mention; he only pruned the exuberance of wonder which delights in relating the most incredible things, apparently put on to impress, while in fact they can only tire. Miracles have ceased to be a religious test; yet the belief in the miraculous powers of the Master still bears witness to the holy awe of the first disciples and reflects their religious enthusiasm.

Lest the fundamental idea of Buddha's doctrines be misunderstood, the reader is warned to take the term 'self' in the sense in which Buddha uses it. The 'self' of man can be and has been understood in a sense to which Buddha would never have made any objection. Buddha denies the existence of 'self' as it was commonly understood in his time; he does not deny man's mentality, his spiritual constitution, the importance of his personality, in a word, his soul. But he does deny the mysterious ego-entity, the âtman, in the sense of a kind of soul-monad which by some schools was supposed to reside behind or within man's bodily and psychical activity as a distinct being, a kind of thing-in-itself, and a metaphysical agent assumed to be the soul.* This philosophical superstition, so common not only in India but all over the world, corresponds to man's habitual egotism in practical life; both are illusions growing out of the same root, which is the vanity fair of worldliness, inducing man to believe that the purpose of his life lies in his self. Buddha proposes to cut off entirely all thought of self, so that it will no longer bear fruit. Thus Buddha's Nirvâna is an ideal state, in which man's soul, after being cleansed from all selfishness and sin, has become a habitation of the truth, teaching him to distrust the allurements of pleasure and confine all his energies to attending to the duties of life.

Buddha's doctrine is no negativism. An investigation into the nature of man's soul shows that while there is no âtman or ego-identity, the very being of man consists in his karma, and his karma remains untouched by death and continues to live. Thus, by denying the existence of that which appears to be our soul and for the destruction of which in death we tremble, Buddha actually opens (as he expresses it himself) the door of immortality to mankind; and here lies the cornerstone of his ethics and also of the comfort as well as the enthusiasm which his religion imparts. Any one who does not see the positive aspect of Buddhism, will be unable to understand how it could exercise such a powerful influence upon millions and millions of people.

The present volume is not designed to contribute to the solution of historical problems. The compiler has studied his subject as well as he could under given circumstances, but he does not intend here to offer a scientific production. Nor is this book an attempt at popularizing the

---

* The translation of 'âtman' by 'soul', which implies that Buddha denied the existence of the soul, is extremely misleading.

Buddhist religious writings, nor at presenting them in a poetic shape. If this 'Gospel of Buddha' helps people to comprehend Buddhism better, and if in its simple style it impresses the reader with the poetic grandeur of Buddha's personality, these effects must be counted as incidental; its main purpose lies deeper still. The present book has been written to set the reader a-thinking on the religious problems of today. It presents a picture of a religious leader of the remote past with the view of making it bear upon the living present and become a factor in the formation of the future.

All the essential moral truths of Christianity are, in our opinion, deeply rooted in the nature of things, and do not, as is often assumed, stand in contradiction to the cosmic order of the world. They have been formulated by the Church in certain symbols, and since these symbols contain contradictions and come in conflict with science, the educated classes are estranged from religion. Now, Buddhism is a religion which knows of no supernatural revelation, and proclaims doctrines that require no other argument than the 'come and see'. Buddha bases his religion solely upon man's knowledge of the nature of things, upon provable truth. A comparison of Christianity with Buddhism will be a great help to distinguish in both the essential from the accidental, the eternal from the transient, the truth from the allegory in which it has found its symbolic expression. We are anxious to press the necessity of distinguishing the symbol and its meaning, between dogma and religion, between man-made formulas and eternal truth. This is the spirit in which we offer this book to the public, cherishing the hope that it will help to develop in Christianity not less than in Buddhism the cosmic religion of truth.

It is a remarkable fact that these two greatest religions of the world, Christianity and Buddhism, present so many striking coincidences in their philosophical basis as well as in the ethical applications of their faith, while their modes of systematizing them in dogmas are radically different. The strength as well as the weakness of original Buddhism lies in its philosophical character, which enabled a thinker, but not the masses, to understand the dispensation of the moral law that pervades the world. As such the original Buddhism has been called by Buddhists the little vessel of salvation, or Hinayâna; for it is comparable to a small boat on which a man may cross the stream of worldliness so as to reach the shore of Nirvâna. Following the spirit of a missionary propaganda, so natural to religious men who are earnest in their convictions, later Buddhists popularized Buddha's doctrines and made them accessible to the multitudes. It is true that they admitted many mythical and even fantastical notions, but they succeeded nevertheless in bringing its moral truths home to the people who could but incompletely grasp the philosophical meaning of Buddha's religion. They constructed, as they called it, a large vessel of salvation, the Mahâyâna, in which the multitudes would find room and could be safely carried over. Although the Mahâyâna unquestionably has its shortcomings, it must not be condemned offhand, for it serves its purpose. Without regarding it as the final stage of the religious development of the nations among which it prevails, we must concede that it resulted from an adaptation to their condition and has accomplished much to educate them. The Mahâyâna is a step forward in so far as it changes a philosophy into a religion and attempts to preach doctrines that were negatively expressed, in positive propositions.

Far from rejecting the religious zeal which gave rise to the Mahâyâna in Buddhism, we can still less join those who denounce Christianity on account of its dogmatology and mythological ingredients. Christianity is more than a Mahâyâna, and Christian dogmatology too had a mission in the religious evolution of mankind. Christianity is more than a large vessel fitted to carry over the multitudes of those who embark in it; it is a grand bridge, a Mahâsêtu, on which a child can safely cross the stream of selfhood and worldly vanity with the same safety as the sage. There is no more characteristic saying of Christ's than his words: 'Suffer little children to come unto me.'

A comparison of the many striking agreements between Christianity and Buddhism may prove fatal to a sectarian conception of Christianity, but will in the end only help to mature our insight into the essential nature of Christianity, and to elevate our religious convictions. It will bring out that nobler Christianity which aspires to be the cosmic religion of universal truth.

Let us hope that this Gospel of Buddha will serve both Buddhists and Christians as a help to penetrate further into the spirit of their faith, so as to see its full width, breadth and depth.

Above any Hinayâna, Mahâyâna, and Mahâsêtu is the Religion of Truth.

INTRODUCTION

I. Rejoice

Rejoice at the glad tidings! Buddha, our Lord, has found the root of all evil. He has shown us the way of salvation.

Buddha dispels the illusions of our minds and redeems us from the terrors of death.

Buddha, our Lord, brings comfort to the weary and sorrow-laden; he restores peace to those who are broken down under the burden of life. He gives courage to the weak when they would fain give up self-reliance and hope.

Ye that suffer from the tribulations of life, ye that have to struggle and endure, ye that yearn for a life of truth, rejoice at the glad tidings!

There is a balm for the wounded, and there is bread for the hungry. There is water for the thirsty, and there is hope for the despairing. There is light for those in darkness, and there is inexhaustible blessing for the upright.

Heal your wounds, ye wounded, and eat your fill, ye hungry. Rest, ye weary, and ye who are thirsty quench your thirst. Look up to the light, ye that sit in darkness; be full of good cheer, ye that are forlorn.

Trust in truth, ye that love the truth, for the kingdom of righteousness is founded upon earth. The darkness of error is dispelled by the light of truth. We can see our way and make firm and certain steps.

Buddha, our Lord, has revealed the truth.

The truth cures our diseases and redeems us from perdition; the truth strengthens us in life and in death; the truth alone can conquer the evils of error.

Rejoice at the glad tidings!

II. Samsâra and Nirvâna

Look about you and contemplate life!

Everything is transient and nothing endures. There is birth and death, growth and decay; there is combination and separation.

The glory of the world is like a flower: it stands in full bloom in the morning and fades in the heat of the day.

Wherever you look, there is a rushing and a pushing, an eager pursuit of pleasures, a panic flight from pain and death, a vanity fair, and the flames of burning desires. The world is full of changes and transformations. All is Samsâra.

Is there nothing permanent in the world? Is there in the universal turmoil no resting-place where your troubled heart can find peace? Is there nothing everlasting?

Is there no cessation of anxiety? Can the burning desires not be extinguished? When shall the mind become tranquil and composed?

Buddha, our Lord, was grieved at the ills of life. He saw the vanity of worldly happiness and sought salvation in the one thing that will not fade or perish, but will abide forever and ever.

Ye who long for life, know that immortality is hidden in transiency. Ye who wish for a happiness that contains not the seeds of disappointment or of regret, follow the advice of the great Master and lead a life of righteousness. Ye who yearn for riches, come and receive treasures that are eternal.

The truth is eternal; it knows neither birth nor death; it has no beginning and no end. Hail the truth, O mortals! Let the truth take possession of your souls.

The truth is the immortal part of mind. The possession of truth is wealth, and a life of truth is happiness.

Establish the truth in your mind, for the truth is the image of the eternal; it portrays the immutable; it reveals the everlasting; the truth gives unto mortals the boon of immortality.

Buddha is the truth; let Buddha dwell in your heart. Extinguish in your soul every desire that antagonizes Buddha, and in the end of your spiritual evolution you will become like Buddha.

That of your soul which cannot or will not develop into Buddha must perish, for it is mere illusion and unreal; it is the source of your error; it is the cause of your misery.

You can make your soul immortal by filling it with truth. Therefore become like unto vessels fit to receive the ambrosia of the Master's words. Cleanse yourselves of sin and sanctify your lives. There is no other way of reaching the truth.

Learn to distinguish between Self and Truth. Self is the cause of selfishness and the source of sin; truth cleaves to no self; it is universal and leads to justice and righteousness.

Self, that which seems to those who love their self as their being, is not the eternal, the everlasting, the imperishable. Seek not self, but seek the truth.

If we liberate our souls from our petty selves, wish no ill to others, and become clear as a crystal diamond reflecting the light of truth, what a radiant picture will appear in us mirroring things as they are, without the admixture of burning desires, without the distortion of erroneous illusion, without the agitation of sinful unrest.

He who seeks self must learn to distinguish between the false self and the true self. His ego and all his egotism are the false self. They are unreal illusions and perishable combinations. He only who identifies his self with the truth will attain Nirvâna; and he who has entered Nirvâna has attained Buddhahood; he has acquired the highest bliss; he has become that which is eternal and immortal.

All compound things shall be dissolved again, worlds will break to pieces and our individualities will be scattered; but the words of Buddha will remain forever.

The extinction of self is salvation; the annihilation of self is the condition of enlightenment; the blotting out of self is Nirvâna. Happy is he who has ceased to live for pleasure and rests in the truth. Verily his composure and tranquility of mind are the highest bliss.

Let us take our refuge in Buddha, for he has found the everlasting in the transient. Let us take our refuge in that which is the immutable in the changes of existence. Let us take our refuge in the truth that is established through the enlightenment of Buddha.

III. Truth the Saviour

The things of the world and its inhabitants are subject to change; they are products of things that existed before; all living creatures are what their past actions made them; for the law of cause and effect is uniform and without exceptions.

But in the changing things truth lies hidden. Truth makes things real. Truth is the permanent in change.

And truth desires to appear; truth longs to become conscious; truth strives to know itself.

There is truth in the stone, for the stone is here; and no power in the world, no God, no man, no demon, can destroy its existence. But the stone has no consciousness.

There is truth in the plant and its life can expand; the plant grows and blossoms and bears fruit. Its beauty is marvellous, but it has no consciousness.

There is truth in the animal; it moves about and perceives its surroundings; it distinguishes and learns to choose. There is consciousness, but it is not yet the consciousness of truth. It is a consciousness of self only.

The consciousness of self dims the eyes of the mind and hides the truth. It is the origin of error, it is the source of illusion, it is the germ of sin.

Self begets selfishness. There is no evil but what flows from self. There is no wrong but what is done by the assertion of self.

Self is the beginning of all hatred, of iniquity and slander, of impudence and indecency, of theft and robbery, of oppression and bloodshed. Self is Mâra, the tempter, the evil-doer, the creator of mischief.

Self entices with pleasures. Self promises a fairy's paradise. Self is the veil of Mâyâ, the enchanter. But the pleasures of self are unreal, its paradisian labyrinth is the road to hell and its fading beauty kindles the flames of desires that never can be satisfied.

Who shall loosen us from the power of self? Who shall save us from misery? Who shall restore us to the life of blessedness?

There is misery in the world of Samsâra; there is much misery and pain. But greater than all the misery is the bliss of truth. Truth gives peace to the yearning mind; it conquers error; it quenches the flames of desire and leads to Nirvâna.

Blessed is he who has found the peace of Nirvâna. He is at rest in the struggles and tribulations of life; he is above all changes; he is above birth and death; he remains unaffected by the evils of life.

Blessed is he who has become an embodiment of truth, for he has accomplished his purpose and is one with himself and truth. He conquers although he may be wounded; he is glorious and happy, although he may suffer; he is strong, although he may break down under the burden of his work; he is immortal, although he may die. The essence of his soul is immortality.

Blessed is he who has attained the sacred state of Buddhahood, for he is fit to work out the salvation of his fellow-beings. The truth has made its abode in him. Perfect wisdom illumines his understanding, and righteousness ensouls the purpose of all his actions.

The truth is a living power for good, indestructible and invincible! Work the truth out in your mind, and spread it among mankind, for Truth alone is the saviour from sin and misery. The Truth is Buddha, and Buddha is the Truth! Blessed be Buddha!

Paul Carus, Preface and Introduction to *The Gospel of Buddha According to Old Records*, 2nd edition (Chicago: Open Court Publishing Company, 1895), pp. v–x, 1–6.

Shaku Sōen

Shaku Sōen (1859–1919) was ordained as a novice of the Rinzai Zen sect in Japan at the age of twelve. He studied at the famous Engakuji monastery in Kamakura, under the Rinzai master Imakita Kōsen (1816–92), one of the proponents of a more universal and socially engaged Buddhism during the Meiji period. He attended Keiō University and then travelled to Ceylon to study Pali and live as a Theravada monk. Upon his return, he became chief abbot of Engakuji in 1892. He gave instruction in Zen meditation to lay men and women, both in Kamakura and Tokyo. One of his students was D. T. Suzuki. In 1893 he was chosen to represent Zen at the World's Parliament of Religions in Chicago, his lecture having been translated into English by Suzuki. While in the US, he met Paul Carus and later arranged for Suzuki to work with Carus in La Salle, Illinois. After serving as Buddhist chaplain to the First Army Division during the Russo-Japanese War of 1904–5, Sōen embarked on a world tour, lecturing on Zen in Europe, America, India and Ceylon. He spent the remainder of his life lecturing extensively on Zen to lay audiences, not only in Japan but in the Japanese colonies of Taiwan, Korea and Manchuria. He served as president of Rinzai College of Hanazono University in Kyoto from 1914 to 1917, before returning as abbot of Engakuji. His 1906 *Sermons of a Buddhist Abbot* (published by Carus's press, Open Court) was the first book on Zen to appear in English.

Two of those sermons appear here, both delivered in Washington, DC, in 1906. In them, Sōen addresses topics essential to modern Buddhism in Japan in the early decades of the twentieth century. In the first, he argues that Mahayana Buddhism, especially as practised in Japan, is the most complete and perfect form of Buddhism. In the second, he declares the allegiance of Buddhism to the Japanese state.

WHAT IS BUDDHISM?
(Read before the National Geographic Society, Washington, DC, April, 1906)

It seems to be very appropriate and even necessary at the outset to draw a well-defined line of demarcation between what is understood as Hînayâna Buddhism and what is known as Mahâyâna Buddhism. Most people imagine that there is only one school of Buddhism and that that one school is no other than the Buddhism they have learned from the Buddhist books written or compiled or translated by Western Orientalists – Orientalists who are in many respects prejudiced against the doctrine which they propose to study most impartially. Owing to these unhappy circumstances, the outsiders are either generally ignorant or altogether misinformed of the true character of Buddhism. For what is understood by the Western people as Buddhism is no more than one of its main divisions, which only partially expresses the spirit of its founder.

I said here 'divisions', but it may be more proper to say 'stages of development.' For Buddhism, like so many other religions, has gone through several stages of development before it has attained the present state of perfection among the Oriental nations. And it will be evident to you that if we catch only a glimpse of an object and try to judge the whole from this transient impression, we place ourselves in a most awkward position, and shall be at a loss how to extricate ourselves from it. Therefore, let me try in the beginning to take a comprehensive view of the subject we here propose to expound.

Properly speaking, Hînayâna Buddhism is a phase of Mahâyâna Buddhism. The former is preparatory for the latter. It is not final, but merely a stepping stone which leads the walker to the hall of perfect truth. Hînayânism is therefore more or less pessimistic, ascetic, ethical (to be distinguished from religious), and monastical. It fails to give a complete satisfaction to a man's religious yearnings. It does not fully interpret the spirit of Buddha. The Buddhism now prevailing in Ceylon, Burma, and Siam may be considered to be betraying in a certain way a Hînayâna tendency.

The Buddhism of present Japan, on the other hand, is Mahâyânistic. It is more comprehensive, more religious, more humanistic, and more satisfying to the innermost needs of the religious consciousness. It cannot be said to be absolutely free from superstition, error, prejudice, etc., for it is a constantly growing, ever-living faith which knows no ossification or fossilization. Some pious people are apt to consider their religious belief to be absolutely fixed and unchanging since the dawn of human consciousness; but they have forgotten, in my opinion, the fact that the human mind is still keeping on unfolding itself, that it has not yet exhausted all its possibilities, that it is constantly coming to a clearer consciousness as to its own nature, origin, and destiny. But what I firmly believe is that in the Buddhism of Japan today are epitomized all the essential results reached through the unfolding of the religious consciousness during the past twenty or thirty centuries of Oriental culture.

In a word, what has been known in the West as the teaching of the Buddha does not represent it in its true, unadulterated color, for it is Hînayânistic in tendency; that is, it is exclusive and not comprehensive, narrow and limited, and not all absorbing and assimilating. What I propose to expound in this lecture tonight is the Mahâyâna Buddhism, so called by Buddhist scholars of the East.

Let me point out in this connection what is most characteristic of Buddhism as distinguished from any other religion. I refer to a predominant tendency of Buddhism toward intellectuality, and it seems to me that the reason why Buddhism is always ready to stand before the tribunal of science and let her pass a judgment upon its merits or demerits is due to this intellectual tenor. It goes without saying that the intellect does not constitute the most essential element of religion, but we must not forget that a religious system too much given up to sentimentalism (understanding it in its purely psychological sense) is generally prone to accede to unwarranted mysticism, ignoring altogether the legitimate claim of the intellect. Buddhism is fortunately saved from this grievous blunder, and always endeavors not to give a free rein to the wantonness of imagination and the irrationality of affection. Love without enlightenment excludes, discriminates, and contradicts itself. Love is not love unless it is purified in the mill of spiritual insight and intellectual discrimination.

What are, then, the fundamental teachings of Buddhism? I deem it best to consider it from two standpoints, ethical and philosophical, or practical and speculative, or affective and intellectual. The philosophical or speculative is preparative for the ethical or practical, for religion is not a system of metaphysics which plays with verbalism and delights in sophistry, but its aim is pre-eminently practical and spiritual. It must bear fruit in this our everyday life.

To begin with the metaphysical side of Buddhism:

1. We Buddhists believe that as far as phenomenality goes, things that exist are all separate and discrete, they are subject to the law of individuation and therefore to that of limitation also. All particular things exist in time and space and move according to the law of cause and effect, not only physically but morally. Buddhism does not, though sometimes understood by Western people to do so, advocate the doctrine of emptiness or annihilation. It most assuredly recognizes the multitudinousness and reality of phenomena. This world as it is, is real, not void. This life as we live it, is true, and not a dream.

2. We Buddhists believe that all these particular things surrounding us come from one ultimate source which is all-powerful, all-knowing, and all-loving. The world is the expression or manifestation of this reason or spirit or life, whatever you may designate it. However diverse, therefore, things are, they all partake of the nature of the ultimate being. Not only sentient beings, but non-sentient beings, reflect the glory of the Original Reason. Not only man but even the lower animals and inorganic substances manifest the divinity of their source. To use the Christian term, God, it★ is visible and audible not only in one of its highest manifestations, whom Christians call Jesus Christ, but also in the meanest and most insignificant piece of stone lying in a deserted field. God's splendor is seen not only in the Biblical lilies, but also in the mud and mire from which they grow. The melody of divine reason is heard not only in the singing of a bird or in the composition of an inspired musician, but also in the 'slums of life' as Emerson phrases it.

★ Let me remark here that it is not at all proper to refer to God, the ultimate source of everything, as masculine as is usually done. God is above sex. It is neither 'he' nor 'she'. Even 'it' is not appropriate, but will be preferable to the other pronouns.

3. This recognition of the oneness of things naturally leads to our third belief, that the one is the many and the many is the one. God does not dwell in the heavens. It does not direct its affairs in a closed office situated somewhere outside this world. It did not create heaven and earth out of nothingness. According to Buddhism, it is a serious error to seek God outside this life, outside this universe. It is living right among ourselves and directing the course of things according to its innate destiny. Though Buddhists refuse to have God walk out of us, they do not identify it with the totality of existence, they are not willing to cast their lot with pantheists so called. God is immanent, surely enough, but it is greater than the totality of things. For the world may pass away, the universe may be shaken out of its foundation, but God will remain and will create a new system out of the former ruins. The ashes of existence will never be scattered to the winds, but they will gather themselves in the ever designing hand of God and build themselves up to a new order of things, in which it is ever shining with its serene radiance.

To sum up the first part of this discourse, what may be called the metaphysical phase of Buddhism is to recognize: (1) the reality of the phenomenal world, (2) the existence of one ultimate reason, and (3) the immanence of this reason in the universe.

Now to come to the practical side of Buddhism: The aim of Buddhism, to state briefly, is to dispel the clouds of ignorance and to make shine the sun of enlightenment. We are selfish because we are ignorant as to the nature of self. We are addicted to the gratification of the passions, because we are ignorant as to the destiny of humanity. We are quarrelsome and want to make ourselves powerful and predominant at the expense of our fellow-beings, because we are ignorant of the ultimate reason of the universe. Buddhists do not recognize any original sin, but acknowledge the existence of ignorance, and insist on its total removal as the surest means of salvation. Let us, therefore, all be enlightened as to the statement made before. Let us know that we are all one in the reason of the universe, that the phenomenal world is real only to the extent it manifests reason, that egoism has no absolute sway in this life, for it destroys itself when it tries to preserve itself through its arrogant assertion, and that perfect peace is only attained when I recognize myself in you and you in me. Let us all be enlightened as to these things, and our ignorance and egoism are forever departed; the wall that divides is destroyed, and there is nothing which prevents us from loving our enemies; and the source of divine love is open in our hearts, the eternal current of sympathy has now found its unobstructed path. This is the reason why Buddhism is called the religion of enlightenment.

Now that we stand on this eminence of religious sanctity, we know what Buddhist practical faith is. It is threefold: (1) to cease from wrongdoing, (2) to promote goodness, and (3) to enlighten the ignorant. Buddhist ethics is the simplest thing to practice in the world. It has nothing mysterious, nothing superstitious, nothing idolatrous, nothing supernatural. Stop doing anything wrong, which is against the reason of things; do whatever is good, which advances the course of reason in this life; and finally help those who are still behind and weary of life to realize enlightenment: and here is Buddhism in a nutshell. It has nothing to do with prayer and worship and singing and what not. Our simple everyday life of love and sympathy is all that is needed to be a good Buddhist.

I was once asked whether there was such a thing as religious life particularly. To which my answer was simple enough: 'Attend to your daily business, do all you can for the promotion of goodness in this world, and out of fullness of heart help your fellow-beings to gain the path of enlightenment. Outside of this there cannot be anything to be specially called a religious life.'

In the latter part of the T'ang Dynasty in China, there was a famous poet-statesman who is known in Japanese as Hak-Rak-Ten. He learned that there resided in his district a Buddhist monk greatly noted for his saintly life and scholarly learning. The governor went to see him, intending to discuss some deeply religious topics. As soon as he was ushered into the presence of the monk, he inquired what was thought by the saint to be the most fundamental teaching of Buddhism. The monk immediately replied that it is the teaching of all enlightened ones to cease doing anything evil, to promote goodness, and to purify one's own heart.

Hak-Rak-Ten was nonplussed to receive such a commonplace instruction from the mouth of such a scholarly personage professing the faith of Buddha; for he secretly expected to have something highly metaphysical and profoundly speculative, which would naturally lead them to further philosophizing and contentless abstraction. The poet-statesman therefore retorted: 'This is what every child of three summers is familiar with. I desire on the other hand what is most abstruse, most essential, most vital in Buddhism.' The monk, however, coldly replied, 'Every child of three summers may know what I said now, but even a silvery-haired man of eighty winters finds it difficult to put the Buddhist instruction into the practice of everyday life.'

And it is said that thereupon the Governor reverentially bowed and went home wiser.

What is philosophical in Buddhism is no more than a preliminary step toward what is practical in it. Every religion, if it deserves the name, must be essentially practical and conducive to the promotion of the general welfare and to the realization of Reason. Though intellectualism is one of the most characteristic features of Buddhism, making it so distinct from any other religious system, it never forgets the fact that our religious consciousness ever demands something concrete, that which is visible to our senses, that which is observable in our everyday life. Religion does not necessarily consist in talking on such subjects as the continuation after death of individual personality, original sin committed by some mythical personages, the last judgment to be given by an unknown quantity, a special historical revelation which takes place in a congested brain, and what not. At least, practical Buddhism does not trouble itself with solving these problems through speculation or imagination or sophistry. Let those theologians who delight in abstraction and supernaturalism discuss them to their hearts' content, for that is their profession. We, plain ordinary Buddhists, will keep on removing selfishness, seeking the light that is everywhere, practising loving-kindness that does not contradict or discriminate. Says an ancient sage, 'The Way is near, and thou seekest it afar.' Why, then, shall we ever attempt to walk away from the path which extends right in front of us, so wide and well paved?

BUDDHISM AND ORIENTAL CULTURE
(Address at the George Washington University, April, 1906)

One of the features peculiar to Buddhism and which appeals most powerfully to Oriental imagination is that man's life is not limited to this existence only, that if he thinks, feels, and acts truthfully, nobly, virtuously, unselfishly, he will live forever in these thoughts, sentiments, and works; for anything good, beautiful, and true is in accordance with the reason of existence, and is destined to have a life eternal.

It is not the ideal of the Buddhist life to escape worldliness and to enter into eternal stillness, as is sometimes understood by Occidental scholars. Buddhists do not shun struggle and warfare. If a cause is worth contending for or defending, they will not hesitate to sacrifice for it not only this life but all of their future lives. They will appear upon this earth over and again and will not rest until they have gained the end, that is, until they have attained the ideal of life. Man, therefore, lives as long as his ideas and feelings conform to the reason of the universe. This is the Buddhist conception of life eternal.

If I am not mistaken, it was at the time of the Independence War, or it might have occurred somewhere in the Old Country – you will pardon my imperfect memory – but the fact is that a military officer who served as a spy for his native country was caught by the enemy and was sentenced to be hung. At the execution the officer exclaimed, 'The pity is that I have only one life to sacrifice for my country.' Pity indeed it was that the officer did not know the truth and fact that from his very corpse there have risen so many patriotic spirits breathing the same breath that he breathed. He was not dead, he was never hung, he did not vanish into an unknown region; but he is living a life eternal, he is being born generation after generation, not only in his own country, but also in my country, and in your country, and in fact all over the three thousand worlds (as they were believed to be existing in Hindu mythology).

In this respect a Buddhist general quite famous in the history of Japan had a decided advantage over the Christian officer just mentioned. The general is still worshipped in Japan as the type of loyalty and patriotism. He lived about six hundred years ago. Before the Emperor of the time came to know him, he was a rather obscure general and would have died without imprinting his immortal name on the pages of Japanese history. But Fate decreed otherwise, and he was requested by the Emperor to lead his royal army against the invading enemy, who greatly outnumbered his forces and was led by a very able general. Masashigé, which is the name of our hero, had his own plan as to how best to make a stand against the onslaught of the overwhelming enemy. But some ignorant court favorite influenced the Emperor and the hero's proposition could not prevail. He then knew he was going to fight a losing battle, but determined to do his best under the circumstances, if necessary to fight to the bitter end. At last came the day, and the enemy developed the plan as he had calculated. There was nothing for him to do but check the advance of the enemy as long as he could, so that the Emperor could find time enough to make his safe escape from the capital. He fought most gallantly, and repeatedly repulsed the furious attacks of the enemy. But many times outnumbered, and occupying a strategically disadvantageous position, and himself covered with many wounds, he saw the uselessness of further resistance. He then gathered his commanding generals around him and asked them if they had anything to desire in this life before they bid farewell to all things earthly. They replied that they had done everything within their power, their obligations were completely filled, and there was nothing more to be desired. But our hero, Masashigé, made a solemn utterance: 'I pray that I be born seven times on this earth and crush all enemies of our Imperial House.' They all then drew their daggers and put an end to their present lives.

I do not know how this story strikes you Christian audience, but upon us Buddhists it makes a very profound impression. It seems to be pregnant with a great religious significance. It is not altogether necessary to specify how many times we are to be reborn. Let us only have a thought or feeling that is worth preserving and actualizing, and we shall come to this life as many times as is necessary to complete the task, even to the end of the world. Let us only do what is in accordance with the reason of things, and the work, which is no more than the world-reason actualized, will create a new agency as needed through

successive generations. This corporeal existence, this particular tempo-
rary combination of feelings and thoughts and desires, may dissolve,
may not last forever as it is, for it is no more than an agent in the hands
of the world-soul to execute its own end. When it decrees that its agent
must put on a new garment, this will take place as it is willed. 'Let
there be light,' it commands, and behold there it is!

It is not Buddhistic, therefore, to hanker after personal immortality and to construct diversity of theories to satisfy this illegitimate
hankering. Do whatever you think right and be sincere with it and the
work will take care of itself, hankering or not hankering after immortality.

My Japanese hero gave an utterance to his inner feeling and conviction only to make his generals perfectly understand the significance of
his and their work. He did not mean to come to this life exactly seven
times, nor did he mean to continue his personal existence as he was
individually. He did mean this, that his work should find its new
executors in the form of a worshipper or an imitator or a successor or
a disciple or a friend, who would be inspired by that noble example.
And most certainly did he find a legion of his selves following closely
behind his back. Are not all loyal and patriotic soldiers and sailors who
died in the recent war with Russia all the incarnations of our most
beloved hero-general, Masashigé? Did he not find his selves in all those
brave, courageous, self-sacrificing hearts? Was he not leading in spirit
all these soldiers to the execution of the work he once planned? Who
says, then, that the hero breathed his last when he fought this losing
battle some six hundred years ago? Is he not indeed still living in the
heart of every patriotic and loyal citizen of Japan, nay, of any people
that aspires to be a nation?

When the late commander Hirosé went to blockade the entrance
to Port Arthur, he must have been inspired by the same sentiment
which he expressed in his swan song; he must have become conscious
of the immortality of the work in which he has thoroughly incarnated
himself. In his last utterance he put this in verse: 'Though I may die
here while executing this work, I will come back seven times over and
again to discharge my duties for my country. I have nothing to fear,
nothing to desire at the present moment. Calmly and smilingly I

embark on this fated boat.'* Can we not say here that the idea which was our long deceased hero himself, found its conscious expression in this brave Commander? Those who fell in the field and on the water were equally his incarnations, only with this difference that the former gave the utterance to his conscious sentiment, while the latter remained mute, though in their inmost hearts the same sentiment was moving. If otherwise, how could they enjoy that serene contentedness which characterized every stricken warrior of my country in the recent war?

Some may say that this is fatalism or determinism, but every clear-headed thinker would see in this not a fatalistic conception of life but a hopeful solution of existence, a firm belief in the final triumph of good over evil, and the calm assurance that the individual lives as long as it identifies itself with a noble thought, worthy work, exalted sentiment, uplifting impulse, in short, with anything that cements the brotherly tie of all mankind. Those who are used to look at things from the individualistic point of view may not understand very clearly what I have so far endeavored to explain to you; but the fact is, however tenaciously we may cling to our individual existences, we are utterly helpless when that which comprehends everything wills otherwise than our selfish desires; we have but to submit meekly to the ordinance of the unknown power and to let it work out its own destiny regardless of ourselves. When Schleiermacher defines religion as a feeling of absolute dependence, he has rightly laid his hand on that indefinable, uncertain sense which lurks in the dark recesses of every conscious mind – the sense which intuitively recognizes the weakness of individuals as such, but which feels an immense strength in their identification with a supra-individual being or power. In this, it must be evident to you, there is nothing fatalistic nor fantastic.

All sincere Buddhists are firmly convinced of the truth of non-egoism, and they do not think that the value of an individual as such is ultimate. On account of this, they are not at all disturbed at the moment of death; they calmly accept the ordinance and let the world-destiny accomplish what end it may have in view. This freedom from

* From memory.

the individualistic view of life seems to have largely contributed to the perfection of the Japanese military culture known as *Bushido*. Old Japanese soldiers, nobles, and men of letters, therefore, displayed a certain sense of playfulness even at the most critical moment when the question of life and death was to be decided without the least hesitation. This playfulness, as I view it, stands in marked contrast to the pious, prayerful attitude of the Christians in their dying moments.

Ota Dôkwan, a great Japanese statesman-general of some four hundred years ago, was assassinated in his own castle by a band of spies sent by his enemy. They surrounded him when he was altogether unarmed. He was stabbed, and he fell on the ground, covered with wounds and helpless. One of the assassins approached closer, and applying the dagger at the victim's throat to finish their cowardly work, he asked what the unfortunate general had to say before he bade farewell to this world. The general most calmly answered:

> 'At the moment like this
> It must be a struggle indeed
> To part with this life so dear,
> If I had not abandoned altogether
> The thought of ego, which is a non-reality.'

Finding peace of heart in this solution of life, Buddhists, whatever their social positions, are ever ready to sacrifice their lives for a cause which demands them. They know that the present individual existences will come to an end, they will not be able to see the faces dearest to them, to hear the voices tenderest to them, as they depart from this world; but they know at the same time that spiritually they live forever and are in constant communication with their friends, that they never lead a solitary, unconnected life in some invisible region. What Buddhism has contributed to Japanese culture is its higher conception of life and nobler interpretation of death.

Buddhists do not think that 'I' is 'I' and 'you' is 'you' when each of us is separated from the other. 'I' is possible when 'you' exists, so with 'you' who is possible through the existence of 'I.' This consideration is very important, as it constitutes one of the fundamental principles of

Buddhist ethics. For according to Buddhism an unconditional assertion of egoism is due to the ignorance of the significance of the individual. Most people imagine that the individual is a final reality, stands by itself, has nothing to do with other fellow-individuals; in fact their existence is tolerated only so far as it does not interfere with his own interests. They first build a formidable fort around individualism and look down at their surroundings, thinking that the position must be defended at all costs. For it is their conception of life that with the downfall of individualism the universe goes to pieces.

The Oriental mode of thinking, however, differs from this. We take our standpoint first on that which transcends individuals, or we take into our consideration first that which comprehends all finite things, that which determines the destiny of the universe; and then we come down into this world of relativity and conditionality, and believe that the earth will sooner or later pass away according to the will of that which controls it. That is to say, individuals will not stay here forever, though the whole which comprises individuals will. Therefore, Oriental ethics considers it of paramount importance to preserve the whole at all hazards, whatever may be the fate of individuals.

For instance, suppose my country is threatened by a powerful enemy, and I will, when called for, sacrifice everything personal and try to do my best for the conservation of my national honor and safety. This is what is called patriotism. My parents are old and they are not able to take care of themselves, and I will do everything for their comfort and alleviate the loneliness of their declining age. Did they not bring me up to this stage of manhood? Did they not go through all forms of hardship for my sake? Did they not care for me with infinite tenderness of heart? Do I not owe them all that I am today? Did they not help me to this position and enable me to do whatever is within my power for the welfare and preservation of the whole of which I belong? When I think of this, the feeling of gratitude weighs heavily on me, and I endeavor to be relieved of it by doing all acts of loving-kindness to my parents. This is what you call filial piety, and the same consideration will apply to the cases of teachers, elder people, friends, and family.

Whatever be the effects of Oriental ethics – and I think they are not a few – I firmly believe that what makes Oriental culture so unique is due to the emphasis laid upon patriotism, filial piety, faithfulness, and abnegation of self.

Before concluding, I wish to add a few more words as a Buddhist subject of Japan. All the world knows what Japan has achieved so far in the history of mankind, especially what she has accomplished in her gigantic struggle with a most powerful nation of Europe. There must have been many causes and conditions through a happy combination of which Japan was able to do what she has done; and among those conditions I would count the influences of American friendship and sympathy as one of the most powerful. If America had tried to play some high-handed diplomacy, imitating some of the European powers, she could have easily seized my country and held it under subjection since Commodore Perry's entrance into Uraga. The fact that the United States did not stoop to play a mean trick upon Japan helped not a little to lift her to the present position. For that reason, we, people of Japan, owe a great deal to you, people of the United States of America.

As a Buddhist I have been long thinking how best to repay this special favor received from the friendly people among whom I am traveling now. You have everything you need in the line of material, industrial, commercial civilization. By this I do not mean that you are wanting in spiritual culture and moral refinement, but I am inclined to think that it would not be altogether inappropriate to ask you to get more and more acquainted with what constitutes Oriental culture and religious belief. And it shall be my duty and pleasure to make such an opportunity of mutual understanding readily possible in every way. Accordingly, I thank you, ladies and gentlemen, for your efforts which have resulted in this enjoyable meeting with each other.

Soyen Shaku [Shaku Sōen], 'What is Buddhism' and 'Buddhism and Oriental Culture' in *Sermons of a Buddhist Abbot* (Chicago: Open Court Publishing Company, 1906), pp. 79–89, 170–81.

Dwight Goddard

Dwight Goddard (1861–1939) was born in Massachusetts and trained as a mechanical engineer. Following the death of his first wife, he enrolled at Hartford Theological Seminary and was ordained as a minister of the Congregational Church. He went to China as a missionary, and it was there that he visited his first Buddhist monastery. Upon his return to the United States, he held pastoral positions in Massachusetts and Chicago before leaving the ministry to work as a mechanical engineer. He invented a device that was sold to the government, yielding Goddard a financial fortune that allowed him to retire in 1913. He travelled to China several times in the 1920s, where he met a Lutheran minister who was seeking to promote understanding between Buddhists and Christians. Goddard first learned of Zen Buddhism from a Japanese friend in New York in 1928 and later travelled to Japan where he met D. T. Suzuki and practised zazen for eight months in Kyoto. Upon his return to America, Goddard, now over seventy years old, attempted to form an American Buddhist sangha, called the Followers of the Buddha, in 1934. With property in Vermont (for the summer) and California (for the winter), the organization was to include a celibate monkhood, the Homeless Brothers, supported by lay members. The organization seems to have foundered due to insufficient numbers of members willing to become Homeless Brothers. Goddard also published a Buddhist magazine, *Zen: A Magazine of Self-Realization*, before bringing out, with his own funds, what would become his most famous work, *A Buddhist Bible*, in 1932. The purpose of the book was to 'show the unreality of all conceptions of the personal ego' and inspire readers to follow the path to buddhahood. It was Goddard's conviction that Buddhism was the religion most capable of solving the problems of European civilization.

Commercially published in 1938, *A Buddhist Bible* was organized according to the original language of the texts that appeared in translation, and contained works that had not been translated into English before. The works came mostly from Chinese, translated by the Chinese monk Wai-tao, in collaboration with Goddard. Tibetan selections were drawn from translations by Evans-Wentz. The new translations included the *Awakening of Faith* and the *Surangama Sūtra* (both Chinese works misidentified as being of Sanskrit origin by Goddard), and an important Tien-tai meditation text. Going against the trend to give excerpts of 'key' passages, Goddard included full translations of these texts. As one of the few anthologies of Buddhist texts, particularly those that included Mahayana works, *A Buddhist Bible* remains widely read decades after its publication, having served as a constant companion to Jack Kerouac, for example.

The work is not without its eccentricities, however. For example, the *Diamond Sūtra* has been rearranged by Goddard into a more 'sensible' order and the Taoist work the *Tao te ching* has been included. Goddard also had the delightful audacity to compose his own treatise, meant to provide guidance in meditation, which he felt was difficult for Europeans and Americans. An extract from the chapter 'Practising the Seventh Stage of Buddha's Noble Path' follows, drawn from one of Goddard's own contributions. He intended this text to be memorized and made part of a daily meditation practice.

Sitting quietly with empty and tranquil mind, breathing gently, deliberately, evenly, slowly; realizing that however necessary the process of breathing is to the life of the organism, it is not the self, neither is it anything that a self can accomplish by volition or effort. It is a spontaneous activity that goes on best as we rest quietly, restraining all rising thoughts, keeping the mind fixed on its pure essence, realizing that the organism and all its activities is only a skillful device, an efficient means, which Buddhahood employs in its fulfillment of its nature to emancipate and enlighten all sentient beings. As such it is a manifestation of Buddhahood's love and wisdom; it is a Buddhahood taking form within one's own mind as a coming Buddha.

Sitting quietly with humble and patient mind, with earnest and disciplined mind, waiting for the clouds of karma and the defilements of the mind to clear away so that the clear brightness within may shine forth, illumining the mind, revealing that self is nothing, that mind-essence is everything. Sitting quietly realizing the mind's pure essence. Realizing its all-embracing wholeness, its inconceivable purity and unity, its boundless potentiality for radiation and integration; radiation going forth in rays and vibrations of cosmic energy; manifesting itself in particles, electrons, and atoms; and by the phenomena of light, heat and electricity. Integration drawing everything inward to purity and unity; the going forth and the drawing inward being so perfectly balanced that all abides in the original emptiness and silence. Sitting quietly with empty and tranquil mind, realizing the universal emptiness and eternal silence; realizing it, but yielding to its radiation potency, continually being reborn in this Saha-world of suffering.

Sitting quietly, breathing gently, deliberately, evenly, slowly; realizing that the organism, if it is to become enlightened and brought to Buddhahood, requires something more than intellectual knowledge, namely, it requires wisdom. Knowledge about Truth is not Truth itself; if one is to attain wisdom, he must realize Truth itself, and that requires another process than intellection, namely, it requires intuition. By intuition the mind becomes identified with Truth and attains wisdom by itself becoming Truth. But this process of transmuting intellection into intuition, and knowledge into wisdom, is not the self, neither are all the processes of the body and mind working together harmoniously a self; they are after all only an aggregation and concatenation of fortuitous causes and conditions and are not a self, nor are they anything that a self can accomplish by volition or effort. It is only a spontaneous activity that goes on best as we rest quietly, restraining all rising thoughts, ignoring all risen thoughts, keeping the mind fixed on its pure essence, realizing that the organism with all its activities, is only a skillful device, an efficient means, which Buddhahood employs in fulfillment of its nature to emancipate and enlighten all sentient beings and bring them to Buddhahood. As such it is a manifestation of Buddhahood's love and wisdom; it is Buddhahood taking form within one's own mind as a coming Buddha.

Sitting quietly with humble and patient mind, with earnest and disciplined mind, waiting for the clouds of karma and the defilements of mind to clear away so that the pure brightness within may shine forth, illumining the mind, revealing that self is nothing, mind-essence is everything. Sitting quietly realizing the mind's pure essence! Realizing that the mind's pure essence is the Universal Essence that is prior to everything, that embraces everything, that is everything; and realizing that what is mind is Buddhahood. Sitting quietly realizing that this life of birth and death with all its greed, anger and infatuation is the pure essence of mind and the Bliss-body of Buddhahood; that all the outer things of manifestation and form and phenomena are unreal and imaginary; that all the inner things of desire and aversion, of fear and anger, of infatuation and pride of egoism are unreal and imaginary; that all the activities of the mind discriminating this and that, big and little, good and bad, self and not-self, are unreal and imaginary; that all the states of the mind, its judgments and feelings and emotions, are unreal and imaginary; that only the mind's pure essence is real and abiding, and that is Buddhahood abiding in blissful Peace.

Sitting quietly realizing that all the changes and processes of the body and mind that are going on with no volition or effort on our part are bringing the organism into perfect Oneness with Buddhahood. Sitting quietly realizing this perfect Oneness:— realizing its all-embracing wholeness, its inconceivable unity and purity, its boundless potentiality for Wisdom and Compassion; Wisdom going forth in individuations of Ignorance and discriminations of knowledge that eventuate in multi-plicities of thought, desires, activities, karma, rebirth in the Saha World of suffering. Compassion drawing everything together eventuating in the patient endurance of suffering, the awakening of faith, mind-control, clearing insight, maturing karma, birth in the Pure Land, attain-ment of Buddhahood. The going forth and drawing into being so perfectly balanced that all abides in the original emptiness and silence.

Sitting quietly, realizing the basic emptiness and eternal silence; realizing its unbornness, its imagelessness, its egolessness. Realizing that in its perfect purity and unity there is neither self nor not-self, neither Ignorance nor Enlightenment, neither a Saha World of Suffering nor a Pure Land of Bliss, but, potentially, all are present in fullness. Realizing that in its perfect unity this Saha World of Suffering is the Pure Land of Bliss; realizing that what is radiation is integration, that what is Wisdom is Compassion. Wisdom-Compassion urging one to yield to its radiating potency that it may go forth for the enlightenment of all sentient beings; Compassion-Wisdom supporting one as he advances along the Bodhisattva Stages, submitting to its integrating potency, for the sake of Buddhahood. In the long last, having yielded to Compassion and submitted to Wisdom, attaining Buddhahood – its highest perfect Wisdom, its unceasing Compassion, its blissful Peace; becoming Pure Essence – its emptiness, its silence.

ALL HAIL! THE BLISS-BODY OF BUDDHAHOOD!

Namo Sambhogakaya Buddhaya

(*To be memorized and repeated daily.*)

Dwight Goddard, *A Buddhist Bible* (Boston, Mass.: Beacon Press, 1966), pp. 634, 640–42.

Anagarika Dharmapala

Anagarika Dharmapala (1864–1933) was born Don David Hewaviratne in Sri Lanka, at that time the British colony of Ceylon. He was raised in the English-speaking middle class of Colombo and was educated in Christian schools run by Anglican missionaries, where he is said to have memorized large portions of the Bible. His family was Buddhist, and he met Madame Blavatsky and Colonel Olcott during their first visit to Ceylon in 1880. In 1884 he was initiated into the Theosophical Society by Colonel Olcott and later accompanied Madame Blavatsky to the headquarters of the society in Adyar, India. Here she encouraged him to study Pali, the language of the Theravada Buddhist scriptures.

In 1881 he had taken the name Dharmapala, Protector of the Dharma. Prior to that time in Ceylon, the leadership in Buddhism had been provided by monks and kings. Dharmapala established a new role for Buddhist laypeople, creating the category of the 'anagarika' or wanderer, a layperson who studied texts and meditated, as monks did, but who remained socially active in the world, as laypeople did. In 1889 he travelled with Colonel Olcott on his lecture tour of Japan. On a trip to India in 1891, he was shocked to see the state of decay of the great pilgrimage sites of India, all under Hindu control, and most especially Bodh Gaya, the site of the Buddha's enlightenment. That same year he founded the Maha Bodhi Society, which called on Buddhists from around the world to work for the restoration of the great sites to Buddhist control, a goal that would only be achieved after his death.

In 1893 Dharmapala attended the World's Parliament of Religions. Although one of several Buddhist speakers, his excellent English and Anglican education made him an effective spokesperson for the dharma, demonstrating what he saw as both its affinities with and superiority to Christianity. In the essay presented below, 'Desire in Buddhism' (originally published in

1917), he takes the offensive against European critics of Buddhism, arguing not only that they misunderstand the dharma but that their misunderstanding stems from the benighted history of their own religion. In his view, Buddhism is more ancient, more civilized and more profound than anything produced by Christianity.

DESIRE IN BUDDHISM

Superficial students of the religion of the Lord Buddha, especially the followers of dogmatic beliefs, find fault with the teachings thereof that they destroy desire, and that a religion that destroys lofty desires is a pessimism, and that European races shall never accept such a religion.

Unfortunately for the cause of Truth no attempt had been made to show the hollowness of such a baseless assertion, and the Bhikkhus have not done their duty to proclaim what the Blessed One taught. The three hundred millions of European peoples were satisfied with the Semitic religion of Canaan, and did not wish for more light. The Buddhist Bhikkhus and the more intelligent lay Buddhists have no idea of the conditions prevalent in Europe. For nearly fifteen centuries the European nations lived isolated, and when they woke up from their long sleep it was not to preach culture or religion that they crossed the oceans, but as apostles of the God of Mammon.

> 'A rabid race fanatically bold,
>   And steeled to cruelty by lust of gold
> Traversed the waves, the unknown world explored;
>   The cross their standard, but their faith the sword;
> Their steps were graves; over prostrate realms they trod
>   They worshipped Mammon while they vowed to God.'

Study of religion and the inquiry into the philosophies of ancient India began after the Upanishads had been translated into Latin, and the first philosophical thinker who investigated the Upanishads was the German philosopher Schopenhauer. He had read of the sublime life of the Buddha and found in the philosophy enunciated by the Great Teacher a resemblance to his own philosophy which was generally known as a philosophy of pessimism. Schopenhauer was more a student of the Upanishads, nevertheless his sympathy with Buddhism was enough for the common man to denounce Buddhism as a pessimism. It proclaimed the Four Noble Truths, and the first Truth was Sorrow, and a religion that proclaimed sorrow as its first principle was not the religion for the materialistic European. He was frightened to think of sorrow, and like the ancient gods who trembled when they heard for the first time from the Blessed One the doctrine of Transiency (anicca), the dogmatists, theologians and hedonists shouted, 'Away with Buddhism; we don't want it, it is a pessimism, and a religion that killed all desires. The pleasure of life, the high hopes were not to be given up, and a religion that killed all desires may be good to the people of India, but not to the virile European.' Since the time of Schopenhauer the baseless assertion is repeated to the great detriment of philosophical enquiry.

Let us make a serious inquiry whether the Great Teacher did actually teach such a gospel to the world. Remember India is a continent, not like Palestine or Arabia, peopled by wild, roving Semitic Bedouins, children of the desert, and that it is a vast country peopled by highly spiritualized races, with a civilization going back to thousands and thousands of years, and the cradle land of religions and philosophies. In a country where religious inquiry is man's birth-right, dogmatism has no place. India never knew in its long record of history to persecute people for their religious opinions. The persecuting spirit of religious tyranny began with the Semitic Jehovahism, and later ruthlessly followed by the founder of Islam. The Semitic spirit was implanted in the Latin and Teuton heart after the introduction of the Semitic doctrine of Palestine into Europe. Never having had a religion with a history and theology among the European races, it was quite easy for the promulgators of the Semitic faith to impress on the European mind the terribleness of the Jealous Jah of Mt Horeb. Europe succumbed, and its future was made a blank by means of terrifying dogmatism ending with hell fire and brimstone to eternity.

Barthelemy St Hilaire in France frightened the people of France by the pronouncement he had made that Buddhism is an annihilation. One hell fire was enough for the people, and if another was to proclaim annihilation, why the people will go mad!

In England the missionary was the sworn enemy of Buddhism. He proclaimed that it was a downright heathenism with devil worship as its complement. It was therefore fit for the cannibals, and the missionary actually proclaimed in his annual report that Buddhist parents did offer their children to crocodiles. With widow burning, infanticide, and the hideous Juggernaut car like the Moloch of the Old Testament demanding human holocausts, and worshipping stocks and stones, which the puritanic people of the British isles were asked to believe by the missionary, there was no hope for the acceptance of the Truth which the Great Teacher proclaimed to the Aryans of ancient India.

Recently a book was published under the title of 'Trade, Politics and Christianity' by Longmans, Green & Co. Its author was one Mr A. J. Macdonald, MA, and the head-hunter of Imperialistic politics, who knows all about the African hippotami and Rhinoceros and the Cannibals of Africa, has contributed a glowing introduction thereto. This head-hunter with the seriousness which makes us blush says 'Perhaps Pity as a cosmic force, was only born with the ministry of Christ.' The history of the Inquisition, the slave trade in the hands of the British for nearly three centuries, the annihilation of the Tasmanians, the introduction of Opium into China at the point of the bayonet, the introduction of firewater into countries where no poisonous drinks were known before, the annihilation of the ancient people of Central America, the partial destruction of the Red Native races of North America, the lynching of helpless Negroes in the United States, the destruction of the feathered tribe for their beautiful plumage to adorn the heads of women, are all due to the birth of pity in the hearts of the followers of Christ. The man has not read the Old Testament seriously and critically to find out what its contents are, and he has not seriously investigated into the dogmatics of Christianity with an eternal hell in flames.

It is the desire to realize the highest happiness that prompts the Buddhist to become an Arhat and realize the highest wisdom; it is desire that prompts the good man to aspire for imperial sovereignty of a Chakravarti; it is desire that prompts the thinking Buddhist to do good deeds and give the merits to others. Meritorious desires prompted the great Buddhist King Asoka to send missionaries to the then civilized countries of Asia; it was desire that prompted the righteous emperor to give his own son and daughter to the Buddha sasana; it was the noble desire to save that prompted the Prince Mahinda and the Princess Sanghmitta to go to Ceylon to preach the Dhamma to the men and women of Ceylon 2,222 years ago. It was desire that made the immortal Buddhaghosa to leave India and go to Ceylon and write the Pali Commentaries.

Desire is of two kinds, the noble and the ignoble. Noble desires prompt man to do works of charity, they make men sober, enlightened and good; ignoble desires make men to adopt the policy of Machiavelli, to distribute opium, intoxicating liquor, and introduce syphilis and create bastards, and murder helpless people for the sake of rubber, gold and land.

Buddhism condemns ignoble desires, and emphasizes on the necessity of cultivating noble desires. Buddha condemned (*Tanha*) craving and lustful desire (*Chandaraga*); and emphasized on the development of (*Chanda iddhipada*) the will to develop lofty desires, and to create (*punnabhisamkharas*) meritorious deeds, words and thoughts. Tanha and chandaraga are born of Ignorance; chanda iddhipada and punnabhisamkharas are born of (*Pragna*) Divine Wisdom.

All good deeds, good words, good thoughts proceed from the element of Noble Desires, the Nekhamma dhatu and the Nekhamma sankappa of the Aryan Noble Path enunciated by the Blessed One the Buddha Sakyamuni.

Section II – Aryadharma of Sakyamuni Guatama Buddha, 1917

Anagarika Dharmapala, *Return to Righteousness: A Collection of Speeches, Essays and Letters of the Anagarika Dharmapala* (Ceylon: Government Press, 1965), pp. 231–4.

Alexandra David-Neel

Alexandra David-Neel (1868–1969) was born Alexandra David in Paris, to a bourgeois family. She ran away from home several times as a child, foreshadowing a life of travel. David-Neel was educated in a Calvinist convent before studying Indian and Chinese philosophy at the Sorbonne and the Collecège de France. In 1888 she travelled to London, where she became interested in Theosophy. She journeyed to Ceylon and India (where she studied Vedanta) in 1891, and reached as far as Sikkim, north-eastern India, during eighteen months of travel. Upon returning to France, she began a career as a singer and eventually was offered the position of female lead in the Hanoi Opera in Vietnam. Some years later, in Tunis, she met and married a railway engineer, Philippe Néel. He insisted that she retire from the stage. She agreed to do so if he would finance a trip to India, to last for one year. He assented but did not see his wife again for fourteen years.

David-Neel became friends with Thomas and Caroline Rhys Davids in London, leading scholars of Theravada Buddhism, and corresponded with D. T. Suzuki, before publishing her first book on Buddhism in 1909, entitled *Le modernisme Bouddhiste et le Bouddhisme du Bouddha* (see also the Introduction). By 'Buddhist Modernism' she meant the rationalist form of Theravada taught by Anagarika Dharmapala, whom she met in Ceylon the following year. She continued to Sikkim, where she encountered the thirteenth Dalai Lama in Darjeeling, where he was living briefly to avoid a Chinese invasion of Tibet. She then spent two years in retreat, receiving instructions from a Nyingma hermit-lama. In 1916 she was expelled from Sikkim by the British and travelled to Japan, where she was the guest of D. T. Suzuki. From there she went to China, travelling west in the company of a young Sikkimese monk named Yongden. Disguised as a pilgrim, she arrived in Lhasa in 1924, presumably the first European woman to reach the Tibetan capital.

When she returned to France the year after, David-Neel had become a celebrity. She published the bestselling *My Journey to Lhasa* (1927), followed by a succession of books based on her travels in Tibet and study and practice of Tibetan Buddhism. She built a home in Digne which she named Samten Dzong ('Fortress of Concentration'). She made another trip to Asia as the Second World War began, but spent the rest of her life writing in Digne, where she died at the age of one hundred.

The extract below, from her popular work *Magic and Mystery in Tibet* (originally published in 1932), provides a description of some of the forms of Tibetan Buddhist practice. Unlike the work of some of the more pious devotees of Tibetan Buddhism, her account has something of an anthropological tone to it, with the author freely providing her own evaluation and comment.

MYSTIC THEORIES AND SPIRITUAL TRAINING

The religious world in Tibet, generally speaking, is divided into two sections. The first includes those who advocate the strict observance of moral precepts and monastic rules as the means of salvation, the second is formed of those who prefer an intellectual method which frees its followers from all laws whatsoever.

Nevertheless there exists no rigid division between these two categories. Though their respective theories are always a favourite subject of controversy between the followers of the two schools, it seldom happens that one stands in the position of a harsh, pugnacious adversary towards those in the opposite camp.

Even the monks attached to morality acknowledge that a virtuous life and the monastic discipline, though of great value and advisable for the many, are but a mere preparation to a higher path. As for the adepts of the second system, they all believe in the beneficial results of a faithful adherence to the moral laws and the rules laid down for members of the religious Order.

Moreover, all are unanimous in declaring the first method the safer of the two. A pure life, the performance of good deeds, righteousness, compassion, detachment from worldly cares, selflessness and quietness of mind act – they say – as a cleaning process which gradually removes the 'impure dust that covers the mental eyes,'* therefore leading to enlightenment which is salvation itself.

As for the method which mystics call the 'Short Path,' the 'Direct Path,'† it is considered as most hazardous. It is – according to the masters who teach it – as if instead of following the road which goes round a mountain ascending gradually towards its summit, one attempted to reach it in a straight line, climbing perpendicular rocks and crossing chasms on a rope. Only first-rate equilibrists, exceptional athletes, completely free from giddiness, can hope to succeed in such a task. Even the fittest may fear sudden exhaustion or dizziness. And there inevitably follows a dreadful fall in which the too presumptuous alpinist breaks his bones.

By this illustration Tibetan mystics mean a spiritual fall leading to the lowest and worst degree of aberration and perversity to the condition of a demon.

I have heard a learned lama maintain that the bold theories regarding complete intellectual freedom and the enfranchisement from all rules whatever, which are expounded by the most advanced adepts of the 'Short Path,' are the faint echo of the teachings that existed from time immemorial in Central and Northern Asia.

The lama was convinced that these doctrines agree completely with the Buddha's highest teaching as it was made evident in various passages of his discourses. However, said the lama, the Buddha was well aware that the majority do better to abide by rules devised to avert the baleful effects of their ignorance and guide them along paths where no disasters are to be feared. For that very reason, the all-wise Master has established rules for the laity and monks of average intelligence.

---

* A favourite Buddhist illustration. We read in the Mahāvagga (I, 10): 'Bhagavan, looking over the world with his eyes of a Buddha, saw beings whose mental eyes were darkened by scarcely any dust and beings whose eyes were covered by much dust, beings sharp of sense and blunt of sense, of good disposition and bad disposition, easy to instruct and difficult to instruct . . .'

† Technically, in mystic parlance: *tse gchig, lus gchig sang rgyais*, to attain Buddhahood in one life, one body. That is to say, in the very life in which one has begun one's spiritual training. Tibetans say also: *lam chung* ('the short road').

The same lama entertained serious doubts as to the Aryan origin of the Buddha. He rather believed that his ancestors belonged to the Yellow race and was convinced that his expected successor, the future Buddha Maitreya, would appear in Northern Asia.

Where did he get these ideas? I have not been able to find out. Discussion is hardly possible with Oriental mystics. When once they have answered: 'I have seen this in my meditations,' little hope is left to the inquirer of obtaining further explanations.

I have also heard similar ideas expressed by Newars from Nepal. Their argument was that the native land of the Buddha was their own country. 'The great Sage of India,' they said, 'belonged to the same stock as ourselves. And as for us, we are of the same race as the Chinese.'

It is, of course, only the learned lamas and mystics who hold the theories just mentioned, regarding the 'Path of Rules' and the 'Short Path.' Now, in Tibet, as elsewhere, scholars and thinkers are few. So while amongst the partisans of the 'rules' the many merely vegetate in the monasteries, the doctrine of 'complete freedom' affords a *raison d'être* to countless people scarcely capable of haunting any summit, but whose originality cannot be denied.

Most magicians shelter themselves under the flag of the latter party. Not that many of them seek rapid spiritual achievement. That which appeals to them in the 'Short Path' is freedom from the bondage of discipline and the permission thus granted to proceed with whatever experiments may be useful for their own advancement. The formula is vague enough to allow interpretations that fit all kinds of characters.

A broad classification of Tibetan professed magicians and students of the magic art divides them into two categories.

The first includes all those who do not seek direct mastery over nature, but only the power of coercing certain gods and demons to secure their help. The men who practise that method believe in the real existence of the beings of the other worlds as entities completely distinct from them. They also think that their own ability and power are much inferior to those of the personalities whom they endeavour to enslave, and that they would be incapable of obtaining the results which they expect from the latter's help by their own efforts.

Again, whatever other means they use: spells, charms, etc., they also implicitly recognize that their active power, though put into motion by the man who uses them, does not emanate from him.

In the second category only a small number of adepts are to be reckoned.

These employ, at times, the very same means as their less enlightened colleagues, but they do it for different reasons. They hold the view that the various phenomena which the vulgar consider as miracles, are produced by an energy arising in the magician himself and depend on his knowledge of the true inner essence of things. Most of them are men of retired habits, even hermits, who do not exhibit any singularity in their ways and appearances. They make no attempt to exhibit their powers and often remain entirely unknown. On the contrary, the magicians of the first group are fond of indulging in many kinds of showy and bewildering eccentricities. Sorcerers, soothsayers, necromancers, occultists from the meanest beggarly class to those of high social standing, can be met with among them. A lover of odd discourses and deeds may enjoy himself listening to the theories regarding 'integral freedom' and its practice that are current in such society. But behind these absurd extravagances there are elements of knowledge regarding old traditions, forgotten history and the handling of psychic forces to be gleaned. But in these circles, as elsewhere in Tibet, the great difficulty is to gain a footing.

It is unnecessary to be an ordained monk to enter the 'Short Path to Deliverance.' According to its adepts, only initiations are of value. So any layman, if recognized as fit to undertake the spiritual climbing, may be accepted by a mystic master and in due time initiated by him. The same rule applies to students of magic. Nevertheless, most mystics and magicians have begun their career as youths in the religious Order.

The choice of the master who is to guide him along the mystic path, arduous and fraught with deceitful mirages, is a momentous decision for the candidate to initiation. The course which his life will follow depends to a great extent upon the character of the lama he elects. •

For having asked admittance at a door from which they ought to have turned away, some have met with fantastic adventures. Yet, if the young monk is satisfied with begging the spiritual guidance of a lama who is neither an anchorite nor an 'extremist' of the 'Short Path,' his novitiate will probably not include any tragic incidents.

During a probation period of undetermined length the master will test the character of his new disciple. Then he may simply explain some philosophical treatises and the meaning of a few symbolic diagrams (*kyilkhors*), teaching him the methodic meditations for which they are used.

If the lama thinks his pupil capable of proceeding farther, he will expound him the programme of the mystic training.

The latter includes three stages, namely:

Tawa – to look, examine.

Gompa – to think, meditate.

Chyöd pa – to practise, realize. This is the fruit of accomplishment through the two former stages.

Another less current enumeration makes use of four terms to convey the same meaning, as follows:

FIRST STAGE:

Tön – 'meaning', 'reason'. That is to say investigation of the nature of things, their origin, their end, the causes upon which they depend.

Lob – 'study' of various doctrines.

SECOND STAGE:

Gom – thinking or meditating on that which one has discovered and learnt. Practising introspective meditation.

THIRD STAGE:

Togs – Understanding.

In order that the novice may practise in perfect quietness the various exercises which the programme requires, it is nearly certain that the lama will command him to shut himself in *tsams*.*

The word *tsams* signifies a barrier, the border of a territory. In religious parlance, to 'stay in tsams' means to live in seclusion, to retire beyond a barrier which must not be passed.

That 'barrier' may be of different kinds. With advanced mystics it becomes purely psychic and it is said that the latter need no material contrivances to isolate themselves while meditating.

---

* Written *mtshams* and pronounced *tsam*.

There exist several categories of *tsams*, each one being subdivided into a number of varieties.

Proceeding from the less austere towards the most severe forms, we find the following ones:

A lama or a lay devotee shuts himself in his room or private apartment. He does not go out or only does so at fixed times, to perform some devotional practices, such as walking around religious edifices making repeated prostrations before sacred objects, or the like.

According to the rule which he has adopted, the *tsamspa*★ either may be seen or must remain invisible. In the first case, he is generally permitted to talk briefly with the members of the household, his relatives or servants, and even to receive a few visitors. In the second case, he may only be seen by those who attend him. If a visitor is admitted, he must remain within hearing *outside* the *tsamspa's* room. A curtain screens the entrance and the interlocutors remain invisible to each other as in some Roman Catholic contemplative Orders of nuns.

A number of Tibetans resort occasionally to one or another of these mild forms of seclusion for non-religious motives, seeking merely to avoid disturbance while engaged in the study of any branch of Tibetan learning: grammar, philosophy, astrology, medicine, etc.

Next comes the recluse who sees but one attendant.

He who renounces speaking and makes known his needs by writing.

He who partly covers his window, so that he cannot see the surrounding landscape, nor any outside object except the sky.

He who renounces the sight of the sky, covering his window entirely or, living in a windowless room which, nevertheless, admits the daylight indirectly.

He who sees no one at all.

In this case, if the *tsamspa* enjoys the use of a suite of rooms, his meals are brought into one of them, while he retires into another. When he lives in a single room, food is placed next to the entrance. Someone knocks at the door to inform the recluse that what he needs is ready, and then the inmates of the house leave the adjacent room or

---

★ He who practises *tsams*. Not to be mistaken for *tsampa*: flour of roast barley, written *rtsampa*.

corridors for a moment to allow the *tsamspa* to come out without being seen. Any object is returned in the same way, the *tsamspa* calling attention by knocking at the door or ringing a bell.

Among those who practise this particular kind of *tsams*, some ask by writing for the things which they require, but others renounce this facility. Consequently, whatever may be their needs, they cannot make them known. Even if those who attend on them forgot to give them their meal, they ought to fast in silence.

Generally *tsams* in one's own house do not last long, especially of the strict kind. One year seems to be an exceptional period. One usually hears of people who live in seclusion for three months, one month and even a few days only. Laymen rarely shut themselves in their apartment for more than one month.

It is easy to understand that prolonged and severe *tsams* cannot be practised in an ordinary residence. There, whatever care is taken, the moving about of people busy with worldly affairs and the noise inevitably reach the *tsamspa*, through the thin barrier of his closed door.

The silence and quiet surroundings which may be enjoyed to a high degree in the monasteries are not even deemed sufficient by some, and many *gompas* own special small houses built for the use of their members who wish to live in strict seclusion.

These houses are called *tsams khang*.* They are sometimes situated in an out-of-the-way spot, inside the monastery's walls, but more frequently stand aloof on some hill, at a little distance outside the walled enclosure. It is not unusual to find groups of these meditation houses standing in the solitude, at a few days' march from their parent monastery.

The plans of the *tsams khangs* correspond to the various rules and requirements here above mentioned.

From the windows of some of them, the recluse may enjoy the sight of beautiful landscapes, while others are surrounded by walls that cut off the view on all sides. In that case, the enclosure often forms a small courtyard or terrace where the *tsamspa* may sit or walk in the open, without being seen, or himself seeing anything of the outside world.

---

* From *mtshams* and *khang*, house: 'a house where to live in seclusion.'

Most *tsams khangs* are divided into two rooms. In one of them, the recluse sits and sleeps, the other one is the kitchen in which an attendant may live.

When the *tsamspa* must see no one and keep the rule of silence, his attendant lives in a separate hut. A double wicket is then built in the wall or the door of the recluse's room, and through it meals are given to him.

Solid food is generally served only once a day, but buttered tea is brought several times. If the lama belongs to one or another of the 'Red cap' sects, beer★ alternates with the tea. Tibetans having the custom of keeping a small bag of barley flour at hand, the recluse is at liberty to eat some with his tea or beer, whenever he likes.

Only members of the religious Order retire in the cottages specially built to be used as meditation houses. Some remain in seclusion during several consecutive years. A canonic period is three years three months three weeks and three days. Some repeat that long retreat twice or thrice in the course of their life, and a few shut themselves in *tsams* for life.

Alexandra David-Neel, 'Mystic Theories and Spiritual Training' in *Magic and Mystery in Tibet* (New York: Dover, 1971), pp. 242–51.

★ Though drinking fermented beverages is strictly prohibited by Buddhism, Tibetan 'Red caps' declare that Padmasambhava, their founder, allowed it. Nevertheless, some of them seem to know better. Padmasambhava, they say, allowed the drinking of alcohol when performing certain rites, and then the quantity to be drunk was that which fills the hollow of the palm. Padmasambhava, who was a Western Indian and an adept of Tantrism, taught his Tibetan converts the form of worship of his sect and, as with many *tantrikas*, the two drops of wine to be drunk in a sacramental fashion led to habitual drinking. An Indian saying goes: 'Some drink to perform the rite, and some perform the rite in order to drink.' But Tibetans addicted to drinking do not seek a religious excuse any more than their Western brethren in drunkenness.

D. T. Suzuki

Daisetz Teitaro Suzuki (1870–1966) was born in Kanazawa, Japan, the son of a physician. He taught English in primary schools before enrolling in what is now Waseda University in Tokyo. While a university student, he travelled to Kamakura to practise Zen meditation at Engakuji monastery under the direction of Shaku Sōen. He became his disciple and translated into English Sōen's lecture for the 1893 World's Parliament of Religions. Sōen arranged for Suzuki to travel to America to work with Paul Carus, editor of *The Gospel of Buddha According to Old Records*. Suzuki lived with Carus's family in La Salle, Illinois, from 1897–1908, producing translations and writing his first book in English, *Outlines of Mahayana Buddhism* (1907). On returning to Japan in 1909, he taught English until 1921, when he accepted a chair in Buddhist philosophy at Otani University in Kyoto. In 1911 he married an American student of Buddhism, Beatrice Lane (1878–1939), who both collaborated with him and published her own studies of Mahayana Buddhism. Suzuki remained in Japan during the war years. He returned to the United States in 1950 and lectured on Zen Buddhism at a number of universities. His lectures at Columbia University, open to the public, attracted a diverse audience of poets, artists and psychoanalysts, including John Cage, Erich Fromm and Karen Horney. He died in Tokyo at the age of ninety-six.

Suzuki was a prolific author in both Japanese and English, with his collected writings in Japanese filling thirty-two volumes. His most influential works in English were his *Essays in Zen Buddhism* (three volumes, 1927–34) and his *Zen and Japanese Culture* (1959). The excerpts below are drawn from an essay entitled 'An Interpretation of Zen-Experience' (originally published in 1939). It offers a clear presentation of Suzuki's claim that Zen, more than being a particular tradition of East Asian Buddhism, with its own texts and history, is, above all, an experience.

AN INTERPRETATION OF ZEN-EXPERIENCE

2

To study Zen means to have Zen-experience, for without the experience there is no Zen one can study. But mere experience means to be able to communicate it to others; the experience ceases to be vital unless it is adequately expressible. A dumb experience is not human. To experience is to be self-conscious. Zen-experience is complete only when it is backed by Zen-consciousness and finds expression in one way or another. In the following I will attempt to give a clue to the understanding of Zen-consciousness.

Daian (died 883), the Zen master of Dai-i San, once gave this to his congregation: '(The conception of) being and non-being is like the wistaria winding round the tree.'

Sozan, hearing this, lost no time in undertaking a long journey, for he wished to find out the meaning of Daian's most enigmatic statement. Seeing the master engaged in making a mud-wall, he approached and asked: '(The conception of) being and non-being is like the wistaria winding around the tree; did you really say that?'

The master said: 'Yes, my friend.'

Sozan queried: 'When the tree is suddenly broken down and the wistaria withers, what happens?'

The master threw up his mud-carrying board and laughing loudly walked away towards his living quarters. Sozan followed and protested: 'O Master, I come from a remote district three thousand *li* away, I have sold my clothing to pay for the travelling expenses, and this for no other purpose than to get enlightened on this subject. Why do you make fun of me?'

The master felt pity for the poor monk and told his attendant to gather up money enough for his return trip. He then turned toward Sozan, saying: 'Some day you may happen to see a master who is known as "One-eyed Dragon" and he will make you see into the matter.'

Later, Sozan came to Myosho and told him about the interview he had with Daian of Dai-i San. Myosho said: 'Daian is all right through and through, only he misses one who really understands his mind.' Sozan now proposed the same question to Myosho, saying: 'What happens when the tree is broken and the wistaria withers?' Myosho said: 'You make Daian renew his laughter!' This made Sozan at once comprehend the meaning of the whole affair, and he exclaimed: 'After all there is a dagger in Daian's laughter.' He reverentially bowed in the direction of Dai-i San.

3

In this account, what strikes one most is the disparity between the question and the answer, for as far as our common sense or logic allows us to see, no connection whatever exists between the statement concerning being and non-being and the master's laughter or, as is given later on, Yengo's repetition of his own master. The question in regard to being and non-being is a philosophical one dealing with abstract ideas. All our thoughts start from the opposition between being and non-being; without this antithesis no reasoning can be carried on, and therefore the question is a fundamental one: 'What will become of our thought-system when the conception of being and non-being is wiped out?' When the tree dies, naturally the wistaria withers. Being is possible only with non-being, and conversely. This world of particulars is comprehensible only when we recognize the fundamental antithesis of being and non-being. Where shall we be when this is no more? An absolute nothingness? This too is inconceivable. Is it an error then to speak at all of the antithesis? But it faces us; we cannot get rid of this world of birth-and-death, which, however, in its present state, is quite unsatisfactory to our moral and spiritual nature. We always have the craving to go beyond the antithesis, which somehow does not seem to be final; it points to something higher and deeper, and this we wish to take hold of. The mutual conditioning of antithesis must be transcended, but how? This is in fact the question raised by Sozan.

As long as we stay with the mutual conditioning of opposites, i.e. in the world of antitheses, we never feel complete; we are always haunted with a feeling of uneasiness. Sozan must have been deeply stirred with the question of being and non-being, or birth and death, or speaking more like a Christian, with the problem of immortality. When he heard of Daian of Dai-i San making the statement about it, he thought that there was the master who could solve the riddle and give him spiritual rest. He sold his scanty possessions and with what little he could realize he managed to travel a long way to Dai-i San. Seeing the master engaged in making the mud-wall, he approached him precipitously and wished to be enlightened on the subject: 'What will become of us, of human souls, of their immortality, when the world with all its multitudinous contents is reduced to ashes at the end of the present *kalpa*?'

The question is metaphysical as well as religious. It is religious as long as it does not attempt to develop its significance along the purely intellectual line; it is metaphysical inasmuch as its approach is by means of abstract concepts. This is a feature peculiar to Zen Buddhism. If we choose, we can call it a kind of practical philosophy, and this practicalness may well be illustrated by the laughter given by Daian of Dai-i San as an answer to Sozan's question. Sozan was metaphysically minded enough to resort to such an abstraction as being and non-being, while his practical-mindedness is shown by transforming this abstraction into the relation between concrete objects such as the wistaria and the pine tree. Even this practical-mindedness of Sozan was thoroughly upset by Daian's ultra-practicalness: the throwing up of the mud-carrier, and the laughter, and the hurried departure for his room. Daian was all action while Sozan was still on the plane of word symbolism; that is, he was still on the conceptual level, away from life itself.

4

As long as we are gregarious animals, and therefore social and rational, everything we experience, be it an idea, an event, or a feeling, we desire to communicate to one another, and this is possible only through a medium. We have developed various mediums of communication, and those who can command them at will are leaders of humankind:

philosophers, poets, artists of all kinds, writers, orators, religionists, and others. But these mediums must be substantiated, must be backed by real personal experiences. Without the latter, mediums are merely utilized and will never vibrate with vitality.

Some mediums are more readily counterfeited than others, being subject to all devices of ingenious simulation. Language as one such medium lends itself most easily to misrepresentation, intentional or otherwise. The highest and most fundamental experiences are best communicated without words; in the face of such experiences we become speechless and stand almost aghast.

Another consideration on the subject of means of communication is that however eloquent a medium may be it will not have the desired effect on anyone who never had an experience somewhat similar in kind although fainter in intensity. Like a pearl thrown before swine, the eloquence is wasted. On the other hand, if two people have had an experience of the same nature, the lifting of a finger will set the whole spiritual mechanism in vibration, and each can read the other's inner thought.

The Zen master is an adept in the use of a medium, either verbal or actional, which directly points to his Zen-experience and by which the questioner, if he is mentally ripe, will at once grasp the master's intention. The medium of this kind functions 'directly' and 'at once', as if it were the experience itself – as when deep calls to deep. This direct functioning is compared to one brightly burnished mirror reflecting another brightly burnished mirror which faces the first with nothing between.

5

In the case of Daian and Sozan, the latter was still a captive in the prison of words and concepts, and not capable of grasping reality at first hand. His mind was filled with ideas of being and non-being, of trees and wistarias, of birth and death, of the absolute and the conditioned, of cause and effect, of *karma* and Nirvana; he had no direct, non-meditated understanding of reality; and this was indeed the reason why he brought himself before the amateur mason, after travelling over a distance of several thousand *li*. The mason master was a master indeed in every sense of the word. He never argued with the logician who was entangled like the wistaria round the problem of being and non-being. He did not talk about the absolute; he never resorted to a dialectic of contradiction; he never referred to a fundamental assumption lying behind the antitheses of being and non-being. What he did was simply throw down his mud-carrier, give a hearty laugh, and hurry to his private quarters.

Now let us ask: Was there anything funny about Sozan's question? We human beings are always worried over the disruption of things we see, especially about the dissolution of this carnal existence, and about the life to come after it, if there should be one. This seems to be quite a natural feeling with us all and why should this excite the Zen master's laughter? Merely laughing was not enough; he even threw down his instrument of work, stopped his wall-making, and made for his quiet retreat. Does he mean by this that it is far better to ask nothing, to enjoy life as it goes on, to take things as they display themselves before us, to laugh when laughable objects are presented, to weep when events excite this feeling; in short, to accept all things and be cheerful about them? Or did he mean that when the world should come to an end, he wanted to enjoy the ending with the world? Or did he mean that there is no such thing as the ending of anything – things are eternal as they are, a world of relativity is mere appearance – and, therefore, that there is in reality no breaking down, no withering, thus barring all conceptual guessings based on the notion of relativity and appearance? Or did he laugh at the questioner's stupidity, which showed that the latter had failed to realize the working of something in himself quite apart from or rather along with his deep concern for the breaking down of the tree and the withering of the wistaria? Such a variety of meaning may be read into Daian's behaviour. But what is desired here from the Zen point of view is to experience the meaning itself and to leave its intellectual interpretation to the elaboration later on the Zen-consciousness which inevitably rises out of the experience.

In any event Sozan could not take in Daian's laughter, or, as we would say, he could not grasp the idea that was behind it or in it. He next visited

Myosho, 'the One-eyed Dragon', wishing to be enlightened about the whole situation, in which he found himself all the more involved. Myosho, however, did not give him any plausible intellectual explanation which might satisfy a philosophical inquirer; he simply remarked that this questioning on the part of Sozan would end in renewing Daian's laughter. This was really an enigmatical confirmation of the predecessor, but, miraculously enough, it helped Sozan to dive into the significance of Daian's puzzle. The whole thing was clarified now and the only step he could take was to bow reverentially in the direction where Daian was and to express his heartfelt appreciation.

6

Through the whole course of this incident there are no metaphysical discussions in any form; nor are there any devotional proceedings such as confession, repentance, or mortification; again, there are no references to sin, God, prayer, shrinking from everlasting fire, or asking for forgiveness. It starts with a kind of philosophical inquiry concerning being and non-being, which is likened to the wistaria winding itself round the tree; but the solution given is not at all along the line suggested by the question – it is absolutely beyond what the ordinary-minded people can expect on such occasions. In the whole history of human thought there is really nothing comparable to this extraordinary Zen transaction. And what is still more extraordinary and incomprehensible is the fact that Sozan, the inquirer, finally grasps the meaning of the strange behaviour of the master, which evidently solves the antithetical entanglements of being and non-being. [. . .]

11

I am not certain whether Zen can be identified with mysticism. Mysticism as it is understood in the West starts generally with an antithesis and ends with its unification or identification. If there is an antithesis, Zen accepts it as it is, and makes no attempt to unify it. Instead of starting with dualism or pluralism, Zen wants us to have a

Zen-experience, and with this experience it surveys a world of such-ness. It has adopted Mahayana terminology, it is true, but it has the tendency to resort to concrete objects and happenings. It does not reduce them to oneness – which is an abstraction. When all things are reduced to oneness, it asks to what this One is reducible. If all comes from God, lives in God, and returns to God, Zen wants to know where this God is or lives. If the whole world with all its multiplicities is absorbed into Brahman, Zen asks us to point out the whereabouts of Brahman. If the soul survives the body, Zen calls on you to locate the soul or to bring it out before us.

A master was asked where he might be found after his death, and he said: 'Lying on my back in the wilderness, my limbs pointing straight up to the sky!' When another master was asked about the immutability of Nirvana, he replied: 'The fallen leaves follow the running stream while the autumnal moon rises above the solitary peak.' Another appeared in the pulpit apparently ready to give a sermon, but as soon as he mounted it, he declared that his discourse was over, saying: 'Fare well!' After a while he resumed: 'If there is any who has no un-derstanding yet, let him come out.' A monk made an advance toward the master and bowed down reverentially, whereupon the master, raising his voice, said, 'How painful!' The monk stood up and was about to propose a question, but the master cried 'Ho!' and drove him out. When another monk approached, saying: 'What is the most won-derful word [expressing the highest truth]?', the master merely re-marked: 'What say you?' Going carefully over all these *mondo* (dia-logues), where do we find traces of mysticism in Zen? The masters give no hint whatever as to the annihilation or absorption of the self in the absolute, or the casting of the world into the abyss of Nirvana.

12

Mystics, I believe, generally agree with this characterization of God: 'God is not an "object" for human understanding. He utterly transcends knowledge, and everything one says of Him is untrue.' ' "Be still," Eckhart says in a sermon, "and prate not of God (i.e. the Godhead), for whatever you prate in words about Him is a lie and is sinful." "If I say God is good, it is not true; for what is good can grow better; what can grow better can grow best. Now these three things (good, better, best) are far from God, for He is above all," i.e. all such distinctions. No word that voices distinctions or characteristics, then, may be spoken of the Godhead. Eckhart's favourite names are: "the Wordless God-head"; "the Nameless Nothing"; "the Naked Godhead"; "the Immovable Rest"; "the Still Wilderness, where no one is at home".' (Rufus Jones, *Studies in Mystical Religion* (London, 1909), pp. 225–226).

However mystical one may be, one cannot avoid using the term 'God' or 'Godhead' or some concept corresponding to it. But this is not so with Zen. Zen avoids, not necessarily deliberately but unavoidably I believe, abstract terms. When the question arises concerning such terms, the Zen master turns them down, making the questioner realize the fact that they have no direct hold on life. Zuigan Shigen asked Ganto (AD 829–87): 'What is the original eternal reason?'

Ganto: 'Moving!'

Zuigan: 'What about it when moving?'

Ganto: 'It is no more the original eternal reason.'

This made Zuigan reflect for some time over the matter. Ganto continued: 'When you assert, you are still in the world of senses; when you do not assert, you sink into the ocean of birth and death!'

Ganto does not wish to see his disciple stay with the original eternal reason, nor does he want him to lose the sight of it. He knows that Zen is neither to assert nor to deny, that Zen is the suchness of things. The Zen masters are not mystics and their philosophy is not mysticism. [. . .]

17

Zen therefore is not mysticism, although there may be something in it reminding one of the latter. Zen does not teach absorption, identification, or union, for all these ideas are derived from a dualistic conception of life and the world. In Zen there is a wholeness of things, which refuses to be analysed or separated into antitheses of all kinds. As they say, it is like an iron bar with no holes or handles to swing it about. You have no way to take hold of it; in other words, it cannot be subsumed under any categories. Thus Zen must be said to be a unique discipline in the history of human culture, religious and philosophical.

Zen often speaks of a flash of lightning as if it valued an instantaneous or instinctive action in dealing with the fundamental problems of life. When somebody asks you about Buddhahood or Godhead, you strike the questioner, saying: 'What a blockheaded fellow of a monk!' There is no time lost between asking and striking, and you may think this is an immediacy, which is Zen. But the fact is far from it. Zen has nothing to do with rapidity or immediacy in the sense of being quick. A flash of lightning refers to the non-mediating nature of Zen-experience.

Zen-experience, one might say, is a kind of intuition which is the basis of mysticism. We have to be careful, however, about the use of the term 'intuition'. If we make it presuppose the existence of an antithesis of some form, Zen is not this kind of intuition, which we may designate as static or contemplative. If Zen-experience is an act of intuition, it must be distinguished from the static form, and let us call it dynamic or actional.

D. T. Suzuki, 'An Interpretation of Zen-Experience (1939)' in *Studies in Zen* (London: Rider and Company, 1955), pp. 62–8, 74–6, 81–2.

W. Y. Evans-Wentz

Walter Wentz (1878–1965) was born in Trenton, New Jersey, the son of a German immigrant and an American Quaker. He took an early interest in the books on spiritualism in his father's library, reading in his teens both *Isis Unveiled* and *The Secret Doctrine* by Madame Blavatsky of the Theosophical Society. These works were to have a profound effect on him.

Wentz moved to California at the turn of the century, where he joined the American Section of the Theosophical Society in 1901. After graduating from Stanford University, he went to Jesus College, Oxford, in 1907, where he studied Celtic folklore and changed his name to Evans-Wentz. After the First World War, he travelled to Ceylon and then India. In 1919 he arrived in the British hill station of Darjeeling on the southern slopes of the Himalayas, where he acquired a worn manuscript of a Tibetan text from a monk (some sources indicate that he acquired it in the bazaar). It was a portion of *The Profound Doctrine of Self-Liberation of the Mind [through Encountering] the Peaceful and Wrathful Deities* (*Zab chos zhi khro dgongs pa rang grol*), said to have been discovered in the fourteenth century by Karma gling pa (1352–1405). Evans-Wentz, who could not read Tibetan, took the text to the English teacher at the Maharaja's Boy's School in Gangtok, one Kazi Dawa Samdup (1868–1922), a scholar and practitioner of Tibetan Buddhism.

Kazi Dawa Samdup provided Evans-Wentz with a translation of a portion of the text, which the latter augmented with his own introduction and notes, publishing it in 1927 as *The Tibetan Book of the Dead*. Since its publication, the various editions have sold over 525,000 copies in English; it has also been translated into numerous European languages, making it the most well-known Tibetan Buddhist text in the world.

The Tibetan text translated in Evans-Wentz's work describes the process of death and rebirth, and especially the intervening period known as the 'bardo' or intermediate state, which may last from one instant to forty-nine days. The text contains instructions on how to recognize reality in the intermediate state and thus gain liberation from rebirth. The departed consciousness is said to be able to do so through listening to the instructions in the text being read aloud. Hence, the Tibetan title of the text, *Bardo Thödol*, may be translated as: 'Liberation in the Intermediate State through Hearing'.

Evans-Wentz draws clear parallels between the Tibetan text and various esoteric traditions of the past. The passage from the introduction presented below should be read with Evans-Wentz's lifelong commitment to Theosophy in mind. It shows how he regards the Tibetan text as a remnant of an esoteric tradition of occult knowledge that had once existed throughout the world but had since been largely lost, while being preserved secretly in remote Tibet.

INTRODUCTION*

'The phenomena of life may be likened unto a dream, a phantasm, a bubble, a shadow, the glistening dew, or lightning flash; and thus they are to be contemplated' – The Buddha, in *The Immutable Sutra*.

* This Introduction is – for the most part – based upon and suggested by explanatory notes which the late Lāma Kazi Dawa-Samdup, the translator of the *Bardo Thödol*, dictated to the editor while the translation was taking shape, in Gangtok, Sikkim. The Lāma was of opinion that his English rendering of the *Bardo Thödol* ought not to be published without his exegetical comments on the more abstruse and figurative parts of the text. This, he thought, would not only help to justify his translation, but, moreover, would accord with the wishes of his late *guru* [. . .] with respect to all translations into a European tongue of works expository of the esoteric lore of the Great Perfectionist School into which that *guru* had initiated him. To this end, the translator's exegesis, based upon that of the translator's *guru*, was transmitted to the editor and recorded by the editor herein.

The editor's task is to correlate and systematize and sometimes to expand the notes thus dictated, by incorporating such congenial matter, from widely separated sources, as in his judgement tends to make the exegesis more intelligible to the Occidental, for whom this part of the book is chiefly intended.

The translator felt, too, that, without such safeguarding as this Introduction is intended to afford, the *Bardo Thödol* translation would be peculiarly liable to misinterpretation and consequent misuse, more especially by those who are inclined to be, for one

I. The Importance of the *Bardo Thödol*

As a contribution to the science of death and the existence after death, and of rebirth, *The Tibetan Book of the Dead*, called, in its own language, *Bardo Thödol* ('Liberation by Hearing on the After-Death Plane'),★ is, among the sacred books of the world, unique. As an epitomized exposition of the cardinal doctrines of the *Mahāyāna* School of Buddhism, it is of very great importance, religiously, philosophically, and historically. As a treatise based essentially upon the Occult Sciences of the *Yoga* Philosophy, which were fundamental in the curriculum of the great Buddhist University of Nālanda, the Oxford of ancient India, it is, perhaps, one of the most remarkable works the West has ever received from the East. As a mystic manual for guidance through the Otherworld of many illusions and realms, whose frontiers are death and birth, it resembles *The Egyptian Book of the Dead* sufficiently to

---

reason or another, inimical to Buddhistic doctrines, or to the doctrines of his particular Sect of Northern Buddhism. He also realized how such an Introduction as is here presented might itself be subject to adverse criticism, perhaps on the ground that it appears to be the outcome of a philosophical eclecticism. However this may be, the editor can do no more than state here, as he has stated in other words in the Preface, that his aim, both herein and in the closely related annotations to the text itself, has been to present the psychology and the teachings peculiar to and related to the *Bardo Thödol* as he has been taught them by qualified initiated exponents of them, who alone have the unquestioned right to explain them.

If it should be said by critics that the editor has expounded the *Bardo Thödol* doctrines from the standpoint of the Northern Buddhist who believes in them rather than from the standpoint of the Christian who perhaps would disbelieve at least some of them, the editor has no apology to offer; for he holds that there is no sound reason adducible why he should expound them in any other manner. Anthropology is concerned with things as they are; and the hope of all sincere researchers into comparative religion devoid of any religious bias ought always to be to accumulate such scientific data as will some day enable future generations of mankind to discover Truth itself – that Universal Truth in which all religions and all sects of all religions may ultimately recognize the Essence of Religion and the Catholicity of Faith.

★ Mr Talbot Mundy, in his interesting Tibetan romance *Om*, in making reference to this title, *The Tibetan Book of the Dead*, has taken it to be a very free translation of *Bardo Thödol*. It should not, however, so be taken; it has been adopted because it seems to be the most appropriate short title for conveying to the English reader the true character of the book as a whole.

suggest some ultimate cultural relationship between the two; although we only know with certainty that the germ of the teachings, as herein made accessible to English readers, has been preserved for us by a long succession of saints and seers of the God-protected Land of the Snowy Ranges, Tibet.

II. The Symbolism

The *Bardo Thödol* is unique in that it purports to treat rationally of the whole cycle of *sangsāric* (i.e. phenomenal) existence intervening between death and birth; the ancient doctrine of *karma*, or consequences (taught by Emerson as compensation), and of rebirth being accepted as the most essential laws of nature affecting human life. Often, however, its teaching appears to be quite the antithesis of rational, because much of it is recorded in an occult cipher. Dr. L. A. Waddell has declared, after careful research, that 'the *lāmas* have the keys to unlock the meaning of much of Buddha's doctrine which has been almost inaccessible to Europeans.'*

Some of the more learned *lāmas*, including the late Lāma Kazi Dawa-Samdup, have believed that since very early times there has been a secret international symbol-code in common use among initiates, which affords a key to the meaning of such occult doctrines as are still jealously guarded by religious fraternities in India, as in Tibet, and in China, Mongolia, and Japan.

In like manner, Occidental occultists have contended that the hieroglyphical writings of ancient Egypt and of Mexico seem to have been, in some degree, a popularized or exoteric outgrowth of the secret language. They argue, too, that a symbol-code was sometimes used by Plato and other Greek philosophers, in relation to Pythagorean and Orphic lore; that throughout the Celtic world the Druids conveyed all their esoteric teachings symbolically; that the use of parables, as in the sermons of Jesus and of the Buddha, and of other Great Teachers, illustrates the same tendency; and that through works like *Aesop's Fables*, and the miracle and mystery plays of medieval Europe, many

---

* L. A. Waddell, *The Buddhism of Tibet or Lāmaism* (London, 1895), p. 17.

of the old Oriental symbols have been introduced into the modern literatures of the West.* Be this as it may, it is certain that none of the great systems of ancient thought, nor even vernacular literatures, have always found the ordinary work-a-day language of the world adequate to express transcendental doctrines or even to bring out the full significance of moral maxims.

The lamb, the dragon (or serpent), the dove above the altar, the triangle enclosing the all-seeing eye (common to Freemasonry as well), the sacred fish-symbol, the ever-burning fire, or the image of the risen sun upon the receptacle for the consecrated wafer in the Roman Mass, the architectural symbols and the orientation of church and cathedral, the cross itself, and even the colours and designs of the robes of priest and bishop and pope, are a few of the silent witnesses of the survival in the modern Christian churches of the symbolism of paganism. But the

---

* There is some sound evidence for supposing that one source of the moral philosophy underlying certain of the *Aesop's Fables* (and, also, by way of comparison, of the Indian *Panchatantra* and *Hitopadesha*) may yet be shown to have been such primitive Oriental folk-tales about animals and animal symbols as scholars now think helped to shape the *Jātaka Tales* concerning the various births of the Buddha (cf. *The Jātaka*, ed. by E. B. Cowell, Cambridge, 1895–1907). Similarly, the Christian mystery plays contain symbolism so much akin to that found in mystery plays still flourishing under ecclesiastical patronage throughout Tibet and the neighbouring territories of Northern Buddhism as to point to another stream of Orientalism having come into Europe (cf. *Three Tibetan Mysteries*, ed. by H. I. Woolf, n.d.). The apparent Romanist canonization of the Buddha, under the medieval character of St Jehoshaphat, is an additional instance of how things Eastern seem to have become things Western (cf. *Baralâm and Yĕwâsĕf*, ed. by E. A. W. Budge, Cambridge, 1923). Furthermore, the once very popular medieval work *De Arte Moriendi* (cf. *The Book of the Craft of Dying*, ed. by F. M. M. Comper, London, 1917), of which there are many versions and variants in Latin, English, French, and other European languages, seems to suggest a still further infiltration of Oriental ideas, concerning death and existence after death, such as underlie both the Tibetan *Bardo Thödol* and the Egyptian *Book of the Dead*; and, in order to show this, a few of the most striking passages, found in the *De Arte Moriendi* cycle, which parallel textually certain parts of the *Bardo Thödol*, have been added in footnotes to the *Bardo Thödol* translation from Mr Comper's excellent edition in *The Book of the Craft of Dying*.

Buddhist and Christian Gospels (Philadelphia, 1908), a pioneer study of the remarkable parallelism which exists between the texts of the *New Testament* and the texts of the Buddhist Canon, by Mr A. J. Edmunds, suggests, likewise, that one of the most promising fields of research, as yet almost virgin, lies in a study of just such correspondences between Eastern and Western thought and literature as is suggested in this note.

key to the interpretation of the inner significance of almost all such Christianized symbols was unconsciously thrown away: uninitiated ecclesiastics, gathered together in heresy-seeking councils, having regarded that primitive Christianity, so deeply involved in symbolism, called Gnosticism, as 'Oriental imagery gone mad', repudiated it as being 'heretical', whereas from its own point of view it was merely esoteric.

Similarly, Northern Buddhism, to which symbolism is so vital, has been condemned by Buddhists of the Southern School for claiming to be the custodian of a esoteric doctrine, for the most part orally transmitted by recognized initiates, generation by generation, direct from the Buddha — as well as for teaching (as, for example, in the *Saddharma-Paṇḍarīka*) recorded doctrines not in agreement with doctrines contained in the *Ti-Pitaka* (Skt. *Tri-Pitaka*), the Pali Canon. And yet, though the Southern Buddhist commonly assumes that there cannot be any but a literal interpretation of the Buddha's teachings, the Pali scriptures contain many parables and metaphorical expressions, some of which the *lāmas* regard as symbolical and confirmatory of their own esoteric tradition, and to which they thus claim to hold — perhaps not without good reason — the initiate's key.

The *lāmas* grant that the *Ti-Pitaka* ('Three *Pitakas*, or Baskets' [of the Law]) are, as the Southern Buddhist holds, the recorded Word (or Doctrine) of the Ancients, the *Theravāda*; but they claim that the *Pitakas* do not contain all the Word, that the *Pitakas* lack much of the Buddha's *yogīc* teachings, and that it is chiefly these teachings which, in many instances, have been handed down esoterically to the present day. 'Esoteric Buddhism', as it has come to be called — rightly or wrongly — seems to depend on large measure upon 'ear-whispered' doctrines of this character, conveyed according to long-established and inviolable rule, from *guru* to *shishya*, by word of mouth alone.

The Pali Canon records that the Buddha held no doctrine secretly 'in a closed fist' (cf. *Mahā Parinibbāṇa Sūttanta, Dīgha Nikāya II*), that is to say, withheld no essential doctrine from the members of the *Saṅgha* (Priesthood), just as no *guru* nowadays withholds a doctrine necessary for the spiritual enlightenment of his initiated or accepted disciples. This, however, is far from implying that all such teachings were intended to be set down in writing for the uninitiated and worldly multitude, or that they ever were so recorded in any of the canons. The Buddha Himself wrote down nothing of His teachings, and His disciples who after His death compiled the Buddhist Scriptures may not have recorded therein all that their Master taught them. If they did not, and there are, therefore, as the *lāmas* contend, certain unwritten teachings of the Buddha which have never been taught to those who were not of the *Saṅgha*, then there is, undoubtedly, an extra-canonical, or esoteric, Buddhism. An esoteric Buddhism thus conceived is not, however, to be regarded as in any wise in disagreement with canonical, or exoteric, Buddhism, but as being related to it as higher mathematics are to lower mathematics, or as being the apex of the pyramid of the whole of Buddhism.

In short, the evidence adducible gives much substantial support to the claim of the *lāmas*, to whom we refer, that there is – as the *Bardo Thödol* appears to suggest – an unrecorded body of orally transmitted Buddhistic teachings complementary to canonical Buddhism.*

W. Y. Evans-Wentz, 'Introduction' to *The Tibetan Book of the Dead* (New York: Oxford University Press, 1960), pp. 1–6.

---

* It is probably unnecessary for the editor to remind his friends who profess the Theravāda Buddhism of the Southern School that, in preparing this Introduction, his aim has necessarily been to present Buddhism chiefly from the standpoint of the Northern Buddhism of the Kargyutpa Sect [. . .] by which the *Bardo Thödol* is accepted as a sacred book and to which the translator belonged. Although the Southern Buddhist may not agree with the *Bardo Thödol* teaching in their entirety, he will, nevertheless, be very apt to find them, in most essentials, based upon doctrines common to all Schools and Sects of Buddhism; and he may even find those of them with which he disagrees interesting and possibly provocative of a reconsideration of certain of his own antagonistic beliefs.

T'ai Hsu

T'ai Hsu (1890–1947) was the most famous figure of the Chinese Buddhist revival of the first decades of the twentieth century. He became a monk at the age of fourteen, reportedly because he wanted to acquire the paranormal powers of buddhas. He studied under the famous Chinese monk Eight Fingers (so called because he had burned off one finger of each hand in reverence to the Buddha) and achieved an awakening when reading a perfection-of-wisdom sutra. In 1908 he joined a group of radicals, including other Buddhist monks, intent on religious revolution. In 1911 he organized the first of many groups (many of which were rather short-lived), the Association for the Advancement of Buddhism. In 1912 T'ai Hsu was involved in a failed attempt to turn the most famous Buddhist monastery in China, Chin Shan, into a modern school for monks. After this disgrace he went into retreat for three years, beginning in 1914, during which time he studied the Buddhist scriptures and formulated plans for the reorganization of the sangha. He drafted a number of such plans over the remainder of his career, although none was implemented. In general, these plans called for improved and modernized education for monks and their participation in community and government affairs. He was involved in the publication of a wide variety of Buddhist periodicals, such as *Masses Enlightenment Weekly*, *Voice of Enlightenment*, *Buddhist Critic*, *New Buddhist Youth*, *Modern Sangha*, *Mind's Light* and the most enduring, *The Voice of the Sea Tide*.

In 1923 T'ai Hsu founded the first of several 'world Buddhist organizations', as a result of which he began to travel widely, becoming well known in Europe and America. In 1928, in Paris, he donated funds for the establishment of the World Buddhist Institute, devoted to the unification of Buddhism and science, which would eventually be renamed Les Amis du Bouddhisme. When the first world Buddhist organization, the World Fellowship of Buddhists, was founded in 1950, T'ai Hsu, who had died three years earlier, was credited with its inspiration.

T'ai Hsu lectured in Ceylon and arranged an exchange programme under which Chinese monks would study there. He had planned to establish a network of seminaries throughout China but was unable to do so because of lack of support. It was his belief that Buddhism had become ossified in China and needed to be reformed in order that it be recognized as a philosophy that had the power both to inspire and improve society.

T'ai Hsu lectured often, both in China and abroad, about a union of Buddhism and science. In the passage here, first published in 1928, he both explains how Buddhism has anticipated some of the discoveries of modern science and argues that the study of Buddhism would be useful to scientists. He concludes, however, that the reality set forth by Buddhism will always remain beyond the reach of scientific investigation.

SCIENCE AND BUDDHISM

Scientific knowledge can prove and postulate the Buddhist doctrine, but it cannot ascertain the realities of the Buddhist doctrine.

Scientific discoveries have brought about a certain doubt as to religious evidence. The old gods and religions seem to have been shaken in the wind of science, and religious doctrines have no longer any defence, and the world at large seems to be handed over to the tyranny of the machine and all those monstrous powers to which Science has given birth.

Buddhism takes quite a different point of view, and holds that Science does not go far enough into the mysteries of Nature, and that if she went further the Buddhist doctrine would be even more evident. The truths contained in the Buddhist doctrine concerning the real nature of the Universe would greatly help Science and tend to bring about a union between Science and Buddhism.

Let us take Astronomy, for instance. In ancient times we only knew the heavens above consisting of the sun, moon and stars, and the earth beneath, consisting of the mountain, rivers and woods, with humanity in between. In the West, Greek and Christian philosophers put forward the theory that the earth was the centre of the solar system, and continued to base all their scientific theories on this foundation until Copernicus discovered the solar system. Today, there are those who consider that there is no centre to the Universe, and that space is filled with an infinite number of fixed stars balancing and counterbalancing one another without any master control, so that the theory of fixed astral centres has to be abandoned.

This only confirms the saying of the Buddhist Sutra that 'Space is endless and the number of worlds is infinite, for all are in mutual counterpoise like a network of innumerable beads'. And again 'The world is maintained on a "wind wheel" (axis) which is suspended in a vast and empty space'. These facts which are recognized by Science, are a point of contact between science and the Buddhist doctrine.

Today the microscope has revealed to us that in every drop of water there are countless numbers of microbes, and in the Inner Canon we are told that 'In a single drop of water Buddha can behold eighty four thousand microbes' a fact which I recognized many years ago with a high-power microscope in Prof. Yang Jens' laboratory in Nanking. This may be considered as a second point of contact. Darwin traces the evolutionary development of man back to the ape and to still lower forms of life, and although there is some difference between this theory and the Buddhist doctrine which shows that 'all life emerges from a certain concentration of matter in the form of a nucleus' both of these statements enunciate a law of change, which is inherent in all forms of life. The physiologist tells us that the body is composed of circulatory organs and that the entire mass is a concentration of innumerable cells growing into and supporting life. Let us compare this with what the Sutra tells us 'Consider the body as a concentration of microbes' and in speaking of the beginnings of life we read 'Life rises from a nucleus body of microbes'. This 'nucleus body' certainly coincides with what the scientists call cells. The materialist tells us that Nature is composed of solids, liquids and gases, and the Sutra speaks of four great forms – solids, liquids, wind and fire, the combination of wind and fire producing all such energies as electricity, light, heat, etc. Such points of contact should suffice.

All these statements were to be found in the Buddhist Sutra twenty-five centuries ago, before any such scientific discoveries had been made and before anyone spoke of them in any way whatsoever. From this it is evident that the more Science advances the more it will be welcome to Buddhism.

The above indicates the first steps in the Buddhist doctrine or dharma, the next steps are those of illustrations.

(a) *By means of superstition* – Not everyone can be expected to understand all the laws of the doctrinal sphere. For this reason it is necessary to use the term 'Nature' in accordance with peoples' beliefs or superstitions which may not be accurate in relation to actual facts. Illustrations and suppositions therefore are necessarily used in line with prevalent ideas or superstitious beliefs. Such was the case in great part during the time when Buddha carried out his propaganda.

(b) *By Expediency* – He who has attained to 'Supreme, absolute and universal perception' must have a real understanding of things which allows him to utilize worldly customs, manners and language so as to give various expressions to what he wishes to propagate.

Even though a person be endowed with the wisdom of Buddha himself, there are instances where ordinary human thought cannot fathom the depths, where language itself is inadequate, and where it is necessary to resort to expedients by the use of illustrations which are nearer to ordinary life.

Comparison in this case is used to establish certain principles, when comparison is incorrect we shall have false inference if correct, it will give us true inference.

This method is that on which Science Principally relies. The Sutra says – How does the disciple seek the wisdom of Buddha? By the five ways of enlightenment – language, logic, art, and philosophy, i.e. by Science.

By the use of such scientific methods the Buddhist scholar is aided in his research. When we go beyond these methods we find that Science is unable to grasp the reality of the Buddhist doctrine. The reality of the Buddhist doctrine is only to be grasped by those who are in the sphere of supreme and universal perception, in which they can behold the true nature of the Universe, but for this they must have attained the wisdom of Buddha himself, and it is not by the use of science or logic that we can expect to acquire such wisdom. Science therefore is only a stepping stone in such matters.

The scientist claims that scientific knowledge is the whole truth and stops there, in this he resembles the blind man who after examining the body of an elephant, declared the ear to be a fan, and the tail to be a broom. If we compare the elephant and all the organs of its body to the Universe, then the blind man may be compared to the Scientist who has never realised an absolute, universal, perception of the universe.

Scientific methods can only corroborate the Buddhist doctrine, they can never advance beyond it.

Here we must refer to two deeply rooted superstitions.

(a) *the Superstition of God or the Restriction of the Ego* – The Ego, or Spiritual Self, known as God is in reality a superstition. The Mahayana doctrine is free from this restriction since it holds that this corporeal form of ours is born from causality and harmony and destroyed or carried on like any other illusion of the Unreal. It may be compared to the interchangeability of the five colours in the flame which flicker here and there in constant change.

(b) *The Superstition of Reality* – To the Materialist, Reality is Matter, it may also be defined as Law. The materialists' theory reduces all Nature to matter, which is a combination of simple elements which, in their turn, are again reduced to atoms or electrons. This theory has now given way to the dynamic conception in which everything is reduced to energy or movement, so that our whole conception of matter is likely to be changed, since energy is something which is not accessible to the eye or ear. In this way Scientific thought is more and more evolving in accordance with the Buddhist doctrine, and tends more and more to confirm the principles of the Inner Canon. It is only after the Boddhisattva has been convinced of the truth of these methods however that Science can be trusted to observe the effects of different emotional processes on the understanding.

The Saddharma Pundarika Sutra tells us that expedients may be used to convince the multitude, and in many of the other Sutras we find that every subject is fully discussed in a manner surpassing that of Science.

Science therefore, can never be the main support of Buddhism although it may act as a valuable auxiliary and much may be expected from uniting the two methods of investigation.

The principles of Buddhism however may enable us to overcome the restriction of the ego and the law and enable us to enter the realm of perfect wisdom. Those who reach this enlightenment are like the blind man, whose vision is suddenly restored, so that he can see clearly and distinctly all that is around him.

The scientist however, is constantly trying to improve his instruments rather than to perfect his inner vision, this is like depending on our bodily senses.

The main principles of the Buddhist doctrine therefore are 'unscientific' and sweep away all the false conclusions at which Science has arrived, otherwise it would be impossible to overcome ignorance and attain enlightenment.

If life however were founded on the six paramitas – the six virtues of the Boddhisattvas, and these in turn, were realised to be in accordance with scientific research, then we might hope to enter into the pure realms of Buddha and emerge from the chaos of fire and brimstone into which we have fallen.

T'ai Hsu, 'Science and Buddhism', in *Lectures in Buddhism* (Paris: 1928), pp. 43–50.

B. R. Ambedkar

Bhimrao Ramji Ambedkar (1891–1956) was the fourteenth child of an 'untouchable' family in the Indian state of Maharashtra, the son of an Indian officer in the British army. He was one of the only members of his caste to receive a secondary-school education, and eventually went on to study in New York and London, receiving a doctorate from Columbia University. Upon his return to India, he worked both for Indian independence from Britain and for the social and political rights of the untouchables. After independence, he served in Nehru's government, chairing the committee that drafted the constitution. Seeking a religious identity for untouchables that would free them from the caste prejudice of Hinduism, he chose Buddhism, after considering also Islam, Christianity and Sikhism. Buddhism had been defunct in India for many centuries, but Ambedkar would eventually conclude that the untouchables were the descendants of Buddhists who had been persecuted by Hindus for their beliefs. In 1956, six weeks before his death, Ambedkar publicly converted to Buddhism and then led an audience of 380,000 in taking refuge in the Buddha, dharma and sangha and in accepting the five precepts (pancha sila) of lay Buddhists. Eventually millions of others, mostly from low-caste and outcaste groups, followed his example.

Ambedkar portrayed the Buddha as a social reformer and saw in Buddhism the foundation for a more egalitarian Indian society. This vision is clearly articulated in the excerpts below, in which he compares the Buddha with Karl Marx. His summary of the teaching of the Buddha in twenty-five points is remarkable for a number of reasons. First, it functions as a critique of contemporary Hinduism, at whose hands the outcastes had so long suffered. Second, it presents the Buddha as a rationalist philosopher and a social reformer, making no mention of the supernatural qualities that Buddhists have ascribed to him over the centuries. Third, it presents Buddhism as focused entirely on this world and the construction of a just and happy society, with no mention of the doctrine of rebirth and the ultimate goal of liberation from rebirth, with suffering caused not by ignorance of the nature of reality but by poverty. In each case Ambedkar adopts the traditional strategy of the Buddhist exegete, citing a Buddhist text to support his point. In so doing, he turns a blind eye to numerous elements of the tradition that do not conform to his vision of a thoroughly modern dharma that is fully compatible with the most modern and egalitarian of European reforms. He is thus able to combine a certain Buddhist triumphalism with a social pro-gramme designed to better the material conditions of his people, finding a critique for what he considered the bigotry of modern Hinduism and the injustices of Indian society not in Christianity or Communism, but in an ancient Indian tradition that had been all but forgotten in the land of its birth.

BUDDHA OR KARL MARX

A comparison between Karl Marx and Buddha may be regarded as a joke. There need be no surprise in this. Marx and Buddha are divided by 2,381 years. Buddha was born in 563 BC and Karl Marx in 1818 AD. Karl Marx is supposed to be the architect of a new ideology-polity – a new Economic system. The Buddha on the other hand is believed to be no more than the founder of a religion which has no relation to politics or economics. The heading of this essay 'Buddha or Karl Marx' which suggests either a comparison or a contrast between two such personalities divided by such a lengthy span of time and occupied with different fields of thought is sure to sound odd. The Marxists may easily laugh at it and may ridicule the very idea of treating Marx and Buddha on the same level. Marx so modern and Buddha so ancient! The Marxists may say that the Buddha as compared to their master must be just primitive. What comparison can there be between two such persons? What could a Marxist learn from the Buddha? What can Buddha teach a Marxist? None-the-less a comparison between the two is attractive and instructive. Having read both and being interested in the ideology of both a comparison between them just forces itself on me. If the Marxists keep back their prejudices and study the Buddha and understand what he stood for I feel sure that they will change their attitude. It is of course too much to expect that having been determined to scoff at the Buddha they will remain to pray. But this much can be said that they will realize there is something in the Buddha's teaching which is worth their while to take note of.

I. The Creed of the Buddha

The Buddha is generally associated with the doctrine of Ahimsa. That is taken to be the be-all and end-all of his teachings. Hardly anyone knows that what the Buddha taught is something very vast; far beyond Ahimsa. It is therefore necessary to set out in detail his tenets. I enumerate them below as I have understood them from my reading of the Tripitaka:

1. Religion is necessary for a free Society.

2. Not every Religion is worth having.

3. Religion must relate to facts of life and not to theories and speculations about God, or Soul or Heaven or Earth.

4. It is wrong to make God the centre of Religion.

5. It is wrong to make salvation of the soul as the centre of Religion.

6. It is wrong to make animal sacrifices to be the centre of Religion.

7. Real Religion lives in the heart of man and not in the Shastras.

8. Man and mortality must be the centre of Religion. If not, Religion is a cruel superstition.

9. It is not enough for Morality to be the ideal of life. Since there is no God it must become the law of life.

10. The function of Religion is to reconstruct the world and to make it happy and not to explain its origin or its end.

11. That the unhappiness in the world is due to conflict of interest and the only way to solve it is to follow the Ashtanga Marga.

12. That private ownership of property brings power to one class and sorrow to another.

13. That it is necessary for the good of Society that this sorrow be removed by removing its cause.

14. All human beings are equal.

15. Worth and not birth is the measure of man.

16. What is important is high ideals and not noble birth.

17. Maitri or fellowship towards all must never be abandoned. One owes it even to one's enemy.

18. Everyone has a right to learn. Learning is as necessary for man to live as food is.

19. Learning without character is dangerous.

20. Nothing is infallible. Nothing is binding forever. Every thing is subject to inquiry and examination.

21. Nothing is final.

22. Every thing is subject to the law of causation.

23. Nothing is permanent or sanatan. Every thing is subject to change. Being is always Becoming.

24. War is wrong unless it is for truth and justice.

25. The victor has duties towards the vanquished.

This is the creed of the Buddha in a summary form. How ancient but how fresh! How wide and how deep are his teachings!

II. The Original Creed of Karl Marx

Let us now turn to the creed of Karl Marx as originally propounded by him. Karl Marx is no doubt the father of modern socialism or Communism but he was not interested merely in propounding the theory of Socialism. That had been done long before him by others. Marx was more interested in proving that his Socialism was scientific. His crusade was as much against the capitalists as it was against those whom he called the Utopian Socialists. He disliked them both. It is necessary to note this point because Marx attached the greatest importance to the scientific character of his Socialism. All the doctrines which Marx propounded had no other purpose than to establish his contention that his brand of Socialism was scientific and not Utopian.

By scientific socialism what Karl Marx meant was that his brand of socialism was *inevitable* and *inescapable* and that society was moving towards it and that nothing could prevent its march. It is to prove this contention of his that Marx principally laboured.

Marx's contention rested on the following theses. They were:

(i) That the purpose of philosophy is to reconstruct the world and not to explain the origin of the universe.

(ii) That the forces which shape the course of history are primarily economic.

(iii) That society is divided into two classes, owners and workers.

(iv) That there is always a class conflict going on between the two classes.

(v) That the workers are exploited by the owners who misappropriate the surplus value which is the result of the workers' labour.

(vi) That this exploitation can be put an end to by nationalization of the instruments of production i.e. abolition of private property.

(vii) That this exploitation is leading to greater and greater impoverishment of the workers.

(viii) That this growing impoverishment of the workers is resulting in a revolutionary spirit among the workers and the conversion of the class conflict into a class struggle.

(ix) That as the workers outnumber the owners, the workers are bound to capture the State and establish their rule which he called the dictatorship of the proletariate.

(x) These factors are irresistible and therefore socialism is inevitable.

I hope I have reported correctly the propositions which formed the original basis of Marxian Socialism. [. . .]

IV. Comparison Between Buddha and Karl Marx

Taking the points from the Marxian Creed which have survived one may now enter upon a comparison between the Buddha and Karl Marx.

On the first point there is complete agreement between the Buddha and Karl Marx. To show how close is the agreement I quote below a part of the dialogue between Buddha and the Brahmin Potthapada.

'Then, in the same terms, Potthapada asked (the Buddha) each of the following questions:

1. Is the world not eternal?
2. Is the world finite?
3. Is the world infinite?
4. Is the soul the same as the body?

5. Is the soul one thing, and the body another?

6. Does one who has gained the truth live again after death?

7. Does he neither live again, nor not live again, after death?

And to each question the exalted one made the same reply: It was this.

'That too, Potthapada, is a matter on which I have expressed no opinion.'

'But why has the Exalted One expressed no opinion on that?'

(Because) 'This question is not calculated to profit, it is not concerned with (the Dhamma) it does not rebound even to the elements of right conduct, nor to detachment nor to purification from lust, nor to quietude, nor to tranquillisation of the heart, nor to real knowledge, nor to the insight (of the higher stages of the Path), nor to Nirvana. Therefore it is that I express no opinion about it.' [. . .]

V. The Means

We must now come to the means. The means of bringing about Communism which the Buddha propounded were quite definite. The means can be divided into three parts.

Part I consisted in observing the Pancha Silas.

The Enlightenment gave birth to a new gospel which contains the solution of the problem which was haunting him.

The foundation of the New Gospel is the fact that the world was full of misery and unhappiness. It was a fact not merely to be noted but to be regarded as being the first and foremost in any scheme of salvation. The recognition of this fact the Buddha made the starting point of his gospel.

To remove this misery and unhappiness was to him the aim and object of the gospel if it is to serve any useful purpose.

Asking what could be the causes of this misery the Buddha found that there could be only two.

A part of the misery and unhappiness of man was the result of his own misconduct. To remove this cause of misery he preached the practice of the Panch Sila.

The Panch Sila comprised the following observations: (1) To abstain from destroying or causing destruction to any living thing; (2) To abstain from stealing i.e. acquiring or keeping by fraud or violence, the property of another; (3) To Abstain from telling untruth; (4) To abstain from lust; (5) To abstain from intoxicating drinks.

A part of the misery and unhappiness of the world was according to the Buddha the result of man's inequity toward man. How was this inequity to be removed? For the removal of man's inequity towards man the Buddha prescribed the Noble Eight-Fold Path. The elements of the Noble Eight-Fold Path are:

(1) Right views i.e. freedom from superstition; (2) Right aims, high and worthy of the intelligent and earnest men; (3) Right speech i.e. kindly, open, truthful; (4) Right Conduct i.e. peaceful, honest and pure; (5) Right livelihood i.e. causing hurt or injury to no living being; (6) Right perseverance in all other seven; (7) Right mindfulness i.e. with a watchful and active mind; and (8) Right contemplation i.e. earnest thought on the deep mysteries of life.

The aim of the Noble Eight-Fold Path is to establish on earth the kingdom of righteousness, and thereby to banish sorrow and happiness from the face of the world [. . .]

Such is the gospel of the Buddha enunciated as a result of his enlightenment to end the sorrow and misery of the world.

It is clear that the means adopted by the Buddha were to convert a man by changing his moral disposition to follow the path voluntarily.

The means adopted by the Communists are equally clear, short and swift. They are (1) Violence and (2) Dictatorship of the Proletariat.

The Communists say that there are only two means of establishing communism. The first is violence. Nothing short of it will suffice to break up the existing system. The other is dictatorship of the proletariat. Nothing short of it will suffice to continue the new system.

It is now clear what are the similarities and differences between the Buddha and Karl Marx. The differences are about the means. The end is common to both.

B. R. Ambedkar, 'Buddha or Karl Marx' in *Writings and Speeches*, vol 3, compiled by Vasant Moon (Bombay: Education Employment Department, 1987), pp. 441–50.

Lama Govinda

Lama Anagarika Govinda (1895–1985) was born Ernst Lothar Hoffmann in Kassel, Germany. He served at the Italian front during the First World War, after which he continued his studies at Freiburg University in Switzerland. Govinda became interested in Buddhism while living with expatriate European and American artists in Capri, publishing his first book, *The Basic Ideas of Buddhism and Its Relationship to Ideas of God*, in 1920, a work that is apparently no longer extant. In 1928 he sailed for Ceylon, where he studied meditation and Buddhist philosophy briefly with the German-born Theravada monk Nyanatiloka Mahathera (who gave him the name Govinda), before leaving to travel in Burma and India. While visiting Darjeeling in the Himalayas in 1931, he was driven by a spring snowstorm to take refuge in a Tibetan monastery at Ghoom, where he met Tomo Geshe Rimpoche, a Gelukpa lama. In his autobiographical *The Way of the White Clouds*, published nearly thirty years later in 1960, Govinda depicts their encounter and his subsequent initiation as a pivotal moment in his life.

After making a pilgrimage to Mount Kailash in south-western Tibet in 1932, he held brief teaching positions at the University of Patna and at Shantiniketan (founded by Rabindranath Tagore), publishing essays in *Mahabodhi*, the journal of Dharmapala's society, as well as various Theosophical journals. His lectures at Patna were compiled as *The Psychological Attitude of Early Buddhist Philosophy* (1937) and those at Shantiniketan as *Psycho-Cosmic Symbolism of the Buddhist Stupa* (1940). While at Shantiniketan he met a Parsi woman, Rati Petit, whom he married in 1947. (She also assumed a new name, Li Gotami, and, like her husband, dressed in Tibetan-style robes of his design.) During the 1930s Govinda founded a number of organizations, including the International Buddhist University Association, the International Buddhist Academy Association and the Arya Maitreya Mandala. In 1942 he was interned by the British at Dehra Dun along with other German nationals, including Heinrich Harrer, the Austrian mountaineer and SS soldier who escaped from the prison camp and made his way to Tibet, later recounting the tale in *Seven Years in Tibet* (1952).

From 1947–8 Govinda and Li Gotami led an expedition sponsored by the *Illustrated Weekly of India* to photograph some of the temples of western Tibet, notably at Tsaparang and Tholing. During their travels they met a lama named Ajorepa Rimpoche at Tsecholing Monastery, who, according to Govinda, initiated them into the Kagyu order. From this point on he described himself as an initiate of the Kagyu order, or, as he often styled himself, 'an Indian National of European descent and Buddhist faith belonging to a Tibetan Order and believing in the Brotherhood of Man'.

Returning from Tibet, Govinda and Li Gotami set up permanent residence in India, living as tenants of a house and property rented to them by Walter Evans Wentz. During the 1960s their home at Kasar Devi became an increasingly obligatory stop for spiritual seekers (including the Beat poets Gary Snyder and Allen Ginsberg in 1961) until they were forced to put up signs around the property warning visitors away. He spent the last two decades before his death in 1985 lecturing in Europe and the United States. His last years were spent in a home in Mill Valley provided by the San Francisco Zen Center.

The passages below are drawn from Lama Govinda's most sustained work of Buddhist philosophy, *Foundations of Tibetan Mysticism* (originally published in 1960). Despite its title, no original Tibetan texts are cited (and it is unclear whether he ever learned to read Tibetan). The 'foundations' to which the title alludes are therefore foundations of which Tibetans would seem unaware, drawn instead from Govinda's wide and eclectic reading. The work is structured as a commentary on the famous mantra *om mani padme hum*. In a reading with strong Theosophical undertones, he presents the syllable *om* as an ancient expression of universal reality that became en-crusted with theology and speculation, only to be restored to its true nature by the Buddha. It, along with other elements of the tantric path, are to be used as tools to bring about mystical experience of an inexpressible reality.

THE DECADENCE OF MANTRIC TRADITION

Mantric knowledge can be called a secret doctrine with as much or as little justification as higher mathematics, physics, or chemistry, which to the ordinary man who is not acquainted with the symbols and formulae of these sciences, appear like a book with seven seals. But just as the ultimate discoveries of these sciences can be misused for purposes of personal or political power and are therefore kept secret by interested parties (like state-governments), in the same way mantric knowledge became a victim of power-politics of certain castes or classes of society at certain times.

In ancient India the Brahmins, the priestly class, made the knowledge of mantras a prerogative or privilege of their caste, thereby forcing all those who did not belong to their class blindly to accept the dictates of tradition. In this way it happened that what once streamed forth from religious ecstasy and inspiration, turned into dogma, and finally reacted even on the originators of this tradition as irresistible compulsion. Knowledge became mere belief; and belief, without the corrective of experience, turned into superstition.

Nearly all superstition in the world can be traced to some truths which, by being separated from their genetic connexions, have lost their meaning. They are, as the word literally says, 'remainders', something that is 'left over' ('super-stitia'). And because the circumstances and the way in which those truths or ideas had been found, i.e. their logical, spiritual, or historical connexions, have been forgotten, they become mere beliefs which have nothing in common with genuine faith or the reasonable confidence in the truth or power of an idea or a person, a confidence which grows into inner certainty through being borne out by experience and in harmony with the laws of reason and reality. This kind of faith is the necessary pre-condition of every mental or spiritual activity, be it science or philosophy, religion or art. It is the positive attitude of our mind and our whole being, without which no spiritual progress can be attained. It is the *saddha* which the Buddha demanded from those who wanted to follow him on his way. *'Aparutā tesam amatassa dvārā, ye sotavantā pamuñcantu saddham.'* 'Opened are the gates of immortality; ye that have ears to hear, release your faith!' These were the words with which the Buddha began his career as a religious teacher, '*Pamuñcantu saddhaṁ*' means: 'let your faith, your inner trust and confidence stream forth, remove your inner obstacles and open yourself to the truth!'

It was this kind of faith, or inner readiness and open-mindedness, which found its spontaneous expression, its liberation from an over-whelming psychic pressure, in the sacred sound OṀ. In this mantric symbol all the positive and forward-pressing forces of the human mind (which are trying to blow up its limitations and burst the fetters of ignorance) are united and concentrated like an 'arrow-point'.

But all too soon this genuine expression of profound experience fell a victim to speculation; because those who had no part in the experience themselves, tried to analyse its results. It was not sufficient to them that by removing the causes of darkness, light would prevail. They wanted to discuss the quality of light before they had even started penetrating the darkness; and while discussing them, they built up an elaborate theology, into which the sacred OṀ was woven so artfully, that it became impossible to extricate it.

Instead of relying on their own forces, they expected the help of some supernatural agent. While speculating about the aim, they forgot that the effort of 'shooting off the arrow' was to be made by themselves and not by some magic power within the arrow or the aim. They adorned and worshipped the arrow instead of using it, charged with all their available energy. They unbent the bow of mind and body instead of training it.

Thus it happened that at the time of the Buddha this great mantric symbol had become so much entangled in the theology of brahmanical faith, that it could not be used in a doctrine which tried to free itself as much from the tutelage of Brahmins as from superfluous dogmas and theories, and which emphasized the self-determination, self-responsibility of man and his independence from the power of gods.

It was the first and most important task of Buddhism 'to bend and re-string the bow of body and mind' by proper training and discipline. And after the self-confidence of man had been restored, the new doctrine firmly established, and the ornaments and cobwebs of theology and speculation had withered and fallen from the sacred arrow-head OM, it could again be attached to the arrow of meditation.

We have mentioned already how closely OM was connected with the development of Yoga which, as a kind of inter-religious system of mental and bodily training methods, received and gave contributions to every school of religious thought. Buddhism, from its very beginning, had accepted and developed the practice of Yoga, and a continuous exchange of experiences between Buddhism and other religious systems took place for nearly two millenniums.

It was therefore not surprising that even though the syllable OM had temporarily lost its importance as a symbol, the religious practice of early Buddhism made use of the mantric formulae, wherever these proved helpful as a means for the awakening of faith (*saddha*), for the liberation from inner hindrances, and for the concentration upon the supreme goal.

[. . .]

THE ANTHROPOMORPHIC SYMBOLISM OF THE *TANTRAS*

The abstractness of philosophical concepts and conclusions requires to be constantly corrected by direct experience, by the practice of meditation and the contingencies of daily life. The anthropomorphic element in the *Vajrayāna* is therefore not born from a lack of intellectual understanding (as in the case of primitive man), but, on the contrary, from the conscious desire to penetrate from a merely intellectual and theoretical attitude to the direct awareness of reality. This cannot be achieved through building up convictions, ideals, and aims based on reasoning, but only through conscious penetration of those layers of our mind which cannot be reached or influenced by logical arguments and discursive thought.

Such penetration and transformation is only possible through the compelling power of inner vision, whose primordial images or 'arche-types' are the formative principles of our mind. Like seeds they sink into the fertile soil of our subconsciousness in order to germinate, to grow and to unfold their potentialities.

One may object that such visions are purely subjective and therefore nothing ultimate. However, words and ideas are nothing ultimate either; and the danger of getting attached to them is all the greater, as words have a limiting, narrowing tendency, while experiences and symbols of true visions are something that is alive, that is growing and ripening within us. They point and grow beyond themselves. They are too immaterial, too 'transparent', too elusive, to become solid or 'thingish', and to arouse attachment. They can neither be 'grasped' nor defined, nor circumscribed exactly. They have the tendency to grow from the formed to the formless – while that which is merely thought-out has the opposite tendency, namely, to harden into lifeless concepts and dogmas.

The subjectivity of inner vision does not diminish its reality-value. Such visions are not hallucinations, because their reality is that of the human psyche. They are symbols, in which the highest knowledge and the noblest endeavour of the human mind are embodied. Their visualization is the creative process of spiritual projection, through which inner experience is translated into visible form, comparable to the creative act of an artist, whose subjective idea, emotion, or vision, is transformed into an objective work of art, which now takes on a reality of its own, independent of its creator.

But just as an artist must gain perfect control over his means of expression and makes use of a variety of technical aids in order to achieve the most perfect expression of his idea, in the same way the spiritually creative man must be able to master the functions of his mind and use certain technical aids in order to embue his vision with the power and value of reality. His technical aids are *yantra*, *mantra*, and *mudrā*: the parallelism of the visible, the audible and the tangible (i.e. what can be felt). They are the exponents of mind (*citta*), speech (*vāk, vācā*), and body (*kāya*).

Here the term '*yantra*' is used in the sense of *maṇḍala* (Tib.: *dkyil-ḥkhor*), the systematic arrangement of the symbols on which the process of visualization is based. It is generally built upon the shape of a four-, eight-, or sixteen-petalled lotus-blossom (*padma*) which forms the visible starting-point of meditation.

Mantra (Tib.: *gzuṅs, sṅags*), the word-symbol, is the sacred sound, transmitted from *guru* to *chela* (disciple) during the ritual of initiation and in the course of the spiritual training. The inner vibrations set up by this sacred sound and its associations in the consciousness of the initiate, open his mind to the experience of higher dimensions.

Mudrā (Tib.: *phyag-rgya*) is the bodily gesture (especially of the hands) which accompanies the ritual act and the mantric word, as well as the inner attitude, which is emphasized and expressed by this gesture.

Only through the co-operation of all these factors can the adept build up his spiritual creation bit by bit and realize his vision. This is not a matter of emotional ecstasy or unrestrained imagination, but a consciously directed creative process of realization, in which nothing is left to chance and in which there is no place for vague emotions and confused thinking.

'The old Buddhist idea, that actions carried out "*kāyena, vācāya uda cetasā*" [in body, speech or thought] produce transcendental effects, in so far as they are *karma*-producing expressions of the human will, gets a new meaning in the *Vajrayāna*. It corresponds to the new conviction of the immense importance of ritual acts: the co-ordination of the actions of body, speech and mind (thought) enables the *sādhaka* to insert himself into the dynamic forces of the cosmos and to make them subservient to his own purposes.' (H. von Glasenapp.)★

The dynamic forces of the universe, however, are not different from those of the human soul, and to recognize and transform those forces in one's own mind – not only for one's own good, but for that of all living beings – is the aim of the Buddhist Tantras.

The Buddhist does not believe in an independent or separately existing world, into whose dynamic forces he could insert himself. The external world and his inner world are for him only the two sides of the same fabric, in which the threads of all forces and of all events, of all forms of consciousness and of their objects, are woven into an inseparable net of endless, mutually conditioned relations.

The word '*tantra*' is related to the concept of weaving and its

---

★ *Die Entstehung des Vajrayāna*, Zeitschrift der Deutschen Morgenländischen Gesellschaft, Band 90.

derivatives (thread, web, fabric, etc.), hinting at the interwovenness of things and actions, the interdependence of all that exists, the continuity in the interaction of cause and effect, as well as in spiritual and traditional development, which like a thread weaves its way through the fabric of history and of individual lives. The scriptures which in Buddhism go under the name of Tantra (Tib.: *rgyud*) are invariably of a mystic nature, i.e. trying to establish the *inner* relationship of things: the parallelism of microcosm and macrocosm, mind and universe, ritual and reality, the world of matter and the world of the spirit.

This is the essence of Tantrism, as it developed with logical necessity from the teachings and the religious practice of *Vijñānavādins* and *Yogācārins* (the former name emphasizes more the theoretical or philosophical, the latter more the practical aspect of the same School of Mahāyāna-Buddhism). Like a gigantic wave, the Tantric conception of the world swept over the whole of India, penetrating and modifying Buddhism and Hinduism alike and obliterating many of their differences.

Lama Anagarika Govinda, *Foundations of Tibetan Mysticism* (New York: Samuel Weiser, 1973), pp. 29–31, 91–4.

R. H. Blyth

Reginald H. Blyth (1898–1964) was born near London into a working-class family. During the First World War he was a conscientious objector and spent three years in prison as a result. He left England shortly thereafter and travelled to India, moving on eventually to Korea where he took a university position teaching English. Blyth returned to England briefly to complete his undergraduate education, receiving a degree in English literature, before again taking up his position at the University of Seoul. While in Korea – which had been a Japanese colony since 1905 – he met and befriended a Japanese Zen monk and began to study the Japanese language and to practise Zen meditation. In 1940 he and his Japanese wife moved to Japan. With the entry of England and then America into the Pacific War, Blyth was interned for its duration, along with other Europeans and Americans living in Japan. Although kept under guard, conditions for these internees were less brutal than those for Allied prisoners of war, and Blyth was allowed to have books and weekly visits from his wife. He remained in Japan after the war, working as a translator, author and teacher of English literature at Gakushuin, the university for the children of the aristocracy and the Japanese royal family.

In 1943, while interned, Blyth published his most famous work, *Zen in English Literature and Oriental Classics*. As one of the few books on Zen (apart from the works of D. T. Suzuki) available in English after the Second World War, it had a great influence on the Beat poets. His subsequent four-volume translation of Japanese haiku, the seventeen-syllable poem, served as model for much of their poetry. As is clear from the extract below, Blyth found Zen absolutely everywhere. He was strongly influenced by D. T. Suzuki, especially his *Zen Buddhism and its Influence on Japanese Culture* (1938; republished in 1959 as *Zen and Japanese Culture*). Suzuki's work (and by extension that of Blyth) cannot be fully understood without some insight into the political climate from which they emerged. Suzuki went to some lengths in his work to identify Zen with the warrior spirit (*bushido*) of Japan, arguing that it was Zen that provided the Japanese warrior with his will. For Suzuki, Zen was not a religion or a philosophy but an intuition that could be deployed in all circumstances. Suzuki was just one of many Zen authors during this period seeking to identify Zen with the Japanese invasion and occupation of the Asian mainland. The works of Suzuki and Blyth promote a kind of Zen universalism that had very different connotations in 1943 than it would have in subsequent decades.

DIRECTNESS IS ALL

Zen is above all things direct; no intermediaries, no mediators between God and man, no symbolism. Emerson says in *Self Reliance*,

The relations of the soul to the divine spirit are so pure that it is profane to seek to interpose helps.

Zen would not say it is profane or holy to do anything, nor would it say that the so-called helps are hindrances. All things are ends in themselves. This truth is easy to grasp, difficult to retain; a moment's inattention and we do as Prof. Suzuki does in his *Buddhist Philosophy and its Effects on the Life and Thought of the Japanese People*, where he says, explaining the meaning of a Buddhist *kuyô* in regard to a painter's worn-out brushes,

It is no doubt a lifeless instrument constructed by human hands, and we can say that there is no 'soul' in it, whatever we may mean by this term. But the fact is that the brush is an extension of the painter's own arm, as every human instrument is, and as such it is endowed with life, for with it the painter can express himself and give spirit to his works. The brush in the hands of the painter is surely possessed of life and spirit.

This is not so. The brush has its own existence; it exists for and of itself, whether used or usable or not. When worn out and thrown into the dustbin, its absolute value is unchanged. So Wordsworth, speaking of the Thames, says,

It glideth *at its own sweet will,*

apart from whether it is used to float vessels, to create electricity, as drinking water, or as the subject of Wordsworth's poem. This was the opinion of Kant and of Goethe.

Die Ansicht, dass jedes Geschöpf um sein selbst willen existiert, und nicht etwa der Korkbaum gewachsen ist, damit wir unsere Flaschen pfropfen können: dieses hatte Kant mit mir gemein, und ich fruete mich, ihm hierin zu begegnen.
(Eckermann, *Gespräche mit Goethe*, April, 1827)

Dean Inge makes precisely the same mistake but at the other end of the scale. He says in *Personal Idealism and Mysticism,*

It seems to me that Truth and Beauty are ideals too august to be ever regarded as means only. Science and Art are both false to themselves if they suffer themselves to be mere handmaids of morality.

As I said above, the corpse of a bed-bug, the parings of the fingernails, are too august to be treated as means. There are no means in this or any other world. But from another point of view we must say that Truth and Beauty are nothing in themselves; they can never be ends. What is the end of man? Wordsworth says, rushing in where angels fear to tread,

Our destiny, our being's end and home
Is with infinitude and only there.

Maybe; but also,

Closer is He than breathing, and nearer than hands and feet, says Tennyson; then let Wordsworth himself amend it to

> With hope it is, hope that can never die,
> Effort and expectation and desire,
> *And something evermore about to be.*

But hear what the angel said one thousand three hundred years before Wordsworth was born:

> Plucking chrysanthemums along the east fence;
> Gazing in silence at the Southern Hills;
> The birds flying home in pairs
> Through the soft mountain air of dusk –
> In these things there is a deep meaning,
> But when we are about to express it,
> We suddenly forget the words.

Truth, Reality, is inexpressible in words – and yet it is expressed in words! It is expressed, if we can hear it, in all the sounds and sights of this world. Blake says,

The roaring of lions, the howling of wolves, the raging of the stormy sea, and the destructive sword, are portions of eternity too great for the eye of man.

It is expressed also in the simplest conversation, if only we can forget, for even a moment, the purely intellectual content of the words, and listen to the voice of eternity.

> A certain monk said to Hôgen,
> 'I, E-chô, ask you, "What is the Buddha?" '
> Hôgen answered, 'You are E-chô.'

The monk wanted to understand the Nature of the Universe, the Secret of Life, its Meaning. Hôgen says, 'All these things will be added unto you, once you know, "Who is E-Chô? Who am I?" And I will tell you the answer at once, without beating about the bush, the answer to the whole Riddle of Existence:

You are E-Chô!'

As Engo says,

How the spiritual war-horses of past times sweated blood to attain this state!

It is just this directness, this perfect sincerity, which is so difficult to attain. In order to reach this state, two things are necessary, one negative, the other positive. First, we must realise that for the understanding of the meaning of Life (which is no different from that of our own life) it is useless to rely on the intellect working alone; and that since the intellect has got into the habit of working by itself, acting like a dictator to the rest of the personality, it must, temporarily, be put into a strait waistcoat. Second, that we are to do what Confucius said in *The Great Learning*, that the superior man does,

In all things, he does his utmost.

Here is an example of how the superior man plays billiards for the first and last time:

Once only do I remember seeing him play a game of billiards, and a truly remarkable performance it was. He played with all the fire and dramatic intensity that he was apt to put into things. The balls flew wildly about, on or off the table as the case might be, but seldom indeed ever threatened a pocket or got within a hand's breadth of a cannon. 'What a fine thing a game of billiards is,' he remarked to the astonished onlookers, ' – once a year or so!'

(*Life of Stevenson*, by Graham Balfour)

Let us take the first poem in the *Golden Treasury*, Nash's *Spring*, from *Summer's Last Will and Testament*:

Spring, the sweete spring, is the yeres pleasant King,
Then bloomes eche thing, then maydes daunce in a ring,
Cold doeth not string, the pretty birds doe sing,
    Cuckow, jugge, jugge, puwe, towittawoo.

The Palme and May make countrey houses gay.
Lambs friske and play, the Shepherds pype all day,
And we heare aye birds tune this merry lay,
    Cuckow, jugge, jugge, puwe, towittawoo.

The fields breath sweete, the dayzies kisse our feete,
Young lovers meete, old wives a-sunning sit:
In every streete, these tunes our ears doe greete,
Cuckow, jugge, jugge, puwe, towittawoo.
    Spring the sweete spring.

Several times, when collecting best pieces of English Poetry (the intelligent young man's substitute for a diary) I hesitated over this poem, but finally, not following my instincts, excluded it. It has no purple patches, no exquisite epithets, nothing to mark the chooser of it as a poetical highbrow. And look at the last line of each verse! Who would dare to read such a poem aloud? But it breathes the spirit of spring as no other poem in the English language. Let us take another on the same subject by Blake:

O thou with dewy locks, who lookest down
Thro' the clear windows of the morning, turn
Thine angel eyes upon our western isle,
Which in full choir hails thy approach, O Spring!

The Hills tell each other, and the list'ning
Vallies hear, all our longing eyes are turned
Up to thy bright pavillions: issue forth,
And let thy holy feet visit our clime.

> Come o'er the eastern hills, and let our winds
> Kiss thy perfumed garments; let us taste
> Thy morn and evening breath: scatter thy pearls
> Upon our love-sick land that mourns for thee.
>
> O deck her forth with thy fair fingers; pour
> Thy soft kisses on her bosom; and put
> Thy golden crown upon her languished head,
> Whose modest tresses were bound up for thee!

Comparing Nash's poem with Blake's, is like comparing bread and butter with a chocolate éclair. The éclair has its virtues no doubt, but éclairs are bad for the complexion; what is more important, they spoil the appetite; and what is most important, they spoil the taste. Zen reminds us that 'directness is all.' It is with Zen as with virtue; according to Bacon,

> It is like a rich stone, – best plain set.

Look at the end of Francis Thomson's *Ode after Easter*:

> Reintegrated are the heavens and Earth!
>   From sky to sod,
> The world's unfolded blossom smells of God.

That's the trouble. Everything is spiced up until it fairly stinks of God. They can't leave it alone, they can't just take it as it is. I dread the coming of the day when everything will smell of Zen; tongues in trees, books in the running brooks, sermons in stones, and Zen in everything.

When we say Zen is vitally concerned with directness we must not make the mistake of supposing that Zen has any objection to such a poem as Keats' *Ode to a Nightingale*, on the ground that there is practically nothing, in eighty lines, concerning the nightingale itself. Take, for example, the second verse:

O, for a draught of vintage! that hath been
    Cool'd a long age in the deep-delved earth,
Tasting of Flora and the country green,
    Dance and Provençøal song, and sunburnt mirth!
O for a beaker full of the warm South,
    Full of the true, the blushful Hippocrene,
       With beaded bubbles winking at the brim,
         And purple-stained mouth;
    That I might drink, and leave the world unseen,
    And with thee fade away into the forest dim.

What is the subject of this verse? It is an unreal, so-called poetical world, in which life is beauty and joy everlasting. This is expressed as directly, as concretely, as Nash's *Spring*, perhaps more so. The *subjects*, then of Nash's poem and Keats', are different; one is the Spring of this world, of England: the other is the Eternal Spring, the Eternal Nightingale – which sings

Not a senseless trancèd thing
But divine melodious truth;
Philosophic numbers smooth,
Tales and golden histories
Of heaven and its mysteries.

The directness of Nash and Keats is undoubted, but the subject of Keats' poem is a dangerous one indeed. The road where

daisies are rose-scented,

is a road that leadeth to destruction, and that nightingale

Procuress to the Lords of Hell.

The Nightingale Ode is Keats' answer to the question, 'What can Art and beauty do for the pains of life?' and concludes that beauty, that is,

> the fancy, cannot cheat so well
> As she is famed to do.

What then becomes of

> Beauty is truth, truth beauty?

In the history of Zen itself we find the cult of directness carried so far, that Tai-E in the 12th century actually burned and destroyed the great text book of Zen, the *Hekiganroku*. This may seem like the Burning of the Books by Shi-kô-tei in BC 213, but was utterly different. The Zen monks of that time were people who knew everything, they knew what life and death, God and man were,

> And why the sea is boiling hot
> And whether pigs have wings.

They were the people of whom it is written,

> They went to the sea in a sieve they did,
>   In a sieve they went to the sea;
> In spite of all their friends could say,

but they were anxious lest their friends should mistake the finger for the moon it was pointing at, so they cut it off. To prevent people from mistaking the expression in words of the truth, for the truth itself, they went to the same extreme as the Jews did in regard in graven images. This was in accordance with an over-literal interpretation of the Four Statements of the Zen Sect,

1. A special transmission outside the scriptures.
2. No depending on books or words.

This is the condition of the poet. Keats writes of himself,

A poet is the most unpoetical thing in existence, – *because he has no identity.*

The setting sun will always set me to rights, and if a sparrow come before my window, I take part in its existence and pick about the gravel.

His books, his body, his soul – all is gone; he so empty that he can contain anything, everything. He has got to the state of

3. Direct pointing to the soul of man.
4. Seeing into one's nature and the attainment of Buddhahood.

that is seeing into the nature of the Sun and attainment of Sparrowhood. If you ask, 'What is the connection between Buddhahood and Sparrowhood?' remember Tennyson's

> Flower in the crannied wall,
> I pluck you out of the crannies; –
> Hold you here, root and all, in my hand,
> Little flower – but if I could understand
> What you are, root and all, and all in all,
> I should know what God and man is.

But a Zen master might take the flower and crush it, and ask, '*Now* do you know what God and man is?' The crushing of the flower is like the burning of the text book.

Reginald H. Blyth, 'Directness is All' in *Zen in English Literature and Oriental Classics* (Tokyo: Hokuseido Press, 1948), pp. 59–68. Blyth's footnotes have been omitted.

Mahasi Sayadaw

Mahasi Sayadaw (1904–82) was born in a village in northern Burma. He began his studies at a local monastery at the age of six and became a novice monk at twelve. Rather than return to lay life at the end of his adolescence, as many novices did, he became a fully ordained monk at the age of nineteen. After passing government examinations on the Buddhist scriptures, he went to Mandalay for advanced study, before becoming a teacher at a monastery in the countryside. At a nearby monastery he met and became the disciple of Mingun Jetavan Sayadaw, a famous meditation teacher, who instructed him in a technique derived from a text called *The Discourse on the Establishment of Mindfulness* (*Satipatthana Sutta*). When Mahasi Sayadaw returned to his native village in 1941, he began to teach this method of insight (vipassana) meditation to both monastic and lay disciples. His fame as a teacher spread widely, and in 1947 he was invited by the prime minister of Burma to serve as chief instructor in a new meditation centre in the capital, Rangoon. The practice of insight meditation, also called 'the Burmese method', proved very popular, and centres were established throughout Burma, as well as in Thailand, Ceylon, Cambodia and India, giving training to hundreds of thousands of people.

Mahasi Sayadaw was also a distinguished scholar of the Buddhist scriptures, providing critical editions, analyses and translations of many important texts, which together filled over sixty volumes. He played a prominent role at the Sixth Buddhist Council in 1954 and in 1957 joined the Burmese Buddhist delegation to Japan. Later he went to Europe and America to teach.

The extracts below, drawn from his 'Practical Vipassana Meditation Exercises', illustrate the simplicity and precision of his exercises in mindfulness.

BASIC PRACTICE

Preparatory Stage

If you sincerely desire to develop contemplation and attain insight in this your present life, you must give up worldly thoughts and actions during the training. This course of action is for the purification of conduct, the essential preliminary step towards the proper development of contemplation. You must also observe the rules of discipline prescribed for laymen (or for monks as the case may be) for they are important in gaining insight. For lay people, these rules comprise the eight precepts which Buddhist devotees observe on Sabbath days (*uposatha*) and during periods of meditation. An additional rule is not to speak with contempt, in jest, or with malice to or about any of the noble ones who have attained states of sanctity. If you have done so, then personally apologize to him or her or make an apology through your meditation instructor. If in the past you have spoken contemptuously to a noble one who is at present unavailable or deceased, confess this offence to your meditation instructor or introspectively to yourself.

The old masters of Buddhist tradition suggest that you entrust yourself to the Enlightened One, the Buddha, during the training period, for you may be alarmed if it happens that your own state of mind produces unwholesome or frightening visions during contemplation. Also place yourself under the guidance of your meditation instructor, for then he can talk to you frankly about your work in contemplation and give you the guidance he thinks necessary. These are the advantages of placing trust in the Enlightened One, the Buddha, and practising under the guidance of your instructor. The aim of this practice and its greatest benefit is release from greed, hatred and delusion, which are the roots of all evil and suffering. This intensive course in insight training can lead you to such release. So work ardently with this end in view so that your training will be successfully completed. This kind of training in contemplation, based on the foundations of mindfulness (*satipattana*), had been taken by successive Buddhas and noble ones who attained release. You are to be congratulated on having the opportunity to take the same kind of training they had undergone.

It is also important for you to begin your training with a brief contemplation on the 'four protections' which the Enlightened One, the Buddha, offers you for reflection. It is helpful for your psychological welfare at this stage to reflect on them. The subjects of the four protective reflections are the Buddha himself, loving-kindness, the loathsome aspects of the body, and death. First, devote yourself to the Buddha by sincerely appreciating his nine chief qualities in this way:

Truly, the Buddha is holy, fully enlightened, perfect in knowledge and conduct, a welfarer, world-knower, the incomparable leader of men to be tamed, teacher of gods and mankind, the awakened one and the exalted one.

Secondly, reflect upon all sentient beings as the receivers of your loving-kindness and identify yourself with all sentient beings without distinction, thus:

May I be free from enmity, disease and grief. As I am, so also may my parents, preceptors, teachers, intimate and indifferent and inimical beings be free from enmity, disease and grief. May they be released from suffering.

Thirdly, reflect upon the repulsive nature of the body to assist you in diminishing the unwholesome attachment that so many people have for the body. Dwell on some of its impurities, such as stomach, intestines, phlegm, pus, blood. Ponder on these impurities so that the absurd fondness for the body may be eliminated.

The fourth protection for your psychological benefit is to reflect on the phenomenon of ever-approaching death. Buddhist teachings stress that life is uncertain, but death is certain; life is precarious but death is sure. Life has death as its goal. There is birth, disease, suffering, old age, and eventually, death. These are all aspects of the process of existence.

To begin training, take the sitting posture with the legs crossed. You might feel more comfortable if the legs are not inter-locked but evenly placed on the ground, without pressing one against the other. If you find that sitting on the floor interferes with contemplation, then obtain a more comfortable way of sitting. Now proceed with each exercise in contemplation as described.

Basic Exercise I

Try to keep your mind (but not your eyes) on the abdomen. You will thereby come to know the movements of rising and falling of it. If these movements are not clear to you in the beginning, then place both hands on the abdomen to feel these rising and falling movements. After a short time the upward movement of exhalation will become clear. Then make a mental note of *rising* for the upward movement, *falling* for the downward movement. Your mental note of each movement must be made while it occurs. From this exercise you learn the actual manner of the upward and downward movements of the abdomen. You are not concerned with the form of the abdomen. What you actually perceive is the bodily sensation of pressure caused by the heaving movement of the abdomen. So do not dwell on the form of the abdomen but proceed with the exercise. For the beginner it is a very effective method of developing the faculties of attention, concentration of mind and insight in contemplation. As practice progresses, the manner of the movements will be clearer. The ability to know each successive occurrence of the mental and physical processes at each of the six sense organs is acquired only when insight contemplation is fully developed. Since you are only a beginner whose attentiveness and power of concentration are still weak, you may find it difficult to keep the mind on each successive rising movement and falling movement as it occurs. In view of this difficulty, you may be inclined to think, 'I just don't know how to keep my mind on each of these movements.' Then simply remember that this is a learning process. The rising and falling movements of the abdomen are always present and therefore there is no need to look for them. Actually it is easy for a beginner to keep his or her mind on these two simple movements. Continue with this exercise in full awareness of the abdomen's rising and falling movements. Never verbally repeat the words, rising, falling, and do not think of rising and falling as words. Be aware only of the actual process of the rising and falling movements of the abdomen. Avoid deep or rapid breathing for the purpose of making the abdominal movements more distinct, because this procedure causes fatigue that interferes with the practice. Just be totally aware of the movements of rising and falling as they occur in the course of normal breathing.

Basic Exercise II

While occupied with the exercise of observing each of the abdominal movements, other mental activities may occur between the noting of each rising and falling. Thoughts or other mental functions, such as intentions, ideas, imaginings, are likely to occur between each mental note of rising and falling. They cannot be disregarded. A mental note must be made of each as it occurs.

If you imagine something, you must know that you have done so and make a mental note, *imagining*. If you simply think of something, mentally note, *thinking*. If you reflect, *reflecting*. If you intend to do something, *intending*. When the mind wanders from the object of meditation, which is the rising and falling of the abdomen, mentally note, *wandering*. Should you imagine you are going to a certain place, note *going*. When you arrive, *arriving*. When, in your thoughts, you meet a person, note *meeting*. Should you speak to him or her, *speaking*. If you imaginarily argue with that person, note *arguing*. If you envision or imagine a light or colour, be sure to note *seeing*. A mental vision must be noted on each occurrence of its appearance until it passes away. After its disappearance continue with Basic Exercise I, by being fully aware of each movement of the rising and falling abdomen. Proceed carefully, without slackening. If you intend to swallow saliva while thus engaged, make a mental note *intending*. While in the act of swallowing, *swallowing*. If you spit, *spitting*. Then return to the exercise of noting rising and falling.

Suppose you intend to bend the neck, note *intending*. In the act of bending, *bending*. When you intend to straighten the neck, *intending*. In the act of straightening the neck, *straightening*. The neck movements of bending and straightening must be done slowly. After mentally making a note of each of these actions, proceed in full awareness with noticing the movements of the rising and falling abdomen.

Basic Exercise III

Since you must continue contemplating for a long time while in one position, that of sitting or lying down, you are likely to experience an intense feeling of fatigue, stiffness in the body or in the arms and legs. Should this happen, simply keep the knowing mind on that part of the body where such feelings occur and carry on the contemplation, noting tired or stiff. Do this naturally; that is, neither too fast nor too slow. These feelings gradually become fainter and finally cease altogether. Should one of these feelings become more intense until the bodily fatigue or stiffness of joints is unbearable, then change your position. However, do not forget to make a mental note of *intending*, before you proceed to change your position. Each movement must be contemplated in its respective order and in detail.

If you intend to lift the hand or leg, make a mental note *intending*. In the act of lifting the hand or leg, *lifting*. Stretching either the hand or the leg, *stretching*. When you bend it, *bending*. When putting it down, *putting*. Should either the hand or leg touch, *touching*. Perform all of these actions in a slow and deliberate manner. As soon as you are settled in the new position, continue with the contemplation in another position keeping to the procedure outlined in this paragraph.

Should an itching sensation be felt in any part of the body, keep the mind on that part and make a mental note, *itching*. Do this in a regulated manner, neither too fast nor too slow. When the itching sensation disappears in the course of full awareness, continue with the exercise of noticing the rising and falling of the abdomen. Should the itching continue and become too strong and you intend to rub the itchy part, be sure to make a mental note, *intending*. Slowly lift the hand, simultaneously noting the actions of *lifting*; and *touching*, when the hand touches the part that itches. Rub slowly in complete awareness of rubbing. When the itching sensation has disappeared and you intend to discontinue rubbing, be mindful by making the usual mental note of *intending*. Slowly withdraw the hand, concurrently making a mental note of the action, *withdrawing*. When the hand rests in its usual place touching the leg, *touching*. Then again devote your time to observing the abdominal movements.

If there is pain or discomfort, keep the knowing mind on that part of the body where the sensation arises. Make a mental note of the specific sensation as it occurs, such as *painful, aching, pressing, piercing, tired, giddy*. It must be stressed that the mental note must not be forced nor delayed but made in a calm and natural manner. The pain may eventually cease or increase. Do not be alarmed if it increases. Firmly continue the contemplation. If you do so, you will find that the pain will almost always cease. But if, after a time, the pain has increased and becomes unbearable, you must ignore the pain and continue with the contemplation of rising and falling.

As you progress in mindfulness you may experience sensations of intense pain: stifling or choking sensations, such as pain from the slash of a knife, the thrust of a sharp-pointed instrument, unpleasant sensations of being pricked by sharp needles, or of small insects crawling over the body. You might experience sensations of itching, biting, intense cold. As soon as you discontinue the contemplation you may also feel that these painful sensations cease. When you resume contemplation you will have them again as soon as you gain in mindfulness. These painful sensations are not to be considered as something wrong. They are not manifestations of disease but are common factors always present in the body and are usually obscured when the mind is normally occupied with more conspicuous objects. When the mental faculties become keener, you are more aware of these sensations. With the continued development of contemplation the time will come when you can overcome them and they will cease altogether. If you continue contemplation, firm in purpose, you will not come to any harm. Should you lose courage, become irresolute in contemplation and discontinue for some time, you may encounter these unpleasant sensations again and again as your contemplation proceeds. If you continue with determination you will most likely overcome these painful sensations and may never again experience them in the course of contemplation.

Should you intend to sway the body, then knowingly note *intending*. While in the act of swaying, *swaying*. When contemplating you may occasionally discover the body swaying back and forth. Do not be alarmed; neither be pleased nor wish to continue to sway. The swaying will cease if you keep the knowing mind on the action of swaying and continue to note *swaying* until the action ceases. If swaying increases in spite of your making a mental note of it, then lean against a wall or post or lie down for a while. Thereafter proceed with contemplation. Follow the same procedure if you find yourself shaking or trembling. When contemplation is developed you may sometimes feel a thrill or chill pass through the back or the entire body. This is a symptom of the feeling of intense interest, enthusiasm or rapture. It occurs naturally in the course of good contemplation. When your mind is fixed in contemplation you may be startled at the slightest sound. This takes place because you feel the effect of sensory impression more intensely while in a state of concentration.

If you are thirsty while contemplating, notice the feeling, *thirsty*. When you intend to stand, *intending*. Keep the mind intently on the act of standing up, and mentally note *standing*. When you look forward after standing up straight, note *looking, seeing*. Should you intend to walk forward, *intending*. When you begin to step forward, mentally note each step as *walking, walking*, or *left, right*. It is important for you to be aware of every moment in each step from the beginning to the end when you walk. Adhere to the same procedure when strolling or when taking walking exercise. Try to make a mental note of each step in two sections as follows: *lifting, putting, lifting, putting*. When you have obtained sufficient practice in this manner of walking, then try to make a mental note of each step in three sections; *lifting, pushing, putting*; or *up, forward, down*.

When you look at the tap or water-pot on arriving at the place where you are to take a drink, be sure to make a mental note, *looking, seeing*.

When you stop walking, *stopping*.
When you stretch out the hand, *stretching*.
When you touch the cup, *touching*.
When you take the cup, *taking*.
When dipping the cup into the water, *dipping*.
When bringing the cup to the lips, *bringing*.

When the cup touches the lips, *touching*.
When you swallow, *swallowing*.
When returning the cup, *returning*.
When withdrawing the hand, *withdrawing*.
When you bring down the hand, *bringing*.
When the hand touches the side of the body, *touching*.
If you intend to turn round, *intending*.
When you turn round, *turning*.
When you walk forward, *walking*.
On arriving at the place where you intend to stop, *intending*.
When you stop, *stopping*.

If you remain standing for some time continue the contemplation of rising and falling. But if you intend to sit down, note *intending*. When you go to sit down, *walking*. On arriving at the place where you will sit, *arriving*. When you turn to sit, *turning*. While in the act of sitting down, *sitting*. Sit down slowly, and keep the mind on the downward movement of the body. You must notice every movement in bringing the hands and legs into position. Then resume the practice of contemplating the abdominal movements.

Should you intend to lie down, note *intending*. Then proceed with the contemplation of every movement in the course of lying down: *lifting*, *stretching*, *putting*, *touching*, *lying*. Then take as the object of contemplation every movement in bringing the hands, legs and body into position. Perform these actions slowly. Thereafter, continue with noting rising and falling. Should pain, fatigue, itching, or any other sensation be felt, be sure to notice each of these sensations. Notice all feelings, thoughts, ideas, considerations, reflections; all movements of hands, legs, arms and body. If there is nothing in particular to note, put the mind on the rising and falling of the abdomen. When sleepy, make a mental note, *sleepy*. After you have gained sufficient concentration in contemplating, you will be able to overcome drowsiness and you will feel refreshed as a result. Take up again the usual contemplation of the basic object. If you are unable to overcome the drowsy feeling, you must continue contemplating drowsiness until you fall asleep.

The state of sleep is the continuity of sub-consciousness. It is similar to the first state of rebirth consciousness and the last state of conscious-ness at the moment of death. This state of consciousness is feeble and, therefore, unable to be aware of an object. When you awake, the continuity of sub-consciousness occurs regularly between moments of seeing, hearing, tasting, smelling, touching, and thinking. Because these occurrences are of brief duration they are not usually clear and therefore not noticeable. Continuity of sub-consciousness remains during sleep – a fact which becomes obvious when you wake up; for it is in the state of wakefulness that thoughts and sense objects become distinct.

Contemplation should start at the moment you wake up. Since you are a beginner, it may not be possible yet for you to start contemplating at the very first moment of wakefulness. But you should start with it when you remember that you are to contemplate. For example, if on awakening you reflect on something, you should become aware of the fact and begin your contemplation by a mental note, *reflecting*. Then proceed with the contemplation of rising and falling. When getting up from the bed, mindfulness should be directed to every detail of the body's activity. Each movement of the hands, legs and rump must be performed in complete awareness. Are you thinking of the time of day when awakening? If so, note *thinking*. Do you intend to get out of bed? If so, note *intending*. If you prepare to move the body into position for rising, note *preparing*. As you slowly rise, *rising*. Should you remain sitting for any length of time, revert to contemplating the abdominal movements.

Perform the acts of washing the face or taking a bath in due order and in complete awareness of every detailed movement; for instance, *looking, seeing, stretching, holding, touching, feeling cold, rubbing*. In the acts of dressing, making the bed, opening and closing doors and windows, handling objects, be occupied with every detail of these actions in se-quence.

You must attend to the contemplation of every detail in the action of eating:

When you look at the food, *looking, seeing*.
When you arrange the food, *arranging*.

When you bring the food to the mouth, *bringing*.
When you bend the neck forwards, *bending*.
When the food touches the mouth, *touching*.
When placing the food in the mouth, *placing*.
When the mouth closes, *closing*.
When withdrawing the hand, *withdrawing*.
Should the hand touch the plate, *touching*.
When straightening the neck, *straightening*.
When in the act of chewing, *chewing*.
When you are aware of the taste, *knowing*.
When swallowing the food, *swallowing*.
While swallowing the food, should the food be felt touching the
     sides of the gullet, *touching*.

Perform contemplation in this manner each time you take a morsel of food until you finish your meal. In the beginning of the practice there will be many omissions. Never mind. Do not waver in your effort. You will make fewer omissions if you persist in your practice. When you reach an advanced stage of the practice you will also be able to notice more details than those mentioned here.

Mahasi Sayadaw, 'Practical Vipassana Meditation Exercises', *Insight Meditation Online*, www.buddanet.net.

Shunryu Suzuki

Shunryu Suzuki (1904–71) was born in a village forty miles south west of Tokyo, the son of a poor Zen priest. After primary school, he went to live at a temple run by a disciple of his father and was ordained as a novice monk in 1917. After completing his secondary-school education, in which he excelled at English, he attended Komazawa in Tokyo, the university of the Soto sect of Zen, graduating in 1930. He then went on to train at the head temple of the sect, Eiheiji. In 1932 Suzuki took over as priest of his father's temple, before moving to on to serve as abbot at the larger temple of Rin-soin. He married in 1935.

Suzuki spent the war years at Rinso-in and, unlike many Buddhist priests, did not actively support the war, although his temple was used to house soldiers, Korean labourers and children displaced by the bombing of Tokyo. In 1945 he went to Manchuria, at that time still a Japanese colony, to establish a branch temple of Rinso-in, but returned almost immediately as the end of the war approached. After the war, he engaged in a common occupation of Zen priests – performing services for the dead – while also opening a kindergarten.

In 1952 Suzuki's wife was murdered by a deranged Zen priest and he was left to raise his children alone. After seeing to the education of his children, Suzuki accepted a post offered by the headquarters of the Soto sect to serve as priest at a Japanese-American Zen temple in San Francisco, where he performed religious services for a community of some sixty families. However, his arrival happened to coincide with the peak of the Zen craze in San Francisco, and soon he was invited by American enthusiasts to provide instruction in Zen meditation, something that laypeople rarely practised in Japan. He began to give lectures in English and to lead meditation retreats at the San Francisco temple. In 1963 he granted the request of an American student to be ordained as a Zen priest. He continued to serve as priest to the Japanese community until 1969, when the tensions between his Japanese parishioners and his American disciples resulted in his resignation from his original position. He founded the San Francisco Zen Center, which eventually established both a centre in the city as well as a mountain centre in Tassajara, south of the city. In 1970 an edited version of some of his lectures was published as *Zen Mind, Beginner's Mind*, a work that became a classic of American Zen, selling over one million copies. He died in San Francisco in 1971.

Suzuki Roshi (as he was known to his students) represented a third strand of Zen in the West. The first was the Zen of D. T. Suzuki, the highly intellectualized version that attracted the interest of artists and poets. The second was the Zen of Yasutani (see also the Introduction), who had left the Soto sect to form his own marginal movement in Japan, with a strong emphasis on rapidly gaining the experience of enlightenment, a movement that became mainstream in the West through the efforts of disciples such as Philip Kapleau and Robert Aitken. Suzuki Roshi was a relatively typical Zen priest who had served the traditional role of administrator of a local temple, performing services for the dead, before coming to America to perform similar services for an immigrant community. Once in San Francisco, his simple teachings and emphasis on seated meditation, without striving for enlightenment, attracted a devoted following. The extracts that follow, from *Zen Mind, Beginner's Mind*, provide some of the flavour of Suzuki's practical yet poetic meditation instructions.

CONTROL

'To give your sheep or cow a large, spacious meadow is the way to control him.'

To live in the realm of Buddha nature means to die as a small being, moment after moment. When we lose our balance we die, but at the same time we also develop ourselves, we grow. Whatever we see is changing, losing its balance. The reason everything looks beautiful is because it is out of balance, but its background is always in perfect harmony. This is how everything exists in the realm of Buddha nature, losing its balance against a background of perfect balance. So if you see things without realizing the background of Buddha nature, everything appears to be in the form of suffering. But if you understand the background of existence, you realize that suffering itself is how we live, and how we extend our life. So in Zen sometimes we emphasize the imbalance or disorder of life.

Nowadays traditional Japanese painting has become pretty formal and lifeless. That is why modern art has developed. Ancient painters used to practice putting dots on paper in artistic disorder. This is rather difficult. Even though you try to do it, usually what you do is arranged in some order. You think you can control it, but you cannot; it is almost impossible to arrange your dots out of order. It is the same with taking care of your everyday life. Even though you try to put people under some control, it is impossible. You cannot do it. The best way to control people is to encourage them to be mischievous. Then they will be in control in its wider sense. To give your sheep or cow a large, spacious meadow is the way to control him. So it is with people: first let them do what they want, and watch them. This is the best policy. To ignore them is not good; that is the worst policy. The second worst is trying to control them. The best one is to watch them, just to watch them, without trying to control them.

The same way works for you yourself as well. If you want to obtain perfect calmness in your zazen, you should not be bothered by the various images you find in your mind. Let them come, and let them go. Then they will be under control. But this policy is not so easy. It sounds easy, but it requires some special effort. How to make this kind of effort is the secret of practice. Suppose you are sitting under some extraordinary circumstances. If you try to calm your mind you will be unable to sit, and if you try not to be disturbed, your effort will not be the right effort. The only effort that will help you is to count your breathing, or to concentrate on your inhaling and exhaling. We say concentration, but to concentrate your mind on something is not the true purpose of Zen. The true purpose is to see things as they are, to observe things as they are, and to let everything go as it goes. This is to put everything under control in its widest sense. Zen practice is to open up our small mind. So concentrating is just an aid to help you realize 'big mind,' or the mind that is everything. If you want to discover the true meaning of Zen in your everyday life, you have to understand the meaning of keeping your mind on your breathing and your body in the right posture in zazen. You should follow the rules of practice and your study should become more subtle and careful. Only in this way can you experience the vital freedom of Zen.

Dogen-zenji said, 'Time goes from present to past.' This is absurd, but in our practice sometimes it is true. Instead of time progressing from past to present, it goes backwards from present to past. Yoshitsune was a famous warrior who lived in medieval Japan. Because of the situation of the country at that time, he was sent to the northern provinces, where he was killed. Before he left he bade farewell to his wife, and soon after she wrote in a poem, 'Just as you unreel the thread from a spool, I want the past to become present.' When she said this, actually she made the past time present. In her mind the past became alive and *was* the present. So as Dogen said, 'Time goes from present to past.' This is not true in our logical mind, but it is in the actual experience of making past time present. There we have poetry, and there we have human life.

When we experience this kind of truth it means we have found the true meaning of time. Time constantly goes from past to present and from present to future. This is true, but it is also true that time goes from future to present and from present to past. A Zen master once said, 'To go eastward one mile is to go westward one mile.' This is vital freedom. We should acquire this kind of perfect freedom.

But perfect freedom is not found without some rules. People, especially young people, think that freedom is to do just what they want, that in Zen there is no need for rules. But it is absolutely necessary for us to have some rules. But this does not mean always to be under control. As long as you have rules, you have a chance for freedom. To try to obtain freedom without being aware of the rules means nothing. It is to acquire this perfect freedom that we practice zazen.

MIND WAVES

'Because we enjoy all aspects of life as an unfolding of big mind, we do not care for any excessive joy. So we have imperturbable composure.'

When you are practicing zazen, do not try to stop your thinking. Let it stop by itself. If something comes into your mind, let it come in, and let it go out. It will not stay long. When you try to stop your thinking, it means you are bothered by it. Do not be bothered by anything. It appears as if something comes from outside your mind, but actually it is only the waves of your mind, and if you are not bothered by the waves, gradually they will become calmer and calmer. In five or at most ten minutes, your mind will be completely serene and calm. At that time your breathing will become quite slow, while your pulse will become a little faster.

It will take quite a long time before you find your calm, serene mind in your practice. Many sensations come, many thoughts or images arise, but they are just waves of your own mind. Nothing comes from outside your mind. Usually we think of our mind as receiving impressions and experiences from outside, but that is not a true understanding of our mind. The true understanding is that the mind includes everything; when you think something comes from outside it means only that something appears in your mind. Nothing outside yourself can cause any trouble. You yourself make the waves in your mind. If you leave your mind as it is, it will become calm. This mind is called big mind.

If your mind is related to something outside itself, that mind is a small mind, a limited mind. If your mind is not related to anything else, then there is no dualistic understanding in the activity of your mind. You understand activity as just waves of your mind. Big mind experiences everything within itself. Do you understand the difference between the two minds: the mind which includes everything, and the mind which is related to something? Actually they are the same thing, but the understanding is different, and your attitude towards your life will be different according to which understanding you have.

That everything is included within your mind is the essence of mind. To experience this is to have religious feeling. Even though waves arise, the essence of your mind is pure; it is just like clear water with a few waves. Actually water always has waves. Waves are the practice of the water. To speak of waves apart from water or water apart from waves is a delusion. Water and waves are one. Big mind and small mind are one. When you understand your mind in this way, you have some security in your feeling. As your mind does not expect anything from outside, it is always filled. A mind with waves in it is not a disturbed mind, but actually an amplified one. Whatever you experience is an expression of big mind.

The activity of big mind is to amplify itself through various experiences. In one sense our experiences coming one by one are always fresh and new, but in another sense they are nothing but a continuous or repeated unfolding of the one big mind. For instance, if you have something good for breakfast, you will say, 'This is good.' 'Good' is supplied as something experienced some time long ago, even though you may not remember when. With big mind we accept each of our experiences as if recognizing the face we see in the mirror as our own. For us there is no fear of losing this mind. There is nowhere to come or to go; there is no fear of death, no suffering from old age or sickness. Because we enjoy all aspects of life as an unfolding of big mind, we do not care for any excessive joy. So we have imperturbable composure, and it is with this imperturbable composure of big mind that we practice zazen.

[. . .]

BOWING

'Bowing is a very serious practice. You should be prepared to bow, even in your last moment. Even though it is impossible to get rid of our self-centered desires, we have to do it. Our true nature wants us to.'

After zazen we bow to the floor nine times. By bowing we are giving up ourselves. To give up ourselves means to give up our dualistic ideas. So there is no difference between zazen practice and bowing. Usually to bow means to pay our respects to something which is more worthy of respect than ourselves. But when you bow to Buddha you should have no idea of Buddha, you just become one with Buddha, you are already Buddha himself. When you become one with Buddha, one with everything that exists, you find the true meaning of being. When you forget all your dualistic ideas, everything becomes your teacher, and everything can be the object of worship.

When everything exists within your big mind, all dualistic relationships drop away. There is no distinction between heaven and earth, man and woman, teacher and disciple. Sometimes a man bows to a woman; sometimes a woman bows to a man. Sometimes the disciple bows to the master; sometimes the master bows to the disciple. A master who cannot bow to his disciple cannot bow to Buddha. Sometimes we may bow to cats and dogs.

In your big mind, everything has the same value. Everything is Buddha himself. You see something or hear a sound and there you have everything just as it is. In your practice you should accept everything as it is, giving to each thing the same respect given to a Buddha. Here there is Buddhahood. Then Buddha bows to Buddha, and you bow to yourself. This is the true bow.

If you do not have this firm conviction of big mind in your practice, your bow will be dualistic. When you are just yourself, you bow to yourself in its true sense, and you are one with everything. Only when you are you yourself can you bow to everything in its true sense. Bowing is a very serious practice. You should be prepared to bow even in your last moment; when you cannot do anything except bow you should do it. This kind of conviction is necessary. Bow with this spirit and all the precepts, all the teachings are yours, and you will possess everything within your big mind.

Sen no Rikyu, the founder of the Japanese tea ceremony, committed *hara-kiri* (ritual suicide by disembowelment) in 1591 at the order of his lord, Hideyoshi. Just before Rikyu took his own life he said, 'When I have this sword there is no Buddha and no Patriarchs.' He meant that when we have the sword of big mind, there is no dualistic world. The only thing which exists is this spirit. This kind of imperturbable spirit was always present in Rikyu's tea ceremony. He never did anything in just a dualistic way; he was ready to die in each moment. In ceremony after ceremony he died, and he renewed himself. This is the spirit of the tea ceremony. This is how we bow.

My teacher had a callous on his forehead from bowing. He knew he was an obstinate, stubborn fellow, and so he bowed and bowed and bowed. The reason he bowed was that inside himself he always heard his master's scolding voice. He had joined the Soto order when he was thirty, which for a Japanese priest is rather late. When we are young we are less stubborn, and it is easier to get rid of our selfishness. So his master always called my teacher 'You-lately-joined-fellow,' and scolded him for joining so late. Actually his master loved him for his stubborn character. When my teacher was seventy, he said, 'When I was young I was like a tiger, but now I am like a cat!' He was very pleased to be like a cat.

Bowing helps to eliminate our self-centered ideas. This is not so easy. It is difficult to get rid of these ideas, and bowing is a very valuable practice. The result is not the point; it is the effort to improve ourselves that is valuable. There is no end to this practice.

Each bow expresses one of the four Buddhist vows. These vows are: 'Although sentient beings are innumerable, we vow to save them. Although our evil desires are limitless, we vow to be rid of them. Although the teaching is limitless, we vow to learn it all. Although Buddhism is unattainable, we vow to attain it.' If it is unattainable, how can we attain it? But we should! That is Buddhism.

To think, 'Because it is possible we will do it,' is not Buddhism. Even though it is impossible, we have to do it because our true nature wants us to. But actually, whether or not it is possible is not the point. If it is our inmost desire to get rid of our self-centered ideas, we have to do it. When we make this effort, our inmost desire is appeased and Nirvana is there. Before you determine to do it, you have difficulty, but once you start to do it, you have none. Your effort appeases your inmost desire. There is no other way to attain calmness. Calmness of mind does not mean you should stop your activity. Real calmness should be found in activity itself. We say, 'It is easy to have calmness in inactivity, it is hard to have calmness in activity, but calmness in activity is true calmness.'

After you have practiced for a while, you will realize that it is not possible to make rapid, extraordinary progress. Even though you try very hard, the progress you make is always little by little. It is not like going out in a shower in which you know when you get wet. In a fog, you do not know you are getting wet, but as you keep walking you get wet little by little. If your mind has ideas of progress, you may say, 'Oh, this pace is terrible!' But actually it is not. When you get wet in a fog it is very difficult to dry yourself. So there is no need to worry about progress. It is like studying a foreign language; you cannot do it all of a sudden, but by repeating it over and over you will master it. This is the Soto way of practice. We may say either that we make progress little by little, or that we do not even expect to make progress. Just to be sincere and make our full effort in each moment is enough. There is no Nirvana outside our practice.

[. . .]

ZEN AND EXCITEMENT

'Zen is not some kind of excitement, but concentration on our everyday routine.'

My master died when I was thirty-one. Although I wanted to devote myself just to Zen practice at Eiheiji monastery, I had to succeed my master at his temple. I became quite busy, and being so young I had many difficulties. These difficulties gave me some experience, but it meant nothing compared with the true, calm, serene way of life.

It is necessary for us to keep the constant way. Zen is not some kind of excitement, but concentration on our usual everyday routine. If you become too busy and too excited, your mind becomes rough and ragged. This is not good. If possible, try to be always calm and joyful and keep yourself from excitement. Usually we become busier and busier, day by day, year by year, especially in our modern world. If we revisit old, familiar places after a long time, we are astonished by the changes. It cannot be helped. But if we become interested in some excitement, or in our own change, we will become completely involved in our busy life, and we will be lost. But if your mind is calm and constant, you can keep yourself away from the noisy world even though you are in the midst of it. In the midst of noise and change, your mind will be quiet and stable.

Zen is not something to get excited about. Some people start to practice Zen just out of curiosity, and they only make themselves busier. If your practice makes you worse, it is ridiculous. I think that if you try to do zazen once a week, that will make you busy enough. Do not be too interested in Zen. When young people get excited about Zen they often give up schooling and go to some mountain or forest in order to sit. That kind of interest is not true interest.

Just continue in your calm, ordinary practice and your character will be built up. If your mind is always busy, there will be no time to build, and you will not be successful, particularly if you work too hard on it. Building character is like making bread – you have to mix it little by little, step by step, and moderate temperature is needed. You know yourself quite well, and you know how much temperature you need. You know exactly what you need. But if you get too excited, you will forget how much temperature is good for you, and you will lose your way. This is very dangerous.

Buddha said the same thing about the good ox driver. The driver knows how much load the ox can carry, and he keeps the ox from being overloaded. You know your way and your state of mind. Do not carry too much! Buddha also said that building character is like building a dam. You should be very careful in making the bank. If you try to do it all at once, water will leak from it. Make the bank carefully and you will end up with a fine dam for the reservoir.

Our unexciting way of practice may appear to be very negative. This is not so. It is a wise and effective way to work on ourselves. It is just very plain. I find this point very difficult for people, especially young people, to understand. On the other hand it may seem as if I am speaking about gradual attainment. This is not so either. In fact, this is the sudden way, because when your practice is calm and ordinary, everyday life itself is enlightenment.

Shunryu Suzuki, *Zen Mind, Beginner's Mind* (New York and Tokyo: Weatherhill, 1995), pp. 31–6, 43–6, 57–8.

Buddhadasa

Buddhadasa (1906–93) was born in southern Thailand, the son of a merchant, and was educated at Buddhist temple schools. It was customary for males in Thailand to be ordained as a Buddhist monk for three months at the age of twenty and then return to lay life. Buddhadasa decided to remain a monk and quickly gained a reputation as a brilliant thinker, meditator and teacher. However, rather than moving through the monastic hierarchy in the capital, he returned home in 1932, after several years of study in Bangkok, to establish a meditation and study centre, which he called Wat Suan Mokkhabalarama (the 'Garden of the Power of Liberation'). Buddhadasa spent most of his life at this forest monastery overlooking the sea. Here the resident monks devoted more time to meditation practice and less time to merit-making activities than did many Thai monks. The centre attracted thousands of guests and visitors each year, with more than a thousand receiving meditation instruction annually.

In addition to his activities as a meditation teacher, Buddhadasa was to become the most prolific author in the history of the Theravada Buddhist tradition, his writing in many cases being transcriptions of lectures given at his monastery. Just as Buddhadasa showed little interest in the administrative programmes of the Thai Buddhist sangha, in his writings he eschewed the more formal style of traditional scholastic commentary in favour of a more informal, and in many ways controversial, approach in which he called many of the more popular practices of Thai Buddhism into question. For example, he spoke out strongly against the practice of merit-making in which laypeople offer gifts to monks in the belief that they will receive material reward in the next life. Although this has traditionally been the dominant form of lay practice, Buddhadasa argued that it only keeps the participants in the cycle of rebirth because it is based on attachment, whereas the true form of giving is the giving up of the self. This is not a solitary pursuit, however. Because of dependent origination, people live in a shared environment connected by social and natural relations. This state is originally one of harmony that has fallen out of balance because of attachment to 'me' and 'mine'. By diminishing attachment and craving, both personal and social well-being are achieved in a society in which leaders promote both the physical and spiritual well-being of the people. Buddhadasa calls such a form of government 'dhammic socialism'. In the passage that follows, Buddhadasa argued that the best form of government for small countries such as Thailand is a 'dictatorial socialism' based on classical Buddhist principles, with leadership provided by a king who embodies ten royal virtues.

The Buddha developed a socialist system with a 'dictatorial' method. Unlike liberal democracy's inability to act in an expeditious and timely manner, this dhammic dictatorial socialism is able to act immediately to accomplish what needs to be done. This approach is illustrated by the many rules in the *vinaya* against procrastination, postponement and evasion. Similarly, the ancient legal system was socialistic. There was no way that someone could take advantage of another, and its method was 'dictatorial' in the sense that it cut through confusion and got things done.

Now we need to look more closely at the system of kingship based on the Ten Royal Precepts or Virtues. This is also a form of dictatorial socialism. The best example is King Asoka. Many books about Asoka have been published, in particular concerning the Asokan inscriptions found on rock pillars throughout his kingdom. These were edicts about Asoka's work which reveal a socialist system of government of an exclusively dictatorial type. He purified the *sangha* by wiping out the heretics, and he insisted on right behavior on the part of all classes of people. Asoka was not a tyrant, however. He was a gentle person who acted for the good of the whole society. He constructed wells and assembly halls, and had various kinds of fruit trees planted for the benefit of all. He was 'dictatorial' in the sense that if his subjects did not do these public works as commanded, they were punished.

After King Asoka gave his orders, one of his officials, the Dhammajo or Dhammāmātaya, determined if they had been faithfully followed out through all the districts of the kingdom. If he found a transgressor a 'dictatorial' method was used to punish him. The punishment was socialistic in the sense that it was useful for society and not for personal or selfish reasons.

The final piece of evidence supporting King Asoka's method occurred at the end of his life, when all that remained of his wealth was a half of a tamarind seed. Before he died he gave even this away to a monk. What kind of person does such an act – a tyrant or a socialist? That King Asoka also preserved the ideals of a Buddhist dictatorial socialism is also supported by an examination of his famous rock and pillar edicts.

Socialism in Buddhism, furthermore, is illustrated by the behavior of more ordinary laymen and laywomen. They live moderately, contributing their excess for the benefit of society. For example, take the case of the Buddhist entrepreneur or *śreṣṭhī*. In Buddhism, *śreṣṭhī* are those who have alms houses (Thai: *rong than*). If they have no alms houses they cannot be called *śreṣṭhī*. The more wealth they have the more alms houses they possess. Do capitalists today have alms houses? If not, they are not *śreṣṭhī* as we think of them during the Buddhist era which was socialistic in the fullest sense. The capitalists during the Buddhist era were respected by the proletariat rather than attacked by them. If being a capitalist means simply accumulating power and wealth for oneself, that differs radically from the meaning of *śreṣṭhī* as one who uses his or her wealth to provide for the wellbeing of the world.

Even such terms as slave, servant, and menial had a socialistic meaning during the Buddhist era. Slaves did not want to leave the *śreṣṭhī*. Today, however, 'slaves' hate capitalists. *Śreṣṭhī* during the Buddhist era treated their slaves like their own children. All worked together for a common good. They observed the moral precepts together on Buddhist sabbath days. The products of their common labor were for use in alms houses. If the *śreṣṭhī* accumulated wealth, that would be put in reserve for use later in the alms houses. Today things are very different. In those days slavery was socialistic and did not need to be abolished. Slave and master worked for the common good. The kind of slavery which should be abolished exists under a capitalist system in which a master treats slaves or servants like animals. Slaves under such a system always desire freedom, but slaves under a socialist system want to remain with their masters because they feel at ease. In my own case, for example, it would be easier to be a common monk than to bear the responsibilities of being an abbot. Similarly, a servant in a socialist system has an easier life than a master (Thai: *nai*), and is treated as a younger family member.

In the Buddhist view, *śreṣṭhī* are those who have alms houses and a great *śreṣṭhī* has many of them. They have enough for their own use and share from their excess. Buddhists have espoused socialism since antiquity, whether at the level of king, wealthy merchant or slave. Most slaves were content with their status even though they could not, for instance, be ordained as monks. They could be released from their obligations, or continue them, as they chose. Slaves were recipients of love, compassion, and care. Thus, one can see that the essence of socialism in those days was pure and totally different from the socialism of today.

Let us look again at the Ten Royal Precepts or Virtues (*dasarāja-dhamma*) as a useful form of Buddhist socialism. Most students at secondary and college level have studied the canonical meaning of the *dasarājadhamma*, and did not find it of much interest. In Buddhism this is called the ten *dhamma* of kingship: *dāna* (generosity), *sīla* (morality), *pariccāga* (liberality), *ajjava* (uprightness), *maddava* (gentleness), *tapo* (self-restraint), *akkodha* (non-anger), *avihiṁsa* (non-hurtfulness), *khanti* (forbearance), *avirodhana* (non-opposition).

Dāna is giving or the will to give; *sīla* is morality, those who possess morality (*sīla-dhamma*) in the sense of being the way things are (*prakati*) freed from the forces of defilement (*kilesa*); *pariccāga* means to give up completely all inner evils such as selfishness; *ajjava* is truthfulness; *maddava* is to be meek and gentle toward all citizens; *tapo* or self-control refers to the fact that a king should always control himself; *akkodha* means to be free from anger; *avihiṁsa* is the dhamma which restrains one from causing trouble to others, even unintentionally; *khanti* is being tolerant or assuming the burden of tolerance; *avirodhana* is freedom from guilt. A king who embodies these ten virtues radiates the spirit of socialism. Why need we abolish this kind of kingship? If such a king was a dictator, he would be like Asoka whose 'dictatorial' rule was to promote the common good and to abolish the evil of private, selfish interest.

Let us now look at the way in which the Samuhanimit monastery (*wat*) in Phumriang District was built as an example of Buddhist dictatorial socialism. An inscription in the monastery tells us that the *wat* was built during the third reign under the sponsorship of the Bunnag family, and that it was built in four months. To finish the *wat* in four months called for 'dictatorial' methods. Thousands of people from the city were ordered to help complete the work and occasionally physical punishment was used. The labor force made bricks, brought stones, animals, trees – everything they could. After the work was finished, the head of the monastery in the city who had resided at one of the city *wats* was forced to be the abbot at Wat Samuhanimit. To be sure, dictatorial methods were used in the establishment of this monastery, but the end result benefited everyone.

The character of the ruler is the crucial factor in the nature of Buddhist dictatorial socialism. If a good person is the ruler the dictatorial socialism will be good, but a bad person will produce an unacceptable type of socialism. A ruler who embodies the ten royal virtues will be the best kind of socialistic dictator. This way of thinking will be totally foreign to most Westerners who are unfamiliar with this kind of Buddhist kingly rule. A good king is not an absolute monarch in the ordinary sense of that word. Because we misunderstand the meaning of kingship we consider all monarchial systems wrong. The king who embodies the ten royal virtues, however, is a socialist ruler in the most profound or dhammic sense, such as the King Mahāsammata, the first universal ruler, King Asoka, and the kings of Sukhodaya and Ayudhaya. Kingship based on the ten royal virtues is a pure form of socialism. Such a system should not be abolished, but it must be kept in mind that this is not an absolute monarchy. In some cases this form of Buddhist dictatorial socialism can solve the world's problems better than any other form of government.

People today follow the Western notion that everyone is equal. Educated people think that everyone should have the right to govern, and that this is a democratic system. However, today, the meaning of democracy is very ambiguous. Let us ask ourselves what the kind of democracy we have had for at least one hundred years has contributed to us as citizens. Questioning this kind of worldly democracy may make us suspect. I, myself, am not afraid to be killed because of rejecting this kind of democracy. I favor a Buddhist socialist democracy which is composed of *dhamma* and managed by a 'dictator' whose character exemplifies the ten royal virtues (*dasarājadhamma*). Do not blindly follow the political theories of someone who does not embody the *dasarājadhamma* system, the true socialist system which can save humankind. Indeed, revolution has a place in deposing a ruler who does not embody the *dasarājadhamma*, but not a place within a revolutionary political philosophy which espouses violence and bloodshed.

The dasarājadhammic system is absolute in that it depends essentially on one person. It was developed to the point where an absolute monarch could rule a country or, for that matter, the entire world as in the case of the King (*rāja*) Mahāsammata. The notion of a ruler (*rāja*) needs to be better understood. The title, *rāja*, was given to the first ruler thousands of years ago when people first became interested in establishing a socialist society. We also need to rethink the notion of caste or class (*varṇa*). The ruling class (*kṣatriya*) has come to be despised and people advocate its abolition. Such an attitude ignores the fact that a ruling class of some kind is absolutely necessary; however, it should be defined by its function rather than by birth. For example, there must be magistrates who constitute a part of a special class of respected people.

Caste or class (*varṇa*) should be based on function and duty rather than on birth. *Varṇa* determined by inherited class should be abolished. The Buddha, after all, abolished his own *varṇa* by becoming a monk and prescribing the abolition of others' inherited class statuses. But class by function and responsibility should not be abolished. It is the result of *kamma*. For instance, *kamma* dictates that a king should rule, and that a Brahman should teach or should be a magistrate in order to maintain order (*dhamma*) in the world. Class in this sense should not be abolished. The ruling class (*kṣatriya-varṇa*) should be maintained, but as part of the *dasarājadhammika* system to govern the world.

There was another system of government typical of small countries during the time of the Buddha, e.g. the Sakya and Licchavi, worthy of examination. The Licchavis, for example, were governed by an assembly composed of 220 people of the *kṣatriya* class. The elected head of the assembly acted as a king, having been chosen to rule for a designated period of time, e.g. seven months. The best of those born into the *kṣatriya* class were chosen as members of the assembly. One may imagine how progressive their kingdom was. Such was the Sakya kingdom of the Buddha. Large kingdoms like Kosala could not conquer these small states because they were rooted in dhammic socialism. When they gave up this system of government social harmony was undermined which resulted in their destruction. The Buddha used the Licchavis as an example of a people who followed a socialist style of life – careful in personal habits, attentive to the defense of the nation, and respectful of women – but who departed from this way and were eventually destroyed. Western scholars have not written very much about this ancient type of government in which the king and his assembly ruled by the *dasarājadhamma*. But this type of government, an enlightened ruling class (*kṣatriyavarṇa*) based in the *dasarājadhamma* is, in fact, the kind of socialism which can save the world.

The sort of socialism I have been discussing is misunderstood because of the term, *rāja*. But a ruler who embodies the ten royal virtues represents socialism in the most complete sense – absolute, thorough, effective – like King Asoka and other rulers like him in our Thai history. For example, upon careful study we can see that Rama Khamhaeng ruled socialistically, looking after his people the way a father and mother look after their children. Such a system should be revived today. We should not blindly follow a liberal democratic form of government essentially based on selfish greed.

The last point I want to make and one especially important for the future is that small countries like our own should adhere to a system of 'dictatorial dhammic socialism' or otherwise it will be difficult to survive. An illusory democracy cannot survive. Liberal democracy has too many flaws. Socialism is preferable, but it must be a socialism based on *dhamma*. Such dhammic socialism is by its very nature 'dictatorial' in the sense I have discussed today. In particular, small countries like Thailand should have democracy in the form of a dictatorial dhammic socialism.

An ancient proverb which is rarely heard goes, 'You must ignite the house fire in order to receive the forest fire.' Elders taught their children that they should burn an area around their huts in order to prevent forest fires from burning down their dwellings. If small countries like our own have a dictatorial dhammic socialist form of government it will be like burning the area around the house in order to protect us from the forest fire. The forest fire can be compared to violent forms of socialism or to capitalism both of which encompass the world today. A dictatorial dhammic socialism will protect us from being victimized by either capitalism or violent forms of proletarian revolution.

Bhikkhu Buddhadasa, 'Dictatorial Dhammic Socialism' in *Dhammic Socialism* (Bangkok: Thai Inter-religious Commission for Development, 1986), pp. 189–93.

Philip Kapleau

The American Philip Kapleau (1912–) worked as a court reporter at the war crimes trials after the Second World War, first in Nuremberg and then in Tokyo. He met D. T. Suzuki in Japan in 1948 and later attended his lectures at Columbia University. Kapleau returned to Japan in 1953, where he spent the next thirteen years practising Zen, the last ten of which under Yasutani Kakuun (1885–1973), a Zen priest (see also the Introduction) who had severed his ties to the Soto sect in order to form his own organization, the Sanbokyodan ('Three Treasures Association') which taught Zen meditation to lay people. Yasutani placed particular emphasis on the rapid attainment of an enlightenment experience (kensho) through the use of the koan *mu*. Kapleau returned to the US in 1965 and the following year founded the Zen Center of Rochester, New York. Yasutani permitted Kapleau to translate his instructions on Zen meditation into English, along with recordings of his interviews with students and testimonials of their enlightenment experiences. These were compiled into *The Three Pillars in Zen*, first published in Japan in 1965. Its clear instructions and inspiring accounts from ordinary people made it an indispensable handbook for thousands of people interested in Zen meditation who lacked either the opportunity or the interest to study with a teacher.

One of the first non-Japanese Zen teachers in America, Kapleau set out to adapt some of the forms of Zen practice to an American audience. For example, daily chants were translated into English, disciples were given Buddhist names that were English rather than Japanese, and Western dress could be worn during meditation. Kapleau's modifications included an English translation of the *Heart Sutra*, a brief Buddhist text chanted daily in Zen temples. Originally composed in Sanskrit, it had been translated first into Chinese and then Japanese, the language in which Yasutani knew it.

Yasutani was strongly opposed to the use of the English translation, arguing that the sound of the words was more important than their meaning. Teacher and student broke over this question in 1967 and never spoke again. Yasutani's successor later raised questions about Kapleau's qualifications as a teacher.

Kapleau, however, has remained dedicated to Yasutani, and his compilation of Yasutani's teachings, *The Three Pillars of Zen*, remains a classic of American Zen. The extracts below from Yasutani's lectures illustrate the structured style of his teaching and his emphasis on the experience of kensho.

THEORY AND PRACTICE OF ZAZEN

What I am about to tell you is based upon the teachings of my revered teacher, Daiun★ Harada-roshi. Although he himself was of the Soto sect, he was unable to find a truly accomplished master in that sect and so went to train first at Shogen-ji and then Nanzen-ji, two Rinzai monasteries. At Nanzen-ji he eventually grasped the inmost secret of Zen under the guidance of Dokutan-roshi, an outstanding master.

While it is undeniably true that one must undergo Zen training himself in order to comprehend the truth of Zen, Harada-roshi felt that the modern mind is so much more aware that for beginners lectures of this type could be meaningful as a preliminary to practice. He combined the best of each sect and established a unique method of teaching Zen. Nowhere in Japan will you find Zen teaching set forth so thoroughly and succinctly, so well suited to the temper of the modern mind, as at his monastery. Having been his disciple for some twenty years, I was enabled, thanks to his favor, to open my Mind's eye in some measure. [. . .]

In point of fact, a knowledge of the theory or principles of zazen is not a prerequisite to practice. One who trains under an accomplished

★ A Zen name meaning 'Great Cloud.' [. . .] His other name is Sogaku.

teacher will inevitably grasp this theory by degrees as his practice ripens. Modern students, however, being intellectually more sophisticated than their predecessors in Zen, will not follow instructions unreservedly; they must first know the reasons behind them. Therefore I feel obligated to deal with theoretical matters. The difficulty with theory, however, is that it is endless. Buddhist scriptures, Buddhist doctrine, and Buddhist philosophy are no more than intellectual formulations of zazen, and zazen itself is their practical demonstration. From this vast field I will now abstract what is most essential for your practice.

[. . .]

THE THREE AIMS OF ZAZEN

The aims of zazen are three: (1) development of the power of concentration (*joriki*), (2) satori-awakening (*kensho-godo*), and (3) actualization of the Supreme Way in our daily lives (*mujodo no taigen*). These three form an inseparable unity, but for purposes of discussion I am obliged to deal with them individually.

Joriki, the first of these, is the power or strength which arises when the mind has been unified and brought to one-pointedness in zazen concentration. This is more than the ability to concentrate in the usual sense of the word. It is a dynamic power which, once mobilized, enables us even in the most sudden and unexpected situations to act instantly, without pausing to collect our wits, and in a manner wholly appropriate to the circumstances. One who has developed joriki is no longer a slave to his passions, neither is he at the mercy of his environment. Always in command of both himself and the circumstances of his life, he is able to move with perfect freedom and equanimity. The cultivation of certain supra-normal powers is also made possible by joriki, as is the state in which the mind becomes like clear, still water.

[. . .] Now, although the power of joriki can be endlessly enlarged through regular practice, it will recede and eventually vanish if we neglect zazen. And while it is true that many extraordinary powers flow from joriki, nevertheless through it alone we cannot cut the roots of our illusory view of the world. Mere strength of concentration is not enough for the highest types of Zen; concomitantly there must be satori-awakening. In a little-known document handed down by the Patriarch Sekito Kisen, the founder of one of the early Zen sects, the following appears: 'In our sect, realization of the Buddha-nature, and not mere devotion or strength of concentration, is paramount.'

The second of these aims is kensho-godo, seeing into your True-nature and at the same time seeing into the ultimate nature of the universe and 'all the ten thousand things' in it. It is the sudden realization that 'I have been complete and perfect from the very beginning. How wonderful, how miraculous!' If it is true kensho, its substance will always be the same for whoever experiences it, whether he be the Buddha Shakyamuni, the Buddha Amida, or any one of you gathered in this temple. But this does not mean that we can all experience kensho to the same degree, for in the clarity, the depth, and the completeness of the experience there are great differences. As an illustration, imagine a person blind from birth who gradually begins to recover his sight. At first he can see very vaguely and darkly and only objects close to him. Then as his sight improves he is able to distinguish things a yard or so away, then objects at ten yards, then at a hundred yards, until finally he can recognize anything up to a thousand yards. At each of these passing stages the phenomenal world he is seeing is the same, but the differences in the clarity and accuracy of his views of that world are as great as those between snow and charcoal. So it is with the differences in clarity and depth of our experiences of kensho.

The last of the three objectives is *mujodo no taigen*, the actualization of the Supreme Way throughout our entire being and our daily activities. At this point we do not distinguish the end from the means. Saijojo, which I have spoken of as the fifth and highest of the five types of Zen, corresponds to this stage. When you sit earnestly and egolessly in accordance with the instructions of a competent teacher – with your mind fully conscious yet as free of thought as a pure white sheet of paper is unmarred by a blemish – there is an unfoldment of your intrinsically pure Buddha-nature whether you have had satori or not. But what must be emphasized here is that only with true awakening do you directly apprehend the truth of your Buddha-nature and perceive that saijojo, the purest type of Zen, is no different from that practiced by all Buddhas.

The practice of Buddhist Zen should embrace all three of these objectives, for they are interrelated. There is, for instance, an essential connection between joriki and kensho. Kensho is 'the wisdom naturally associated with joriki,' which is the power arising from concentration. Joriki is connected with kensho in yet another way. Many people may never be able to reach kensho unless they have first cultivated a certain amount of joriki, for otherwise they may find themselves too restless, too nervous and uneasy to persevere with their zazen. Moreover, unless fortified by joriki, a single experience of kensho will have no appreciable effect on your life and will fade into a mere memory. For although through the experience of kensho you have apprehended the underlying unity of the cosmos with your Mind's eye, without joriki you are unable to act with the total force of your being on what your inner vision has revealed to you.

Likewise there is an interconnection between kensho and the third of these aims, *mujodo no taigen*. Kensho when manifested in all your actions is *mujodo no taigen*. With perfect enlightenment (*anuttara samyak-sambodhi*) we apprehend that our conception of the world as dual and antithetical is false, and upon this realization the world of Oneness, of true harmony and peace, is revealed.

The Rinzai sect tends to make satori-awakening the final aim of sitting and skims over joriki and *mujodo no taigen*. Thus the need for continued practice after enlightenment is minimized, and koan study, since it is unsupported by zazen and scarcely related to daily life, becomes essentially an intellectual game instead of a means by which to amplify and strengthen enlightenment.

On the other hand, while the practice advocated in the official quarters of the Soto sect today stresses *mujodo no taigen*, in effect it amounts to little more than the accumulation of joriki, which, as I pointed out earlier, 'leaks' or recedes and ultimately disappears unless zazen is carried on regularly. The contention of the Soto sect nowadays that kensho is unnecessary and that one need do no more than carry on his daily activities with the Mind of the Buddha is specious, for without kensho you can never really know what this Buddha-mind is.

These imbalances in both sects* in recent times have, unfortunately, impaired the quality of Zen teaching.

This concludes the discussion of the three aims of zazen.

[. . .]

THE THREE ESSENTIALS OF ZEN PRACTICE

What I am about to say is especially applicable to daijo Zen, which is specifically directed toward satori, but it also embraces saijojo, though in a lesser degree.

The first of the three essentials of Zen practice is strong faith (*daishinkon*). This is more than mere belief. The ideogram for *kon* means 'root,' and that for *shin*, 'faith.' Hence the phrase implies a faith that is firmly and deeply rooted, immovable, like an immense tree or a huge boulder. It is a faith, moreover, untainted by belief in the supernatural or the superstitious. Buddhism has often been described as both a rational religion and a religion of wisdom. But a religion it is, and what makes it one is this element of faith, without which it is merely philosophy. Buddhism starts with the Buddha's supreme enlightenment, which he attained after strenuous effort. Our deep faith, therefore, is in his enlightenment, the substance of which he proclaimed to be that human nature, all existence, is intrinsically whole, flawless, omnipotent – in a word, perfect. Without unwavering faith in this, the heart of the Buddha's teaching, it is impossible to progress far in one's practice.

The second indispensable quality is a feeling of strong doubt (*diagidan*),† Not a simple doubt, mind you, but a 'doubt-mass' – and this

---

* For a poetic description of the differences between Rinzai and Soto, the following from an unpublished manuscript of the late Nyogen Senzaki may be of interest: 'Among Zen students it is said that "Rinzai's teaching is like the frost of the late autumn, making one shiver, while the teaching of Soto is like the spring breeze which caresses the flower, helping it to bloom." There is another saying: "Rinzai's teaching is like a brave general who moves a regiment without delay, while the Soto teaching is like a farmer taking care of a rice field, one stalk after another, patiently." '

† In Zen, 'doubt' implies not scepticism but a state of perplexity, of probing inquiry, of intense self-questioning.

inevitably stems from strong faith. It is a doubt as to why we and the world would appear so imperfect, so full of anxiety, strife, and suffering, when in fact our deep faith tells us exactly the opposite is true. It is a doubt which leaves us no rest. It is as though we knew perfectly well we were millionaires and yet inexplicably found ourselves in dire need without a penny in our pockets. Strong doubt, therefore, exists in proportion to strong faith.

I can illustrate this state of mind with a simple example. Take a man who has been sitting smoking and suddenly finds that the pipe which was in his hand a moment before has disappeared. He begins to search for it in the complete certainty of finding it. It was there a moment ago, no one has been near, it cannot have disappeared. The longer he fails to find it, the greater the energy and determination with which he hunts for it.

From this feeling of doubt the third essential, strong determination (*dai-funshi*), naturally arises. It is an overwhelming determination to dispel this doubt with the whole force of our energy and will. Believing with every pore of our being in the truth of the Buddha's teaching that we are all endowed with the immaculate Bodhi-mind, we resolve to discover and experience the reality of this Mind for ourselves.

The other day someone who had quite misunderstood the state of mind required by these three essentials asked me: 'Is there more to believing we are Buddhas than accepting the fact that the world as it is is perfect, that the willow is green and the carnation red?' The fallacy of this is self-evident. If we do not question why greed and conflict exist, why the ordinary man acts like anything but a Buddha, no determination arises in us to resolve the obvious contradiction between what we believe as a matter of faith and what our senses tell us is just the contrary, and our zazen is thus deprived of its prime source of power.

I shall now relate these three essentials to daijo and saijojo Zen. While all three are present in daijo, this doubt is the main prod to satori because it allows us no rest. Thus we experience satori, and the resolution of this doubt, more quickly with daijo Zen.

In saijojo, on the other hand, the element of faith is strongest. No fundamental doubt of the kind I mentioned assails us and so we are not driven to rid ourselves of it, for we sit in the unswerving faith that we are inherently Buddhas. Unlike daijo Zen, saijojo, which you will recall is the purest type of zazen, does not involve the anxious striving for enlightenment. It is zazen wherein ripening takes place naturally, culminating in enlightenment. At the same time saijojo is the most difficult zazen of all, demanding resolute and dedicated sitting.

However, in both types of zazen all three elements are indispensable, and teachers of old have said that so long as they are simultaneously present it is easier to miss the ground with a stamp of the foot than to miss attaining perfect enlightenment.

Philip Kapleau, *The Three Pillars of Zen*, revised and expanded edition (Garden City, NY: Anchor Press, 1980), pp. 29–30, 49–52, 64–6.

William Burroughs

William S. Burroughs (1914–97) was born in St Louis, the grandson of the inventor of the Burroughs adding machine, the source of a family fortune that supported Burroughs during much of his life. After graduating from Harvard, he moved to New York, where he met Allen Ginsberg and later Jack Kerouac. Fascinated by the criminal life, Burroughs intentionally became addicted to heroin. He wrote an account of his drug experiences, published in 1953 with the help of Ginsberg as *Junkie: Confessions of an Unredeemed Drug Addict*. Burroughs, together with his common-law wife, Joan Vollmer Adams, and their young son, moved to Texas and then, to evade the authorities, Mexico. In 1951 while attempting to shoot a shotglass off his wife's head, he accidentally shot her in the head and killed her. He was subsequently acquitted.

Burroughs travelled to South America and then Tangier, where he was visited by Kerouac and Ginsberg in 1957. They typed up the assorted handwritten stories that they found in Burroughs's rooms and arranged them into what became his most famous work, *Naked Lunch* (1959; the title provided by Kerouac). Burroughs would go on to write many other works, including plays, film scripts, journals, and collections of essays.

He did not share the enthusiasm for Buddhism of his friends Kerouac, Ginsberg and Snyder. It was somewhat surprising, therefore, that he went on a meditation retreat in 1975 at Tail of the Tiger, a Tibetan Buddhist meditation centre founded by Chögyam Trungpa. But, as he explains in the introduction to *The Retreat Diaries* (1976), presented below, he found certain contradictions between the vocation of the writer and that of the Buddhist.

Last summer in Boulder I was talking to Chogyam Trungpa Rinpoche about doing a retreat at his Vermont center. I asked about taking along a typewriter. He objected that this would defeat the whole purpose of doing a retreat, like a carpenter takes along his tools – and I see we have a very different purpose in mind. That he could make the carpenter comparison shows where the difference lies: the difference being, with all due respect for the trade of Jesus Christ, that a carpenter can always carpenter, while a writer has to take it when it comes and a glimpse once lost may never come again, like Coleridge's Kubla Khan. Writers don't write, they read and transcribe. They are only allowed access to the books at certain times. They have to make the most of these occasions. Furthermore I am more concerned with writing than I am with any sort of enlightenment, which is often an ever-retreating mirage like the fully analyzed or fully liberated person. I use meditation to get material for writing. I am not concerned with some abstract nirvana. It is exactly the vision and fireworks that are useful for me, exactly what all the masters tell us we should pay as little attention to as possible. Telepathy, journeys out of the body – these manifestation, according to Trungpa, are mere distractions. Exactly. Distraction: fun, like hang-gliding or surfboarding or skin diving. So why not have fun? I sense an underlying dogma here to which I am not willing to submit. The purposes of a Boddhisattva and an artist are different and perhaps not reconcilable. *Show me a good Buddhist novelist.* When Huxley got Buddhism, he stopped writing novels and wrote Buddhist tracts. Meditation, astral travel, telepathy, are all means to an end for the novelist. I even got copy out of scientology. It's a question of emphasis. Any writer who does not consider his writing the most important thing he does, who does not consider writing his only salvation, I – 'I trust him little in the commerce of the soul.' As the French say: *pas serieux.*

I was willing to concede the typewriter, but I certainly would not concede pen and paper. A good percentage of my characters and sets come from dreams, and if you don't write a dream, in many cases, you forget it. The actual brain trace of dream memory differs from that of waking memory. I have frequently had the experience of waking from a dream, going over it a number of times, and then forgetting it completely. So during the retreat I kept pen and paper by my bed, and lit a candle and wrote my dreams down when they occurred. As it happens, I got a new episode for the book I am currently writing and solved a problem of structure in a dream recorded in these diaries. I also attempted some journeys out of the body to visit specific people, with results that, while not conclusive (they rarely are), were at least interesting and fruitful. In short, I feel that I get further out through writing than I would through any meditation system. And so far as any system goes, I prefer the open-ended, dangerous and unpredictable universe of Don Juan to the closed, predictable karma universe of the Buddhists.* Indeed existence *is* the cause of suffering, and suffering may be good copy. Don Juan says he is an impeccable warrior and not a master; anyone who is looking for a master should look elsewhere. *I am not looking for a master*; I am looking for the *books*. In dreams I sometimes find the books where it is written and I may bring back a few phrases that unwind like a scroll. Then I write as fast as I can type, because I am reading, not writing.

I will endeavor to summarize the highly complex and sophisticated system of spiritual training outlined by Don Juan in *Tales of Power*. The aim of this training is to produce an impeccable warrior – that is, a being who is at all times completely in possession of himself. The warrior is concerned only with expressing the totality of himself, not with praise or support from others. He neither seeks nor admits a master. The warrior's state is achieved with the aid of a teacher and a benefactor. To understand the respective roles of teacher and benefactor, one must consider the concepts of the *tonal* and the *nagual*, which are basic to the warrior's path. The *tonal* is the sum of any individual's perceptions and knowledge, everything he can talk about and explain, including his own physical being. The *nagual* is everything outside the *tonal*: the inexplicable, the unpredictable, the unknown. The *nagual* is everything that cannot be talked about or explained, but only witnessed. The sudden irruption of the *nagual* into the *tonal* can be lethal unless the student is carefully prepared. The teacher's role is to clean up and strengthen the *tonal*, so that the student is able to deal with the

---

* 'Outside the wheel of conditional karmic existence' would be the Buddhist equivalent of 'unpredictable, open-ended' – Allen Ginsberg

nagual which the benefactor will then demonstrate. The teacher and the benefactor show the student how to reach the unknown, but they cannot predict what will happen when he does reach the *nagual*. The *nagual* is by its nature unpredictable, and the whole training is extremely dangerous. While the *tonal*, the totality of conscious existence, shapes the individual being, the *tonal* is in turn shaped by the *nagual*, by everything it is not, which surrounds it like a mold. The *tonal* tends to shut out and deny the *nagual*, which takes over completely in the moment of death. If we see the *nagual* as the unknown, the unpredictable and unexplainable, the role of the artist is to make contact with the *nagual* and bring a part of it back into the *tonal* in paint or words, sculpture, film or music. The *nagual* is also the area of so-called psychic phenomena which the Buddhists consider as distractions from the way of enlightenment. Buddhism and the teachings of Don Juan are simply not directed towards the same goals. Don Juan does not offer any final solution or enlightenment. Neither does the artist.

During the retreat I wrote down dreams and the elaboration of dreams that takes place spontaneously in the waking state. I used an exercise in association: take a walk and later write down what you were thinking when a deer crossed the road or when you sat down on a rock and killed a biting fly. One of my first acts in my retreat hut was to improvise a fly swatter from an old whisk broom, and I think this no-killing obsession is nonsense. Where do you draw the line? Mosquitoes? Biting flies? Lice? Venomous insects? I'd rather kill a brown recluse spider than get bitten by one. And I will not coexist with flies.* Interesting point here: The Miracle of the Centipede which disappeared as I was about to kill it with a sledge hammer. That was a nice miracle. *Chapeau*, Trungpa Rinpoche. Because that centipede was only half an inch long, and they don't get much bigger in that climate. And that's a bearable size – doesn't keep me awake knowing it is in the room, so why kill it? On the other hand, a centipede three inches long is already an abomination in my eyes. Little spider in web at window. He's all right. But I hear a rustling on the shelf above my bed. I light

---

* Buddhist Tantrics kill insects with Mantras in Dharma teaching places. 'Kill mindfully' – A.G.

the candle and there is a spider about an inch across and a brown spider at that. Might be a brown recluse. Any case, too big to live in my vicinity. I feel better after it is dead, knowing it can't get on my face while I am sleeping.

The Retreat Diaries are not a sequential presentation. By sequential presentation, I mean Monday with all dreams and occurrences noted, then on to Tuesday and so forth. Here Thursday and Friday may be cut in with Monday, or the elaboration of a dream cut in with the dream itself in a grid of past present and future. Like the last words of Dutch Schultz. Some of Dutch's associations cannot be traced or even guessed at. Others quite clearly derive from the known events of his life. The *structure* is that a man is *seeing a film* composed of past present and future, dream and fantasy, a film which the reader cannot see directly but only infer through the words. This is the structure of these diaries.

William S. Burroughs, *The Retreat Diaries* (New York: The City Moon, 1976), unpaginated.

Alan Watts

Alan Watts (1915–73) was born in Kent and educated at public school. Inspired by such works as W. E. Holmes's *The Creed of the Buddha*, he declared himself a Buddhist at the age of fifteen and wrote to the Buddhist Lodge of the Theosophical Society in London. Watts became a student and protégé of the head of the Lodge (later the Buddhist Society), Christmas Humphreys. At the age of nineteen, he wrote his first book, *The Spirit of Zen*, largely a summary of the writings of D. T. Suzuki. Shortly thereafter he assumed the editorship of the Lodge's journal, *Buddhism in England* (later to become *The Middle Way*). In 1938 Watts married an American, Eleanor Everett, the daughter of Ruth Fuller Everett (later, Sasaki), an important early figure in American Zen. They emigrated to the US during the Second World War (Watts, a pacifist, did not serve) and settled in New York, where Watts studied briefly with Shigetsu Sasaki, a Japanese artist and Zen practitioner known as Sokei-an, who would later marry Ruth Fuller Everett. Watts gave seminars in New York and published a book entitled *The Meaning of Happiness* (1940). Inspired by his wife's vision of Christ, Watts decided to become a priest and entered the Seabury-Western Theological Seminary near Chicago. He was ordained as an Episcopal priest and served for five years as chaplain at Northwestern University, resigning from the priesthood shortly after his wife had their marriage annulled on the charge that Watts was a 'sexual pervert'. He was befriended by the American scholar of ancient myth Joseph Campbell, who helped him acquire a grant from the Bollingen Foundation, after which he worked for six years at the newly founded American Academy of Asian Studies in San Francisco. He published *The Way of Zen* in 1957, followed by *Nature, Man, and Woman* (1958) and *Psychotherapy East and West* (1961). Watts supported himself financially as a popular author and speaker until his death in 1973.

In his 1959 essay 'Beat Zen, Square Zen, and Zen' (presented in an abbreviated form below), he offers an erudite analysis of the American Zen scene at the end of the 1950s.

BEAT ZEN, SQUARE ZEN, AND ZEN

It is as difficult for Anglo-Saxons as for the Japanese to absorb anything quite so Chinese as Zen. For though the word 'Zen' is Japanese and though Japan is now its home, Zen Buddhism is the creation of T'ang dynasty China. I do not say this as a prelude to harping upon the incommunicable subtleties of alien cultures. The point is simply that people who feel a profound need to justify themselves have difficulty in understanding the viewpoints of those who do not, and the Chinese who created Zen were the same kind of people as Lao-tzu, who, centuries before, had said, 'Those who justify themselves do not convince.' For the urge to make or prove oneself right has always jiggled the Chinese sense of the ludicrous, since as both Confucians and Taoists – however different these philosophies in other ways – they have invariably appreciated the man who can 'come off it'. To Confucius it seemed much better to be human-hearted than righteous, and to the great Taoists, Lao-tzu and Chuang-tzu, it was obvious that one could not be right without also being wrong, because the two were as inseparable as back and front. As Chuang-tzu said, 'Those who would have good government without its correlative misrule, and right without its correlative wrong, do not understand the principles of the universe.'

To Western ears such words may sound cynical, and the Confucian admiration of 'reasonableness' and compromise may appear to be a weak-kneed lack of commitment to principle. Actually they reflect a marvelous understanding and respect for what we call the balance of nature, human and otherwise – a universal vision of life as the Tao or way of nature in which the good and the evil, the creative and the destructive, the wise and the foolish are the inseparable polarities of existence. 'Tao,' said the *Chung-yung*, 'is that from which one cannot depart. That from which one can depart is not the Tao.' Therefore wisdom did not consist in trying to wrest the good from the evil but in learning to 'ride' them as a cork adapts itself to the crests and troughs of the waves. At the roots of Chinese life there is a trust in the good-and-evil of one's own nature which is peculiarly foreign to those brought up with the chronic uneasy conscience of the Hebrew-Christian cultures. Yet it was always obvious to the Chinese that a man who mistrusts himself cannot even trust his mistrust, and must therefore be hopelessly confused.

For rather different reasons, Japanese people tend to be as uneasy in themselves as Westerners, having a sense of social shame quite as acute as our more metaphysical sense of sin. This was especially true of the class most attracted to Zen, the *samurai*. Ruth Benedict, in that very uneven work *Chrysanthemum and Sword*, was, I think, perfectly correct in saying that the attraction of Zen to the *samurai* class was its power to get rid of an extremely awkward self-consciousness induced in the education of the young. Part and parcel of this self-consciousness is the Japanese compulsion to compete with oneself – a compulsion which turns every craft and skill into a marathon of self-discipline. Although the attraction of Zen lay in the possibility of liberation from self-consciousness, the Japanese version of Zen fought fire with fire, overcoming the 'self observing the self ' by bringing it to an intensity in which it exploded. How remote from the regimen of the Japanese Zen monastery are the words of the great T'ang master Lin-chi:

In Buddhism there is no place for using effort. Just be ordinary and nothing special. Eat your food, move your bowels, pass water, and when you're tired go and lie down. The ignorant will laugh at me, but the wise will understand.

Yet the spirit of these words is just as remote from a kind of Western Zen which would employ this philosophy to justify a very self-defensive Bohemianism.

There is no single reason for the extraordinary growth of Western interest in Zen during the last twenty years. The appeal of Zen arts to the 'modern' spirit in the West, the work of Suzuki, the war with Japan, the itchy fascination of 'Zen stories', and the attraction of a nonconceptual, experimental philosophy in the climate of scientific relativism – all these are involved. One might mention, too, the affinities between Zen and such purely Western trends as the philosophy of Wittgenstein, Existentialism, General Semantics, the metalinguistics of B. L. Whorf, and certain movements in the philosophy of science and in psychotherapy. Always in the background there is our vague disquiet with the artificiality or 'antinaturalness' of both Christianity, with its politically ordered cosmology, and technology, with its imperialistic mechanization of a natural world from which man himself feels strongly alien. For both reflect a psychology in which man is identified with a conscious intelligence and will standing apart from nature to control it, like the architect-God in whose image this version of man is conceived. The disquiet arises from the suspicion that our attempt to master the world from outside is a vicious circle in which we shall be condemned to the perpetual insomnia of controlling controls and supervising supervision ad infinitum.

To the Westerner in search of the reintegration of man and nature there is an appeal far beyond the merely sentimental in the naturalism of Zen – in the landscapes of Ma-yuan and Sesshu, in an art which is simultaneously spiritual and secular, which conveys the mystical in terms of the natural, and which, indeed, never even imagined a break between them. Here is a view of the world imparting a profoundly refreshing sense of wholeness to a culture in which the spiritual and the material, the conscious and the unconscious, have been cataclysmically split. For this reason the Chinese humanism and naturalism of Zen intrigue us much more strongly than Indian Buddhism or Vedanta. These, too, have their students in the West, but their followers seem for the most part to be displaced Christians – people in search of a more plausible philosophy than Christian supernaturalism to carry on the essentially Christian search for the miraculous. The ideal man of Indian Buddhism is clearly a superman, a yogi with absolute mastery of his own nature, according perfectly with the science-fiction ideal of 'men beyond mankind'. But the Buddha or awakened man of Chinese Zen is 'ordinary and nothing special'; he is humorously human like the Zen tramps portrayed by Mu-ch'i and Liang-k'ai. We like this because here, for the first time, is a conception of the holy man and sage who is not impossibly remote, not superhuman but fully human, and, above all, not a solemn and sexless ascetic. Furthermore, in Zen the *satori* experience of awakening to our 'original inseparability' with the universe seems, however elusive, always just around the corner. One has even met people to whom it has happened, and they are no longer mysterious occultists in the Himalayas or skinny yogis in cloistered ashrams. They are just like us, and yet much more at home in the world, floating much more easily upon the ocean of transience and insecurity.

Above all, I believe that Zen appeals to many in the post-Christian West because it does not preach, moralize, and scold in the style of Hebrew-Christian prophetism. Buddhism does not deny that there is a relatively limited sphere in which human life may be improved by art and science, reason and good will. However, it regards this sphere of activity as important but nonetheless subordinate to the comparatively limitless sphere in which things are as they are, always have been, and always will be – a sphere entirely beyond the categories of good and evil, success and failure, and individual health and sickness. On the one hand, this is the sphere of the great universe. Looking out into it at night, we make no comparisons between right and wrong stars, nor between well and badly arranged constellations. Stars are by nature big and little, bright and dim. Yet the whole thing is a splendor and a marvel which sometimes makes our flesh creep with awe. On the other hand, this is also the sphere of human, everyday life which we might call existential.

For there is a standpoint from which human affairs are as much beyond right and wrong as the stars, and from which our deeds, experiences, and feelings can no more be judged than the ups and downs of a range of mountains. Though beyond moral and social valuation, this level of human life may also be seen to be just as marvelous and uncanny as the great universe itself. This feeling may become particularly acute when the individual ego tries to fathom its own nature, to plumb the inner sources of its own actions and consciousness. For here it discovers a part of itself – the inmost and greatest part – which is strange to itself and beyond its understanding and control. Odd as it may sound, the ego finds that its own center and nature is beyond itself. The more deeply I go into myself, the more I am not myself, and yet this is the very heart of me. Here I find my own inner workings functioning of themselves, spontaneously, like the rotation of the heavenly bodies and the drifting of the clouds. Strange and foreign as this aspect of myself at first seems to be, I soon realize that it *is* me, and much more than my superficial ego. This is not fatalism or determinism, because there is no longer anyone being pushed around or determined; there is nothing that this deep 'I' is not doing. The configuration of my nervous system, like the configuration of the stars, happens of itself, and this 'itself' is the real 'myself'.

From this standpoint – and here language reveals its limitations with a vengeance – I find that I cannot help doing and experiencing, quite freely, what is always 'right', in the sense that the stars are always in the 'right' places. As Hsiang-yen put it,

> There's no use for artificial discipline,
> For, move as I will, I manifest the ancient Tao.

At this level, human life is beyond anxiety, for it can never make a mistake. If we live, we live; if we die, we die; if we suffer, we suffer; if we are terrified, we are terrified. There is no problem about it. A Zen master was once asked, 'It is terribly hot, and how shall we escape the heat?' 'Why not,' he answered, 'go to the place where it is neither hot nor cold?' 'Where is that place?' 'In the summer we sweat; in the winter we shiver.' In Zen one does not feel guilty about dying, or being afraid, or disliking the heat. At the same time, Zen does not insist upon this point of view as something which one *ought* to adopt; it does not preach it as an ideal. For if you don't understand it, your very not-understanding is also IT. There would be no bright stars without dim stars and, without the surrounding darkness, no stars at all.

The Hebrew-Christian universe is one in which moral urgency, the anxiety to be right, embraces and penetrates everything. God, the Absolute itself, is good as against bad, and thus to be immoral or in the wrong is to feel oneself an outcast not merely from human society but also from existence itself, from the root and ground of life. To be in the wrong therefore arouses a metaphysical anxiety and sense of guilt – a state of eternal damnation – utterly disproportionate to the crime. This metaphysical guilt is so unsupportable that it must eventually issue in the rejection of God and his laws – which is just what has happened in the whole movement of modern secularism, materialism, and naturalism. Absolute morality is profoundly destructive of morality, for the sanctions which it invokes against evil are far, far too heavy. One does not cure the headache by cutting off the head. The appeal of Zen, as of other forms of Eastern philosophy, is that it unveils behind the urgent realm of good and evil a vast region of oneself about which there need be no guilt or recrimination, where at last the self is indistinguishable from God.

But the Westerner who is attracted by Zen and who would understand it deeply must have one indispensable qualification: he must understand his own culture so thoroughly that he is no longer swayed by its premises unconsciously. He must really have come to terms with the Lord God Jehovah and with his Hebrew-Christian conscience so that he can take it or leave it without fear or rebellion. He must be free of the itch to justify himself. Lacking this, his Zen will be either 'beat' or 'square', either a revolt from the culture and social order or a new form of stuffiness and respectability. For Zen is above all the liberation of the mind from conventional thought, and this is something utterly different from rebellion against convention, on the one hand, or adapting foreign conventions, on the other.

Conventional thought is, in brief, the confusion of the concrete universe of nature and cultural symbolism. For in Taoism and Zen the world is seen as an inseparably interrelated field or continuum, no part of which can actually be separated from the rest or valued above or below the rest. It was in this sense that Huineng, the Sixth Patriarch, meant that 'fundamentally not one thing exists', for he realized that things are *terms*, not entities. They exist in the abstract world of thought, but not in the concrete world of nature. Thus one who actually perceives or feels this to be so no longer feels that he is an ego, except by definition. He sees that his ego is his *persona* or social role, a somewhat arbitrary selection of experiences with which he has been taught to identify himself. (Why, for example, do we say 'I think' but not 'I am beating my heart'?) Having seen this, he continues to play his social role without being taken in by it. He does not precipitately adopt a new role or play the role of having no role at all. He plays it cool.

The 'beat' mentality as I am thinking of it is something much more extensive and vague than the hipster life of New York and San Francisco. It is a younger generation's nonparticipation in 'the American Way of Life', a revolt which does not seek to change the existing order but simply turns away from it to find the significance of life in subjective experience rather than objective achievement. It contrasts with the 'square' and other-directed mentality of beguilement by social convention, unaware of the correlativity of right and wrong, of the mutual necessity of capitalism and communism to each other's existence, of the inner identity of puritanism and lechery, or of, say, the alliance of church lobbies and organized crime to maintain laws against gambling.

Beat Zen is a complex phenomenon. It ranges from a use of Zen for justifying sheer caprice in art, literature, and life to a very forceful social criticism and 'digging of the universe' such as one may find in the poetry of Ginsberg, Whalen, and Snyder, and, rather unevenly, in Kerouac, who is always a shade too self-conscious, too subjective, and too strident to have the flavor of Zen.

When Kerouac gives his philosophical final statement, 'I don't know. I don't care. And it doesn't make any difference' – the cat is out of the bag, for there is a hostility in these words which clangs with self-defense. But just because Zen truly surpasses convention and its values, it has no need to say 'To hell with it,' nor underline with violence the fact that anything goes.

It is indeed the basic intuition of Zen that there is an ultimate standpoint from which 'anything goes.' In the celebrated words of master Yun-men, 'Every day is a good day.' Or as is said in the *Hsin-hsin Ming*:

> If you want to get the plain truth,
> Be not concerned with right and wrong.
> The conflict between right and wrong
> Is the sickness of the mind.

But this standpoint does not exclude and is not hostile toward the distinction between right and wrong at other levels and in more limited frames of reference. The world is seen to be beyond right and wrong when it is not framed: that is to say, when we are not looking at a particular situation by itself – out of relation to the rest of the universe. Within this room there is a clear difference between up and down; out in interstellar space there is not. Within the conventional limits of a human community there are clear distinctions between good and evil. But these disappear when human affairs are seen as part and parcel of the whole realm of nature. Every framework sets up a restricted field of relationships, and restriction is law or rule.

Now a skilled photographer can point his camera at almost any scene or object and create a marvelous composition by the way in which he frames and lights it. An unskilled photographer attempting the same thing creates only messes, for he does not know how to place the frame, the border of the picture, where it will be in relation to the contents. How eloquently this demonstrates that as soon as we introduce a frame anything does *not* go. But every work of art involves a frame. A frame of some kind is precisely what distinguishes a painting, a poem, a musical composition, a play, a dance, or a piece of sculpture from the rest of the world. Some artists may argue that they do not want their works to be distinguishable from the total universe, but if this be so they should not frame them in galleries and concert halls. Above all they should not sign them nor sell them. This is as immoral as selling the moon or signing one's name to a mountain. (Such an artist may perhaps be forgiven if he knows what he is doing and prides himself inwardly, not on being a poet or painter, but a competent crook.) Only destructive little boys and vulgar excursionists go around initialing the trees. [. . .]

The realization of the unswerving 'rightness' of whatever happens is no more manifested by utter lawlessness in social conduct than by sheer caprice in art. As Zen has been used as a pretext for the latter in our time, its use as a pretext for the former is ancient history. Many a rogue has justified himself with the Buddhist formula, 'Birth-and-death (*samsara*) is Nirvana; worldly passions are Enlightenment.' This danger is implicit in Zen because it is implicit in freedom. Power and freedom can never be safe. They are dangerous in the same way that fire and electricity are dangerous. But it is quite pitiful to see Zen used as a pretext for license when the Zen in question is no more than an idea in the head, a simple rationalization. To some extent 'Zen' is so used in the underworld which often attaches itself to artistic and intellectual communities. After all, the Bohemian way of life is primarily the natural consequence of artists and writers being so absorbed in their work that they have no interest in keeping up with the Joneses. It is also a symptom of creative changes in manners and morals which at first seem as reprehensible to conservatives as new forms in art. But every such community attracts a number of weak imitators and hangers-on, especially in the great cities, and it is mostly in this class that one now finds the stereotype of the 'beatnik' with his phony Zen. Yet if Zen were not the pretext for this shiftless existence, it would be something else. [. . .]

Now the underlying protestant lawlessness of beat Zen disturbs the square Zennists very seriously. For square Zen is the Zen of established tradition in Japan with its clearly defined hierarchy, its rigid discipline, and its specific tests of *satori*. More particularly, it is the kind of Zen adopted by Westerners studying in Japan, who will before long be bringing it back home. But it there is an obvious difference between square Zen and the common or garden squareness of the Rotary Club or the Presbyterian Church. It is infinitely more imaginative, sensitive, and interesting. But it is still square because it is a quest for the *right* spiritual experience, for a *satori* which will receive the stamp (*inka*) of approval and established authority. There will even be certificates to hang on the wall.

If square Zen falls into any serious excess it is in the direction of spiritual snobbism and artistic preciousness, though I have never known an orthodox Zen teacher who could be accused of either. These gentlemen seem to take their exalted office rather lightly, respecting its dignity without standing on it. The faults of square Zen are the faults of any spiritual in-group with an esoteric discipline and degrees of initiation. Students in the lower ranks can get unpleasantly uppity about inside knowledge which they are not at liberty to divulge – 'and you wouldn't understand even if I could tell you' – and are apt to dwell rather sickeningly on the immense difficulties and iron disciplines of their task. There are times, however, when this is understandable, especially when someone who is just goofing off claims that he is following the Zen ideal of 'naturalness'.

The student of square Zen is also inclined at times to be niggling in his recognition of parallels to Zen in other spiritual traditions. Because the essentials of Zen can never be accurately and fully formulated, being an experience and not a set of ideas, it is always possible to be critical of anything anyone says about it, neither putting up nor shutting up. Any statement about Zen, or about spiritual experience of any kind, will always leave some aspect, some subtlety, unexpressed. No one's mouth is big enough to utter the whole thing. The Western follower of Zen should also resist the temptation to associate himself with an even worse form of snobbery, the intellectual snobbery so largely characteristic of Far Eastern studies in American universities. In this particular field the fad for making humanistic studies 'scientific' has gone to such wild extremes that even Suzuki is accused of being a 'popularizer' instead of a serious scholar – presumably because he is a little unsystematic about footnotes and covers a vast area instead of confining himself with rigor to a single problem, e.g. 'An Analysis of Some Illegible and Archaic Character-forms in the Tun-huang Manuscript of the Sutra of the Sixth Patriarch.' There is a proper and honorable place in scholarship for the meticulous drudge, but when he is on top instead of on tap his dangerous envy of real intelligence drives all creative scholars from the field.★

In its artistic expression square Zen is often rather tediously studied and precious, a fate which all too easily befalls a venerable aesthetic tradition when its techniques are so highly developed that it takes a lifetime to master any one of them. No one has then the time to go beyond the achievements of the old masters, so that new generations are condemned to endless repetition and imitation of their refinements.

★ Suzuki, incidentally, is a very rare bird among contemporary Asians – an original thinker. He is no mere mouthpiece for any fixed tradition, and has come forth with some ideas about comparative religion and the psychology of religion which are of enormous importance, quite aside from what he has done to translate and interpret the literature of Zen. But it is just for this reason that people in square Zen and academic Sinology have their qualms about accepting him.

The student of *sumi* painting, calligraphy, *haiku* poetry, or tea ceremony can therefore get trapped in a tiresomely repetitious affectation of styles, varied only with increasingly esoteric allusions to the work of the past. When this comes to the point of imitating the old masters' happy accidents in such a way that 'primitive' and 'rough' effects are produced by the utmost practice and deliberation, the whole thing becomes so painful that even the wildest excesses of beat Zen art look refreshing. Indeed, it is possible that beat Zen and square Zen will so complement and rub against one another that an amazingly pure and lively Zen will arise from the hassle.

For this reason I see no really serious quarrel with either extreme. There was never a spiritual movement without its excesses and distortions. The experience of awakening which truly constitutes Zen is too timeless and universal to be injured. The extremes of beat Zen need alarm no one since, as Blake said, 'the fool who persists in his folly will become wise.' As for square Zen, 'authoritative' spiritual experiences have always had a way of wearing thin, and thus of generating the demand for something genuine and unique which needs no stamp.

I have known followers of both extremes to come up with perfectly clear *satori* experiences, for since there is no real 'way' to *satori* the way you are following makes very little difference. [. . .]

Foreign religions can be immensely attractive and highly overrated by those who know little of their own, and especially by those who have not worked through and grown out of their own. This is why the displaced or unconscious Christian can so easily use either beat or square Zen to justify himself. The one wants a philosophy to justify him in doing what he pleases. The other wants a more plausible authoritative salvation than the Church or the psychiatrists seem to be able to provide. Furthermore the atmosphere of Japanese Zen is free from all one's unpleasant childhood associations with God the Father and Jesus Christ – though I know many young Japanese who feel just the same way about their early training in Buddhism. But the character of Zen remains almost incomprehensible to those who have not surpassed the immaturity of needing to be justified, whether before the Lord god or before a paternalistic society.

The old Chinese Zen masters were steeped in Taoism. They saw nature in its total interrelatedness, and saw that every creature and every experience is in accord with the Tao of nature just as it is. This enabled them to accept themselves as they were, moment by moment, without the least need to justify anything. They didn't do it to defend themselves or to find an excuse for getting away with murder. They didn't brag about it and set themselves apart as rather special. On the contrary, their Zen was *wu-shih*, which means approximately 'nothing special' or 'no fuss'. But Zen is 'fuss' when it is mixed up with Bohemian affectations, and 'fuss' when it is imagined that the only proper way to find it is to run off to a monastery in Japan or to do special exercises in the lotus posture for five hours a day. And I will admit that the very hullabaloo about Zen, even in such an essay as this, is also fuss – but a little less so.

Having said that, I would like to say something for all Zen fussers, beat or square. Fuss is all right too. If you are hung on Zen, there's no need to try to pretend that you are not. If you really want to spend years in a Japanese monastery, there is no earthly reason why you shouldn't. Or if you want to spend your time hopping freight cars and digging Charlie Parker, it's a free country.

> In the landscape of Spring there is neither
> > better nor worse;
> The flowering branches grow naturally, some
> > long, some short.

Alan W. Watts. 'Beat Zen, Square Zen, and Zen' in *Visibles and Invisibles: A Primer for New Sociological Imagination* (Boston, Mass.: Little, Brown and Company, 1973), pp. 209–23.

Jack Kerouac

Jack Kerouac (1922–69) was born in Lowell, Massachusetts, to a working-class Quebocois family. His first language was a French-Canadian dialect; he learned English from nuns at the local parish school. Kerouac was an outstanding student and athlete at high school, accepting a scholarship to Columbia University in 1940 and becoming a star football player until a broken leg ended his athletic career. He left university and enlisted in the navy, but was discharged. Kerouac then served as a merchant seaman before returning to Columbia in 1944, where he met Allen Ginsberg, who introduced him to William Burroughs, forming a group of companions that Kerouac would later dub the 'Beat generation'. He made several automobile trips across the United States between 1947 and 1950, in the company of Neal Cassady, providing the basis for his most famous work, *On the Road*, published in 1957. Neal Cassady's enthusiasm for the psychic Edgar Cayce inspired Kerouac to learn about Asian religions. He found Goddard's *A Buddhist Bible* in the public library in San Jose, California, and studied it carefully, memorizing sections of it. Although Kerouac considered himself to be a Roman Catholic throughout his life, his interest in Buddhism grew, in part due to the influence of Gary Snyder, whom he met in San Francisco. At Snyder's urging, he wrote a Buddhist scripture, *The Scripture of the Golden Eternity* (1960), as well as a life of the Buddha. However, his best-known work on the subject is *The Dharma Bums* (1958). He died at the age of forty-seven in his mother's home in Florida due to complications resulting from alcoholism.

The Dharma Bums is a thinly fictionalized account of the experiments in Buddhism by Kerouac and a group of friends in California in 1956. The hero of the story, Japhy Rider, is based closely on Gary Snyder; Alvah Goldbook (author of the poem 'Wail') is Allen Ginsberg; and the narrator, Ray

Smith, is Kerouac. Although the characters speak much of Zen, in the passage below Tibetan tantric Buddhism is introduced with *yab yum* ('father-mother'), a union of the male and female principles which Japhy interprets quite literally.

4

But the next night, about midnight, Coughlin and I and Alvah got together and decided to buy a big gallon jug of Burgundy and go bust in on Japhy in his shack.

'What's he doing tonight?' I asked.

'Oh,' says Coughlin, 'probably studying, probably screwing, we'll go see.' We bought the jug on Shattuck Avenue way down and went over and once more I saw his pitiful English bicycle on the lawn. 'Japhy travels around on that bicycle with his little knapsack on his back all up and down Berkeley all day,' said Coughlin. 'He used to do the same thing at Reed College in Oregon. He was a regular fixture up there. Then we'd throw big wine parties and have girls and end up jumping out of windows and playing Joe College pranks all up and down town.'

'Gee, he's strange,' said Alvah, biting his lip in a mood of marvel, and Alvah himself was making a careful interested study of our strange noisy-quiet friend. We came in the little door again, Japhy looked up from his crosslegged study over a book, American poetry this time, glasses on, and said nothing but 'Ah' in a strangely cultured tone. We took off our shoes and padded across the little five feet of straw to sit by him, but I was last with my shoes off, and had the jug in my hand, which I turned to show him from across the shack, and from his crosslegged position Japhy suddenly roared 'Yaaaaah!' and leaped up into the air and straight across the room to me, landing on his feet in a fencing position with a sudden dagger in his hand the tip of it just barely stabbing the glass of the bottle with a small distinct 'clink.' It was the most amazing leap I ever saw in my life, except by nutty acrobats, much like a mountain goat, which he was, it turned out. Also it reminded me of a Japanese Samurai warrior – the yelling roar, the leap, the position, and his expression of comic wrath his eyes bulging and making a big funny face at me. I had the feeling it was really a complaint against our breaking in on his studies and against wine itself which would get him drunk and make him miss his planned evening of reading. But without further ado he uncapped the bottle himself and took a big slug and we all sat crosslegged and spent four hours screaming news at one another, one of the funniest nights. Some of it went like this:

JAPHY: Well, Coughlin, you old fart, what you been doin?

COUGHLIN: Nothin.

ALVAH: What are all these strange books here? Hm, Pound, do you like Pound?

JAPHY: Except for the fact that that old fartface flubbed up the name of Li Po by calling him by his Japanese name and all such famous twaddle, he was all right – in fact he's my favorite poet.

RAY: Pound? Who wants to make a favorite poet out of that pretentious nut?

JAPHY: Have some more wine, Smith, you're not making sense. Who is your favorite poet, Alvah?

RAY: Why don't people ask me *my* favorite poet, I know more about poetry than all of you put together.

JAPHY: Is that true?

ALVAH: It might be. Haven't you seen Ray's new book of poems he just wrote in Mexico – 'the wheel of the quivering meat conception turns in the void expelling tics, porcupines, elephants, people, stardusts, fools, nonsensense . . .'

RAY: That's not it!

JAPHY: Speaking of meat, have you read the new poem of . . .

Etc., etc., then finally disintegrating into a wild talkfest and yellfest and finally songfest with people rolling on the floor in laughter and ending with Alvah and Coughlin and I going staggering up the quiet college street arm in arm singing 'Eli Eli' at the top of our voices and dropping the empty jug right at our feet in a crash of glass, as Japhy laughed from his little door. But we'd made him miss his evening of study and I felt bad about that, till the following night when he suddenly appeared at our little cottage with a pretty girl and came in and told her to take her clothes off, which she did at once.

5

This was in keeping with Japhy's theories about women and lovemaking. I forgot to mention that the day the rock artist had called on him in the late afternoon, a girl had come right after, a blonde in rubber boots and a Tibetan coat with wooden buttons, and in the general talk she'd inquired about our plan to climb Mount Matterhorn and said 'Can I come with ya?' as she was a bit of a mountainclimber herself.

'Shore,' said Japhy, in his funny voice he used for joking, a big loud deep imitation of a lumberjack he knew in the Northwest, a ranger actually, old Burnie Byers, 'shore, come on with us and we'll all screw ya at ten thousand feet' and the way he said it was so funny and casual, and in fact serious, that the girl wasn't shocked at all but somewhat pleased. In this same spirit he'd now brought this girl Princess to our cottage, it was about eight o'clock at night, dark, Alvah and I were quietly sipping tea and reading poems or typing poems at the typewriter and two bicycles came in the yard: Japhy on his, Princess on hers. Princess had gray eyes and yellow hair and was very beautiful and only twenty. I must say one thing about her, she was sex mad and man mad, so there wasn't much of a problem in persuading her to play yabyum. 'Don't you know about yabyum, Smith?' said Japhy in his big booming voice striding in his boots holding Princess's hand. 'Princess and I come here to show ya, boy.'

'Suits me,' said I, 'whatever it is.' Also I'd known Princess before and had been mad about her, in the City, about a year ago. It was just another wild coincidence that she had happened to meet Japhy and fallen in love with him and madly too, she'd do anything he said. Whenever people dropped in to visit us at the cottage I'd always put my red bandanna over the little wall lamp and put out the ceiling light to make a nice cool red dim scene to sit and drink wine and talk in. I did this, and went to get the bottle out of the kitchen and couldn't believe my eyes when I saw Japhy and Alvah taking their clothes off and throwing them every whichaway and I looked and Princess was stark naked, her skin white as snow when the red sun hits it at dusk, in the dim red light. 'What the hell,' I said.

'Here's what yabyum is, Smith,' said Japhy, and he sat crosslegged on the pillow on the floor and motioned to Princess, who came over and sat down on him facing him with her arms about his neck and they sat like that saying nothing for a while. Japhy wasn't at all nervous and embarrassed and just sat there in perfect form just as he was supposed to do. 'This is what they do in the temples of Tibet. It's a holy ceremony, it's done just like this in front of chanting priests. People pray and recite Om Mani Pahdme Hum, which means Amen the Thunderbolt in the Dark Void. I'm the thunderbolt and Princess is the dark void, you see.'

'But what's she thinking?' I yelled almost in despair, I'd had such idealistic longings for that girl in that past year and had conscience-stricken hours wondering if I should seduce her because she was so young and all.

'Oh this is lovely,' said Princess. 'Come on and try it.'

'But I can't sit crosslegged like that.' Japhy was sitting in the full lotus position, it's called, with both ankles over both thighs. Alvah was sitting on the mattress trying to yank his ankles over his thighs to do it. Finally Japhy's legs began to hurt and they just tumbled over on the mattress where both Alvah and Japhy began to explore the territory. I still couldn't believe it.

'Take your clothes off and join in, Smith!' But on top of all that, the feelings about Princess, I'd also gone through an entire year of celibacy based on my feeling that lust was the direct cause of birth which was the direct cause of suffering and death and I had really no lie come to a point where I regarded lust as offensive and even cruel.

'Pretty girls make graves,' was my saying, whenever I'd had to turn my head around involuntarily to stare at the incomparable pretties of Indian Mexico. And the absence of active lust in me had also given me a new peaceful life that I was enjoying a great deal. But this was too much. I was still afraid to take my clothes off; also I never liked to do that in front of more than one person, especially with men around. But Japhy didn't give a goddamn hoot and holler about any of this and pretty soon he was making Princess happy and then Alvah had a turn (with his big serious eyes staring in the dim light, and him reading poems a minute ago). So I said 'How about me startin to work on her arm?'

'Go ahead, great.' Which I did, lying down on the floor with all my clothes on and kissing her hand, then her wrist, then up, to her body, as she laughed and almost cried with delight everybody everywhere working on her. All the peaceful celibacy of my Buddhism was going down the drain. 'Smith, I distrust any kind of Buddhism or *any* kinda philosophy or social system that puts down sex,' said Japhy quite scholarly now that he was done and sitting naked crosslegged rolling himself a Bull Durham cigarette (which he did as a part of his 'simplicity' life). It ended up with everybody naked and finally making gay pots of coffee in the kitchen and Princess on the kitchen floor naked with her knees clasped in her arms, lying on her side, just for nothing, just to do it, then finally she and I took a warm bath together in the bathtub and could hear Alvah and Japhy discussing Zen Free Love Lunacy orgies in the other room.

'Hey Princess we'll do this every Thursday night, hey?' yelled Japhy. 'It'll be a regular function.'

'Yeah,' yelled Princess from the bathtub. I'm telling you she was actually glad to do all this and told me 'You know, I feel like I'm the mother of all things and I have to take care of my children.'

'You're such a young pretty thing yourself.'

'But I'm the old mother of earth. I'm a Bodhisattva.' She was just a little off her nut but when I heard her say 'Bodhisattva' I realized she wanted to be a big Buddhist like Japhy and being a girl the only way she could express it was this way, which had its traditional roots in the yabyum ceremony of Tibetan Buddhism, so everything was fine.

Alvah was immensely pleased and was all for the idea of 'every Thursday night' and so was I by now.

'Alvah, Princess says she's a Bodhisattva.'

'Of course she is.'

'She says she's the mother of all of us.'

'The Bodhisattva women of Tibet and parts of ancient India,' said Japhy, 'were taken and used as holy concubines in temples and sometimes in ritual caves and would get to lay up a stock of merit and they meditated too. All of them, men and women, they'd meditate, fast, have balls like this, go back to eating, drinking, talking, hike around, live in viharas in the rainy season and outdoors in the dry, there was no question of what to do about sex which is what I always liked about Oriental religion. And what I always dug about the Indians in our country . . . You know when I was a little kid in Oregon I didn't feel that I was an American at all, with all that suburban ideal and sex repression and general dreary newspaper gray censorship of all our real human values but and when I discovered Buddhism and all I suddenly felt that I had lived in a previous lifetime innumerable ages ago and now because of faults and sins in that lifetime I was being degraded to a more grievous domain of existence and my karma was to be born in America where nobody has any fun or believes in anything, especially freedom. That's why I was always sympathetic to freedom movements, too, like anarchism in the Northwest, the old-time heroes of Everett Massacre and all . . .' It ended up with long earnest discussions about all these subjects and finally Princess got dressed and went home with Japhy on their bicycles and Alvah and I sat facing each other in the dim red light.

'But you know, Ray, Japhy is really sharp – he's really the wildest craziest sharpest cat we've ever met. And what I love about him is he's the big hero of the West Coast, do you realize I've been out here for two years now and hadn't met anybody worth knowing really or anybody with any truly illuminated intelligence and was giving up hope for the West Coast? Besides all the background he has, in Oriental scholarship, Pound, taking peyote and seeing visions, his mountainclimbing, and bhikkuing, wow, Japhy Ryder is a great new hero of American culture.'

'He's mad!' I agreed. 'And other things I like about him, his quiet sad moments when he don't say much . . .'

'Gee, I wonder what will happen to him in the end.'

'I think he'll end up like Han Shan living alone in the mountains and writing poems on the walls of cliffs, or chanting them to crowds outside his cave.'

'Or maybe he'll go to Hollywood and be a movie star, you know he said that the other day, he said "Alvah you know I've never thought of going to the movies and becoming a star, I can do anything you know, I haven't tried that yet," and I believe him he *can* do anything. Did you see the way he had Princess all wrapped around him?'

'Aye indeed' and later that night as Alvah slept I sat under the tree in the yard and looked up at the stars or closed my eyes to meditate and tried to quiet myself down back to my normal self.

Alvah couldn't sleep and came out and lay flat on his back in the grass looking up at the sky, and said 'Big steamy clouds going by in the dark up there, it makes me realize we live on an actual planet.'

'Close your eyes and you'll see more than that.'

'Oh I don't know what you mean by all that!' he said pettishly. He was always being bugged by my little lectures on Samadhi ecstasy, which is the state you reach when you stop everything and stop your mind and you actually with your eyes closed see a kind of eternal multiswarm of electrical Power of some kind ululating in place of just pitiful images and forms of objects, which are, after all, imaginary. And if you don't believe me come back in a billion years and deny it. For what is time? 'Don't you think it's much more interesting just to be like Japhy and have girls and studies and good times and really be doing something, than all this silly sitting under trees?'

'Nope,' I said and meant it, and I knew Japhy would agree with me. 'All Japhy's doing is amusing himself in the void.'

'I don't think so.'

'I bet he is. I'm going mountainclimbing with him next week and find out and tell you.'

'Well' (sigh), 'as for me, I'm just going to go on being Alvah Goldbook and to hell with all this Buddhist bullshit.'

'You'll be sorry some day. Why don't you ever understand what I'm trying to tell you: it's with your six senses that you're fooled into believing not only that you have six senses, but that you contact an actual outside world with them. If it wasn't for your eyes, you wouldn't see me. If it wasn't for your ears, you wouldn't hear that airplane. If it wasn't for your nose, you wouldn't smell the midnight mint. If it wasn't for your tongue taster, you wouldn't taste the difference between A and B. If it wasn't for your body, you wouldn't feel Princess. There is no me, no airplane, no mint, no Princess, no nothing, you for krissakes do you want to go on being fooled every damn minute of your life?'

'Yes, that's all I want, I thank God that something has come out of nothing.'

'Well, I got news for you, it's the other way around nothing has come out of something, and that something is Dharmakaya, the body of the True Meaning, and that nothing is this and all this twaddle and talk. I'm going to bed.'

'Well sometimes I see a flash of illumination in what you're trying to say but believe me I get more of a satori out of Princess than out of words.'

'It's a satori of your foolish flesh, you lecher.'

'I know my redeemer liveth.'

'What redeemer and what liveth?'

'Oh let's cut this out and just live!'

'Balls, when I thought like you, Alvah, I was just as miserable and graspy as you are now. All you want to do is run out there and get laid and get beat up and get screwed up and get old and sick and banged around by samsara, you fucking eternal meat of comeback you you'll deserve it too, I'll say.'

'That's not nice. Everybody's tearful and trying to live with what they got. Your Buddhism has made you mean Ray and makes you even afraid to take your clothes off for a simple healthy orgy.'

'Well, I did finally, didn't I?'

'But you were coming on so hincty about – Oh let's forget it.'

Alvah went to bed and I sat and closed my eyes and thought 'This thinking has stopped' but because I had to think it no thinking had stopped, but there did come over me a wave of gladness to know that all this perturbation was just a dream already ended and I didn't have to worry because I wasn't 'I' and I prayed that God, or Tathagata, would give me enough time and enough sense and strength to be able to tell people what I knew (as I can't even do properly now) so they'd know what I know and not despair so much. The old tree brooded over me silently, a living thing. I heard a mouse snoring in the garden weeds. The rooftops of Berkeley looked like pitiful living meat sheltering grieving phantoms from the eternality of the heavens which they feared to face. By the time I went to bed I wasn't taken in by no Princess or no desire for no Princess and nobody's disapproval and I felt glad and slept well.

Jack Kerouac, *The Dharma Bums* (New York: The New American Library, 1959), pp. 22–30.

Ayya Khema

Ilse Ledermann (1923–97) was born to Jewish parents in Berlin. In 1938 she escaped to Scotland along with two hundred other German-Jewish children. Her parents went to Shanghai, where Ilse joined them two years later. Shortly thereafter, the family was imprisoned by the Japanese for the duration of the war. Ilse emigrated to the United States four years after the war and spent several years travelling in Asia with her husband in the early 1960s. During this period she began to practise meditation. She began to teach meditation in Europe and Australia in the 1970s, and in 1979 Ilse became a Theravada 'nun', taking the name Ayya Khema ('Noble Safety'). She helped to establish a Theravada forest monastery in Australia in 1978 and in Germany in 1989. In Sri Lanka she established the International Buddhist Women's Centre as well as a meditation centre for women on Parappuduwa Island (since closed), attracting both Sinhalese and Western women, some of whom sought ordination as Buddhist nuns. She was one of the organizers of the first international conference of Buddhist nuns in 1987 at Bodh Gaya.

As discussed in the Introduction, one of the most important issues for women in modern Buddhism has been the question of the admission of women to the order of fully ordained nuns, especially for those women from the Theravada tradition of Sri Lanka and Southeast Asia, in which the order of nuns disappeared centuries ago. A number of Buddhist women from Theravada countries have been frustrated in their attempts to re-establish the order of nuns in their homelands, due to resistance from the monastic hierarchy. The Dalai Lama, however, has encouraged women from the Tibetan tradition (where the order of nuns was never established) to seek ordination from Chinese nuns. Like Kabilsingh (see the Introduction), Ayya Khema sought ordination from Chinese nuns, but not in Taiwan or Hong Kong. Instead, she participated in the ceremony at an opulent Chinese Buddhist temple in Los Angeles, receiving an extensive set of vows in a language that she did not understand. She describes the event in the following extract from her autobiography, *I Give You My Life* (1998).

An interesting year for me was 1987. The first thing was that I was invited by the delegate to the United Nations from Sri Lanka to give a talk at the United Nations in New York. Almost all the representatives of the smaller countries came, but those of the large countries were absent. The United States and Russia were not represented. At the time, the Iron Curtain had not yet been lifted.

I spoke about peace in the heart as a prerequisite for bringing peace to the world, and there were also a great number of questions afterward. But it seemed that those present believed that religion and politics do not go together. In the Buddha's time, he taught many kings and high ministers. Today this is still quite difficult. At the end, I was awarded a small medal for peace, which pleased me a great deal.

The second event of that year was the international Conference for Buddhist Nuns in Bodh Gaya, in India. The Dalai Lama presided over the conference. This was the first time that anything of this nature had taken place, and I was one of the three women who organized the event. The other two were an American nun from the Tibetan tradition and a Thai professor. We founded Sakyadhita (Daughters of the Buddha), an international organization for Buddhist nuns and women. Since then the organization has held a conference nearly every year and has brought about improvements for nuns and relieved some of the difficulties they face, particularly those from Asia.

Above all this organization provides an opportunity for exchange among Buddhist women from more than thirty countries. We learn from each other and about each other. Another very important function is providing support for women who want to become fully ordained *bhikkhunis*.

The year 1988 was marked by an extraordinary event. I flew to California to participate in a *bhikkhuni* ordination ceremony at Hsi Lai Temple in Los Angeles. This was the first time that a ceremony of this nature was possible in the West, and it was even done in the traditional manner with a double platform. This means that we nuns received ordination from both nuns and monks. Two hundred and fifty Chinese nuns, fifty monks, and twelve Western nuns came to the ordination. The Hsi Lai temple is built in the style of the 'Forbidden Palace' in Peking, and many of the assemblies took place in the inner court of the temple. The temple itself had just been finished at a cost of twenty-five million US dollars, as one could learn from a plaque on one of its walls.

We received a rigorous, almost military-style training, almost all in Chinese. We were treated most generously and did not have to pay anything for lodging, food, and clothing. It would have been better if they had immediately established some Western nuns there, since only one of the Chinese nuns spoke English and the temple was intended for the spreading of the Teaching in the West.

After we had received training daily for four weeks, many hours a day, the great day of the ordination arrived. This meant both the day and the night for the nuns, because we had to be ordained twice – once by ten monks, who had all been monks for at least thirty years; and again by ten *bhikkhunis*, who had all been *bhikkhunis* for at least twenty years. We all completed the process successfully, although the Western monks and nuns often had no idea what was going on, because the proceedings were not translated. But we understood the essential. I was glad when it was over, since every bone in my body ached.

One curious thing has remained in my memory. In China and of course in Taiwan also, nuns and monks are required to be vegetarians. But every day in the temple fabulous food was provided. Once it seemed to be chicken, another time, fish, another time liver. Until one day I got my courage up and asked the English-speaking nun why vegetarian food was not being provided. She looked at me in amazement and told me that of course all the food was vegetarian. When I told her about the chicken and fish, she was highly amused. She explained to me that everything had been made from soy flour and flown in from Taiwan daily, since such things were not available in the West.

Before I flew back to the nuns' island, I stayed for a while with [my daughter] Irene, whom I had not seen for a rather long time. It was lovely for the two of us to be together again. I also have a particular memory from this visit.

Irene asked me why I was a nun. She could understand being a Buddhist, but why a nun? Then I asked her if it made her feel good when she went to church with her husband, Ronny, on Sundays. She said yes. Then I told her that I wanted to feel that way every day. This answer seemed to satisfy her completely.

Ayya Khema, *I Give You My Life* (Boston, Mass., and London: Shambhala Press, 1998), pp. 180–84.

Sangharakshita

Sangharakshita (1925–) was born Dennis Lingwood, in London. His first exposure to Oriental wisdom came from reading Madame Blavatsky's *Isis Unveiled*. Upon reading the *Diamond Sutra*, a perfection-of-wisdom sutra, and the *Platform Sutra*, a Chan text, he determined to be a Buddhist and took refuge vows from a Burmese monk in London. Stationed in Ceylon at the end of the Second World War, he felt little connection with the Buddhist monks there, finding more affinity with the Hindu monks of the Ramakrishna Mission, who worked on behalf of the poor. At the end of the war he remained in India and in 1946 gave away all of his possessions and donned the ochre robes of a renunciate. He eventually received ordination as a Buddhist novice from a Burmese monk living at Kushinagara, the site of the Buddha's passage into nirvana. In 1950 he moved to the Himalayan town of Kalimpong, where he became friends with Lama Govinda, with whom he shared a belief in the affinity of art and religious practice. Sangharakshita's period in Kalimpong coincided with the arrival of the first wave of Tibetan refugees after the uprising against the Chinese in Lhasa in March 1959. Among the refugees were many of the most distinguished lamas of Tibetan Buddhism. Sangharakshita received teachings from many of them. In 1952 he met B. R. Ambedkar and joined him in his campaign to bring the teachings of the Buddha to the untouchables. After Ambedkar's death in 1956, Sangharakshita remained committed to this work. Returning to England and finding that the traditional bifurcation of Buddhist practitioners into monks and laity was not fully suited to the West, he founded the Friends of the Western Buddhist Order in 1968.

Sangharakshita placed great emphasis on the practice that has tradition-ally defined one as a Buddhist, whether as a monk or layperson: going for refuge to the Buddha, dharma and sangha (the 'three jewels'). His wide ex-perience with Buddhist communities in South Asia has led Sangharakshita to perceive a unity in the dharma beyond its cultural and historical specifics. As a result, he has sought to introduce a form of Buddhism that is not tied to a single sect or tradition. He has interpreted the classical doctrine of dependent origination both as an explanation of the cycle of negativity that afflicts so much human life, and as a key to a steady progression out of that cycle towards enlightenment. Again, refuge, regarded not simply as a formula to be recited but a life-changing event, is seen as the key to movement from the negative to the positive. Among the three jewels, Sangharakshita places particular emphasis on the sangha as a community of friends committed to the greater good of society.

In the extract below, from *The Priceless Jewel* (1993), he addresses some of the misconceptions about Buddhism, before presenting a succinct description of what he considers the essence of Buddhism, drawing from the Theravada, Mahayana and Vajrayana traditions.

The historical and the spiritual importance of Buddhism is, of course, beyond dispute. It is the major cultural and spiritual tradition of Asia, and what we most readily think of when mention is made of the Wisdom of the East. The image of the Buddha, seated in meditation beneath the Tree of Enlightenment, is one of the best known of all the religious symbols of mankind. Together with Christianity and Islam, which are younger than Buddhism by five and eleven centuries respectively, Buddhism is one of the three great 'universal' religions of the world, that is to say, it is not an ethnic religion, like Confucianism or Shinto, but a religion whose message is in principle addressed to every human being *qua* human being, irrespective of caste, race, sex, social position, nationality, or culture. For centuries together Buddhism was, in fact, the religion of between one quarter and one third of the human race. As distinct from both Christianity and Islam, however, Buddhism is not a theistic but a non-theistic religion. In Buddhism there is no personal God, the creator and ruler of the universe. There is no divine revelation, in the sense of a communication of God's will to mankind either through the life and sacrificial death of his incarnate son or through the inspired utterance of his chosen messenger. There is no sacred book in the sense of an inerrant and authoritative record of that communication. There is no prayer in the sense of petition to, or communion with, a Heavenly Father. Such being the case, some people have doubted whether Buddhism is a religion at all. To them religion is essentially theistic, and a non-theistic religion therefore a contradiction in terms. Perhaps in the last analysis the question is simply one of definition. In any case, one nowadays hears talk, in some quarters, of non-theistic Christianity, of religionless Christianity, and even of Christian Buddhism, whatever that might mean.

Since Buddhism is certainly non-theistic, and possibly not a religion, some people, again, have not only doubted whether it was a religion but have even wondered whether it was not a form of Science. Thus one occasionally hears talk of something called Scientific Buddhism. Buddhism is supposed to be 'scientific', or even a 'scientific religion'. This misunderstanding is sufficiently serious, even though not sufficiently widespread, to warrant correction. Buddhism is certainly not scientific in the sense that anticipations of modern scientific thought, and even of actual scientific discoveries, are to be found in ancient Buddhist texts, thereby somehow 'proving' the truth of Buddhism, as Scientific Buddhism at its most naive has been known to assert. Such an assertion is little more than a clumsy attempt to appropriate, on behalf of Buddhism, some of the immense prestige of modern Science, and betrays a lack of confidence in Buddhism as a spiritual tradition. Buddhism is 'scientific' only in the very limited and indeed metaphorical sense of being imbued with the scientific spirit, i.e. with that spirit of open-minded inquiry that in the modern West is associated with Science rather than with religion, as well as in the sense of being empirical rather than dogmatic in its approach to the problems of existence – which in the case of Buddhism means strictly human or, more correctly, strictly sentient existence. Buddhism is *non*-scientific to the extent that it recognizes the 'existence' of a transcendental Reality with regard to which Modern Science, in the person of its official representatives, is at best agnostic. (There are, of course, signs that the monolithic materialist unity of Science is beginning to crack, as this conference itself bears witness.) This transcendental Reality can actually be experienced by man, a human being who experiences it in the highest degree being known as a Buddha, or Enlightened One. Buddhism also differs from science in making use not only of the intellect but also of the emotions. Indeed, according to Buddhism the problems of existence can be solved, and transcendental Reality be experienced, only when reason and emotion unite and there comes into existence a higher spiritual faculty variously known as Vision, Insight, and Imagination. In other words, transcendental Reality is to be experienced by the *whole man*, functioning with the utmost intensity at the height of his unified being.

Risking an oversimplification, one might say Science represents the extreme of objectivity and reason, whereas Mysticism represents the extreme of subjectivity and emotion – in this context, emotion purified by spiritual discipline. Science seeks to reduce the subject to the object, Mysticism to absorb the object in the subject. Buddhism, following here as elsewhere a Middle Way, represents a dissolution of the subject–object duality itself in a blissful, non-dual Awareness wherein that which, without, is beyond the object, coincides with that which, within, is beyond the subject, or, in other words, wherein that which is most exterior coincides with that which is most interior. When expressed in terms of objectivity, this blissful, non-dual Awareness appears as Wisdom; when expressed in terms of subjectivity, it manifests as Compassion – Wisdom and Compassion being the twin 'attributes' of Buddhahood or Enlightenment.

Besides the one represented by 'Scientific Buddhism', there are other misunderstandings of Buddhism. As I discovered on my return to England in 1964, after spending twenty years uninterruptedly in the East, mainly in India, such misunderstandings are extremely persistent and very difficult to account for. Though Buddhism has been known in the West for well over a hundred years, the blurred and shifting 'image' of Buddhism that flickers on the screen of public consciousness is hardly a positive one. More often than not Buddhism appears as cold, bleak, inhuman, and anti-social. It is seen as a system of rigid asceticism which, by means of a great mass of prohibitions and restrictions, seeks to bring about the extinction of all human desires and the achievement of a state of passionless calm indistinguishable from death. For some people the mere mention of its name immediately brings to mind high

walls surmounted by rows of spikes, darkened rooms, and joyless lives.
'Are you allowed to go out of the monastery?' 'Are you allowed to
speak to other people?' 'Who sent you to England?' These were some
of the questions which, on my return to England, I was asked by editors
of women's magazines and members of the general public. When I
explained that I could go out of the monastery whenever I wished, and
speak to whoever I thought fit, and that I had come to England entirely
on my own initiative, my questioners were clearly surprised. (I should
mention that in those days I was shaven-headed, and wore my yellow
robes constantly, not just for ceremonial purposes as I do now.) At the
same time, Buddhism is also seen as strange, exotic, colourful, weird,
and mysterious. Indeed, in recent years the image of Buddhism as a
system of rigid asceticism has been partly overlaid – perhaps in the
United States more than in Britain – by more fascinating images of
absurdity (= 'Zen') and erotic abandon (= 'Tantra') – thus adding to
the confusion. But rather than spend any more time correcting misunderstandings, or telling you what Buddhism is not, let me try to tell
you, in the clearest and most general terms, what Buddhism *is*. Let me
try to draw for you a picture of Buddhism that will obliterate, once
and for all, the old misleading images. This will give us a means of
approach to the Bodhisattva Ideal, and enable us to see why it is the
key to the Evolution of Consciousness.

Speaking in the clearest and most general terms, then, Buddhism
is a Path or Way. It is a Path leading from the impermanent to the
permanent, from sorrow to happiness, from the darkness of ignorance
to the light of perfect wisdom. This is the Path for which the Buddha
himself, in the days before his Enlightenment, is represented as searching. For the sake of this Path he went forth from home into home-
lessness. For the sake of this Path he sat at the foot of the Bodhi Tree.
This is the Path he discovered at the time of his Supreme Enlightenment, this is the Path which, after initial hesitation, he made known
to mankind. In his own words, as recorded in the *Dhammapada*,

> Walking this Path you shall make an end of suffering.
> This is the Path made known by me when I had learnt to
> remove all darts.

This Path it was that, for the forty-five years of his teaching life, in one formulation or another made up the principal content of the Buddha's message. The formulations were indeed very numerous. Perhaps the most basic was that of the Path as consisting of the three great stages of right conduct (*śīla*), meditation (*samādhi*), and wisdom (*prajñā*).

> Great becomes the fruit, great the advantages of meditation, when it is set round with (i.e. supported by) upright conduct.
> Great becomes the fruit, great the advantage of wisdom, when it is set round with meditation.

Such was the gist of the 'comprehensive religious talk' which the Buddha delivered in eleven out of the fourteen places he visited in the course of the last six months of his life. No less important, and even better known, is the formulation of the Path as Eightfold, that is to say, as consisting in the gradual extension of Perfect Vision – the vision of the transcendental – successively to one's emotional attitude, one's communication with other people, one's actions, one's means of livelihood, one's energy, one's recollection, and one's overall state of being and consciousness. Much rarer is a formulation which in fact occurs only once in the Pāli Canon. This is the formulation of the Path in terms of the Seven Stages of Purification – ethical, emotional, intellectual, and so on. Together with right conduct, meditation, and wisdom, this formulation provides the double framework of Buddhaghosha's great exegetical work, the *Visuddhimagga* or 'Path of Purity', the standard work of Theravāda Buddhism, i.e. of the Pāli-Buddhism of Sri Lanka, Burma, Thailand, Cambodia, and Laos.

In the Mahāyāna scriptures many other formulations are found. Some of these extremely comprehensive in scope, so that with them the Path begins to take on a more universal character. Among these more comprehensive formulations the most important, both historically and spiritually, is that of the Path of the Ten Perfections, the Ten Perfections being Generosity, Right Conduct, Patience and Forbearance, Vigour, Meditation, Wisdom, Skilful Means (= Compassion), Salvific Vow, Strength or Power, and Knowledge or Transcendental

Awareness. This Path of the Ten Perfections is, of course, the Path of the Bodhisattva, 'he whose nature or essence is Bodhi' (interpretations vary), the great spiritual hero who instead of aiming at the inferior goal of individual Enlightenment, i.e. Enlightenment for oneself alone, out of compassion seeks to attain the universal Enlightenment of a Buddha, so as to be able to deliver all sentient beings from suffering. For the accomplishment of this sublime purpose he practises the Ten Perfections not for one lifetime only but for an unthinkable number of lifetimes, being reborn in many different worlds, and on many different planes of existence. In this way he traverses the ten great 'levels' (*bhūmis*) of spiritual progress – another formulation – from that called 'the Joyful' right up to 'the Cloud of Dharma', at which stage he becomes a Buddha. Thus he fulfils the Bodhisattva Ideal, as it is called – an ideal which the Mahāyāna regards the historical Buddha as himself exemplifying. Yet another formulation of the Path found in Mahāyāna scriptures is that of the eleven 'abodes' (*vihāras*), which are, also, stages of spiritual progress traversed by the Bodhisattva, and which coincide to some extent with the ten 'levels'. Perhaps the most comprehensive of all formulations of the Path is that of the Nyingmapa School of Tibetan Buddhism, according to which the total Path consists of nine 'ways' (*yānas*) which between them cover all the three major *yānas*, i.e. the Hīnayāna, the Mahāyāna, the Vajrayāna, conceived not only as stages in the historical development of Indian Buddhism but as stages in the spiritual evolution of the individual Buddhist.

The number and importance of these abstract formulations of the Path should not blind us to the fact that the Path also finds vivid concrete embodiment in actual human lives, whether as depicted in the scriptures or as recorded by profane history. The Path in truth *is* the pilgrim, and the pilgrim the Path, so that 'Thou canst not travel on the Path before thou hast become the Path itself.' Travelling on a path implies a journey, and it is of a journey that both the scriptures and history often speak. Thus in the *Gaṇḍavyūha* or 'Flower-Array' *Sūtra* the youth Sudhana, in order to achieve what the text calls 'the highest knowledge of Enlightenment,' goes on a journey that takes him to various parts of India and in the course of which he visits more than fifty spiritual teachers. Similarly, in the *Prajñāpāramitā* or

'Perfection of Wisdom' *Sūtra* (the version in 8,000 lines), the Bodhisattva Sadāprarudita or 'Ever-Weeping', advised by a divine voice, goes east in search of the perfection of wisdom, encountering many adventures on the way until, in the city of Gandhavatī, he meets with the Bodhisattva Dharmodgata and hears his demonstration of the Dharma. On a more mythic level, in the *Saddharma-puṇḍarīka* or 'White Lotus of the True Dharma' *Sūtra* the journey is a *return* journey not unlike that of the king's son in the Gnostic 'Hymn of the Pearl'. In more strictly geographical terms there is Yuan Chwang's famous pilgrimage from China to the West, i.e. to India – and Monkey's. There is also Basho's 'Journey to the Far North.'

Sangharakshita, 'The Bodhisattva Principle' in *The Priceless Jewel* (Glasgow: Windhorse Publications, 1993), pp. 141–6.

Allen Ginsberg

Allen Ginsberg (1926–97) was born in Newark, New Jersey. His father, Louis, was a poet and high-school teacher. His mother, Naomi, was a committed Communist who suffered attacks of paranoia, eventually being hospitalized for mental illness. He attended Columbia University with plans to become a labour lawyer, but soon fell in with a group that included students such as Jack Kerouac and non-students such as William Burroughs who shared interests, both literary and otherwise, in sex, drugs and various criminal activities. In 1948, he had a transformative vision while reading William Blake in his Harlem apartment. After briefly working for an advertising agency in the Empire State Building, he moved to San Francisco where he joined the burgeoning poetry movement there. In October 1955 Ginsberg performed his most famous work, 'Howl', at the Six Gallery. ('I saw the best minds of my generation destroyed by madness, starving hysterical naked, dragging themselves through the negro streets at dawn looking for an angry fix, angelheaded hipsters burning for the ancient heavenly connection to the starry dynamo in the machinery of night . . .')

According to his own account, Ginsberg had first been introduced to Buddhism in letters from Kerouac, in which he wrote of suffering as the fundamental fact of existence. Kerouac sang the refuge formula ('I go for refuge to the Buddha, I go for refuge to the dharma, I go for refuge to the sangha') in Sanskrit to Ginsberg in 1952, sounding 'like Frank Sinatra'. Ginsberg began to read the works of D. T. Suzuki, whom he later met in New York in the company of Kerouac. He was intimately involved in the various cultural movements of the 1960s, collaborating with Timothy Leary, Bob Dylan and Ken Kesey, and protesting actively against the Vietnam War. In 1962 he travelled to India with Gary Snyder, visiting the site of the Buddha's enlightenment and first sermon, and having an audience with the Dalai Lama, who had arrived from Tibet just three years earlier.

After experimenting with various forms of Hindu practice, Ginsberg met the Tibetan lama Chögyam Trungpa in 1970, and remained his disciple until Trungpa's death, helping to found the Jack Kerouac School of Disembodied Poetics at Trungpa's Naropa Institute in Boulder, Colorado. In his last years Ginsberg became a disciple of another Tibetan lama, Gelek Rinpoche.

Buddhism figures in much of Ginsberg's poetry. The extracts here include one of his earliest 'Buddhist' poems, describing a Chinese painting of the Buddha coming down from the mountain on the eve of his enlightenment after years of asceticism. The other poems that follow derive from his later work, the final two devoted to Trungpa Rinpoche.

SAKYAMUNI COMING OUT FROM THE MOUNTAIN

Liang Kai, Southern Sung

He drags his bare feet
        out of a cave
                under a tree,
eyebrows
        grown long with weeping
                and hooknosed woe,
In ragged soft robes
        wearing a fine beard,
                unhappy hands
clasped to his naked breast –
        humility is beatness
                humility is beatness –
faltering
        into the bushes by a stream,
                all things inanimate

but his intelligence –
    stands upright there
      tho trembling:
Arhat
   who sought Heaven
     under a mountain of stone,
sat thinking
   till he realized
     the land of blessedness exists
in the imagination –
   the flash come:
     empty mirror –
how painful to be born again
   wearing a fine beard,
     reentering the world
a bitter wreck of a sage:
   earth before him his only path.
    We can see his soul,
he knows nothing
   like a god:
    shaken
meek wretch –
   humility is beatness
    before the absolute World.
     NY Public Library 1953

Allen Ginsberg, *Reality Sandwiches* (San Francisco: City Lights Books, 1966;
first published 1963), pp. 9–10.

FIFTH INTERNATIONALE

To Billy MacKeever

Arise ye prisoners of your mind-set
Arise Neurotics of the Earth

For Insight thunders Liberation
A sacred world's in birth

No more Attachment's chains shall bind us
Mind's Aggression no more rules
The Earth shall rise on new foundations
We have been jerks we shall be Fools

'Tis the Path of Accumulation
Let each sit on his place
The International Crazy Wisdom School
Could save the Human Race

July 1986 Naropa

ON CREMATION OF CHÖGYAM TRUNGPA, VIDYADHARA

I noticed the grass, I noticed the hills, I noticed the highways,
I noticed the dirt road, I noticed car rows in the parking lot
I noticed ticket takers, I noticed the cash and checks & credit
    cards,
I noticed buses, noticed mourners, I noticed their children in
    red dresses,
I noticed the entrance sign, noticed retreat houses, noticed
    blue & yellow Flags –
noticed the devotees, their trucks & buses, guards in Khaki
    uniforms
I noticed crowds, noticed misty skies, noticed the all-pervading
    smiles and empty eyes –
I noticed pillows, colored red & yellow, square pillows and
    round –
I noticed the Tori Gate, passers-through bowing, a parade of
    men & women in formal dress –
noticed the procession, noticed the bagpipe, drum, horns,

noticed high silk head crowns & saffron robes, noticed the
three piece suits,
I noticed the palanquin, an umbrella, the stupa painted with
jewels the colors of the four directions –
amber for generosity, green for karmic works, noticed the
white for Buddha, red for the heart –
thirteen worlds on the stupa hat, noticed the bell handle and
umbrella, the empty head of the cement bell –
noticed the corpse to be set in the head of the bell –
noticed the monks chanting, horn plaint in our ears, smoke
rising from atop the firebrick empty bell –
noticed the crowds quiet, noticed the Chilean poet, noticed a
Rainbow,
I noticed the Guru was dead, I noticed his teacher bare breasted
watching the corpse burn in the stupa,
noticed mourning students sat crosslegged before their books,
chanting devotional mantras,
gesturing mysterious fingers, bells & brass thunderbolts in their
hands
I noticed flame rising above flags & wires & umbrellas &
painted orange poles
I noticed the sky, noticed the sun, a rainbow round the sun,
light misty clouds drifting over the Sun –
I noticed my own heart beating, breath passing thru my nostrils
my feet walking, eyes seeing, noticing smoke above the
corpse-fir'd monument
I noticed the path downhill, noticed the crowd moving toward
buses
I noticed food, lettuce salad, I noticed the Teacher was absent,
I noticed my friends, noticed our car the blue Volvo, a young
boy held my hand
our key in the motel door, noticed a dark room, noticed a
dream
and forgot, noticed oranges lemons & caviar at breakfast,
I noticed the highway, sleepiness, homework thoughts, the
boy's nippled chest in the breeze

as the car rolled down hillsides past green woods to the water,
I noticed the houses, balconies overlooking a misted horizon,
     shore & old worn rocks in the sand
I noticed the sea, I noticed the music, I wanted to dance.

                              May 28, 1987, 2:30–3.15 A.M.

SUPPLICATION FOR THE REBIRTH OF THE VIDYADHARA CHÖGYAM TRUNGPA, RINPOCHE

Dear Lord Guru who pervades the space of my mind
permeates the universe of my consciousness,
still empties my balding head and's stabilized my wand'ring
     thought
to average equanimity in Manhattan & Boulder

Return return reborn in spirit & knowledge in human body
my own or others as continual teacher of chaotic peace,
Return according to your vow to pacify magnetize enrich
     destroy
grasping angry stupidity in me my family friends & Sangha

Return in body speech & mind to enlighten my labors
& the labors of your meditators, thousands from L.A. to Halifax
to relieve sufferings of our brothers, lovers
family, friends, fellow citizens, nations, and planet.

Remember your vow to be with us on our deathbeds
in living worlds where we dwell in your tender perspective
breathe with your conscious breath, catch ourselves thinking
& dissolve bomb dream, fear of our own skin & yelling
     argument
                              in the sky of your mind

Bend your efforts to regroup our community within your
    thought-body
& mind-space, the effects of your non-thought,
Turbulent ease of your spontaneous word & picture
nonmeditative compassion your original mind

These slogans were writ on the second day of June 1991
a sleepless night my brother's 70th birthday on Long Island
my own sixty-fifth year in the human realm visiting his house
by the Vajra Poet Allen Ginsberg supplicating protection of his
                    Vajra Guru Chögyam Trungpa
                            June 2, 1991, 2:05 A.M.

Allen Ginsberg, *Cosmopolitan Greetings* (New York: HarperCollins, 1994),
pp. 15, 25–6, 67.

Thich Nhat Hanh

Thich Nhat Hanh (1926–   ) was born in South Vietnam, the son of a government bureaucrat. He entered a Buddhist monastery as a novice at the age of seventeen where he studied with a Vietnamese Zen master, receiving full ordination as a monk in 1949. His interests in philosophy, literature and foreign languages led him to leave the Buddhist seminary to study at Saigon University. While teaching in a secondary school, he served as editor of the periodical *Vietnamese Buddhism*, the organ of the Association of All Buddhists in Vietnam. He studied in the US in the early 1960s, returning in 1964 after the overthrow of the government of President Diem, who had actively persecuted Buddhists, leading to widespread public protests, remembered in the West through the photographs of self-immolation of Buddhist monks. Thich Nhat Hanh founded the School of Youth for Social Service, a Buddhist university, a new order of his Buddhist sect (the Order of Interbeing), and helped establish a publishing house, all of which promoted what he called Engaged Buddhism during the Vietnam War, involving both non-violent resistance and aid to the victims of the war. A collection of his pacifist poetry was banned by the governments of both North Vietnam and South Vietnam. In 1966 he set forth a five-point peace plan during an international lecture tour, meeting with Martin Luther King (who would later nominate him for the Nobel Peace Prize) and Thomas Merton in the US, addressing the House of Commons in Britain, and having an audience with Pope Paul VI in Rome. The book that resulted from his lecture tour, *Vietnam: Lotus in a Sea of Fire* (1967), was banned by the government of South Vietnam. Fearing that he would be arrested or assassinated if he returned to Vietnam after the lecture tour, his supporters urged him to remain abroad and he has lived in exile ever since, residing in France. He continued to work for peace over the next decade. He founded a Buddhist centre, Plum Village, in southern France, and has worked both to assist Vietnamese refugees and political prisoners and to teach En-gaged Buddhism to large audiences in Europe and the Americas.

In his teachings Thich Nhat Hanh calls for a clear recognition and analysis of suffering, identifying its causes, and then working to relieve present suffering and prevent future suffering through non-violent action. Such action in bringing peace can only truly succeed when the actor is at peace or, in his words, is 'being peace'. Thich Nhat Hanh therefore advocates the practice of mindful awareness in all activities, focusing especially on breathing.

The excerpt below is the first chapter of his most famous book, *Being Peace* (originally published in 1987), in which he describes the importance of dwelling in the moment and of smiling as techniques for bringing peace to oneself and others.

SUFFERING IS NOT ENOUGH

Life is filled with suffering, but it is also filled with many wonders, like the blue sky, the sunshine, the eyes of a baby. To suffer is not enough. We must also be in touch with the wonders of life. They are within us and all around us, everywhere, any time.

If we are not happy, if we are not peaceful, we cannot share peace and happiness with others, even those we love, those who live under the same roof. If we are peaceful, if we are happy, we can smile and blossom like a flower, and everyone in our family, our entire society, will benefit from our peace. Do we need to make a special effort to enjoy the beauty of the blue sky? Do we have to practice to be able to enjoy it? No, we just enjoy it. Each second, each minute of our lives can be like this. Wherever we are, any time, we have the capacity to enjoy the sunshine, the presence of each other, even the sensation of our breathing. We don't need to go to China to enjoy the blue sky. We don't have to travel into the future to enjoy our breathing. We can be in touch with these things right now. It would be a pity if we are only aware of suffering.

We are so busy we hardly have time to look at the people we love, even in our own household, and to look at ourselves. Society is organized in a way that even when we have some leisure time, we don't know how to use it to get back in touch with ourselves. We have millions of ways to lose this precious time – we turn on the TV or pick up the telephone, or start the car and go somewhere. We are not used to being with ourselves, and we act as if we don't like ourselves and are trying to escape from ourselves.

Meditation is to be aware of what is going on – in our bodies, in our feelings, in our minds, and in the world. Each day 40,000 children die of hunger. The superpowers now have more than 50,000 nuclear warheads, enough to destroy our planet many times. Yet the sunrise is beautiful, and the rose that bloomed this morning along the wall is a miracle. Life is both dreadful and wonderful. To practice meditation is to be in touch with both aspects. Please do not think we must be solemn in order to meditate. In fact, to meditate well, we have to smile a lot.

Recently I was sitting with a group of children, and a boy named Tim was smiling beautifully. I said, 'Tim, you have a very beautiful smile,' and he said, 'Thank you.' I told him, 'You don't have to thank me, I have to thank you. Because of your smile, you make life more beautiful. Instead of saying, "Thank you," you should say, "You're welcome."'

If a child smiles, if an adult smiles, that is very important. If in our daily life we can smile, if we can be peaceful and happy, not only we, but everyone will profit from it. This is the most basic kind of peace work. When I see Tim smiling, I am also happy. If he is aware that he is making other people happy, he can say, 'You are welcome.'

From time to time, to remind ourselves to relax, to be peaceful, we may wish to set aside some time for a retreat, a day of mindfulness, when we can walk slowly, smile, drink tea with a friend, enjoy being together as if we are the happiest people on Earth. This is not a retreat, it is a treat. During walking meditation, during kitchen and garden work, during sitting meditation, all day long, we can practice smiling. At first you may find it difficult to smile, and we have to think about why. Smiling means that we are ourselves, that we have sovereignty over ourselves, that we are not drowned into forgetfulness. This kind of smile can be seen on the faces of Buddhas and Bodhisattvas.

I would like to offer one short poem you can recite from time to time, while breathing and smiling.

> Breathing in, I calm my body.
> Breathing out, I smile.
> Dwelling in the present moment
> I know this is a wonderful moment.

'Breathing in, I calm my body.' This line is like drinking a glass of ice water – you feel the cold, the freshness, permeate your body. When I breathe in and recite this line, I actually feel the breathing calming my body, calming my mind.

'Breathing out, I smile.' You know the effects of a smile. A smile can relax hundreds of muscles in your face, and relax your nervous system. A smile makes you master of yourself. That is why Buddhas and Bodhisattvas are always smiling. When you smile, you realize the wonder of the smile.

'Dwelling in the present moment.' While I sit here, I don't think of somewhere else, of the future or the past. I sit here, and I know where I am. This is very important. We tend to be alive in the future, not now. We say, 'Wait until I finish school and get my PhD degree, and then I will be really alive.' When we have it, and it's not easy to get, we say to ourselves, 'I have to wait until I have a job in order to be *really* alive.' And then after the job, a car. After the car, a house. We are not capable of being alive in the present moment. We tend to postpone being alive to the future, the distant future, we don't know when. Now is not the moment to be alive. We may never be alive at all in our entire life. Therefore, the technique, if we have to speak of technique, is to *be* in the present moment, to be aware that we are here and now, and the only moment to be alive is the present moment.

'I know this is a wonderful moment.' This is the only moment that is real. To be here and now, and enjoy the present moment is our most important task. 'Calming, Smiling, Present moment, Wonderful moment.' I hope you will try it.

★

Even though life is hard, even though it is sometimes difficult to smile, we have to try. Just as when we wish each other, 'Good morning,' it must be a real 'Good morning.' Recently, one friend asked me, 'How can I force myself to smile when I am filled with sorrow? It isn't natural.' I told her she must be able to smile at her sorrow, because we are more than our sorrow. A human being is like a television set with millions of channels. If we turn the Buddha on, we are the Buddha, If we turn sorrow on, we are sorrow. If we turn a smile on, we really are the smile. We cannot let just one channel dominate us. We have the seed of everything in us, and we have to seize the situation in our hand, to recover our own sovereignty.

When we sit down peacefully, breathing and smiling, with awareness, we are our true selves, we have sovereignty over ourselves. When we open ourselves up to a TV program, we let ourselves be invaded by the program. Sometimes it is good, but often it is just noisy. Because we want to have something other than ourselves enter us, we sit there and let a noisy TV program invade us, assail us, destroy us. Even if our nervous system suffers, we don't have the courage to stand up and turn it off, because if we do that, we will have to return to our self.

Meditation is the opposite. It helps us return to our true self. Practicing meditation in this kind of society is very difficult. Everything seems to work in concert to try to take us away from our true self. We have thousands of things, like video tapes and music, which help us be away from ourselves. Practicing meditation is to be aware, to smile, to breathe. These are on the opposite side. We go back to ourselves in order to see what is going on, because to meditate means to be aware of what is going on. What is going on is very important.

Suppose you are expecting a child. You need to breathe and smile for him or her. Please don't wait until your baby is born before beginning to take care of him or her. You can take care of your baby right now, or even sooner. If you cannot smile, that is very serious. You might think, 'I am too sad. Smiling is just not the correct thing to do.' Maybe crying or shouting would be correct, but your baby will get it – anything you are, anything you do, is for your baby.

Even if you do not have a baby in your womb, the seed is already there. Even if you are not married, even if you are a man, you should be aware that a baby is already there, the seeds of future generations are already there. Please don't wait until the doctors tell you that you are going to have a baby to begin to take care of it. It is already there. Whatever you are, whatever you do, your baby will get it. Anything you eat, any worries that are on your mind will be for him or her. Can you tell me that you cannot smile? Think of the baby, and smile for him, for her, for the future generations. Please don't tell me that a smile and your sorrow just don't go together. It's your sorrow, but what about your baby? It's not his sorrow, it's not her sorrow.

Children understand very well that in each woman, in each man, there is a capacity of waking up, of understanding, and of loving. Many children have told me that they cannot show me anyone who does not have this capacity. Some people allow it to develop, and some do not, but everyone has it. This capacity of waking up, of being aware of what is going on in your feelings, in your body, in your perceptions, in the world, is called Buddha nature, the capacity of understanding and loving. Since the baby of that Buddha is in us, we should give him or her a chance. Smiling is very important. If we are not able to smile, then the world will not have peace. It is not by going out for a demonstration against nuclear missiles that we can bring about peace. It is with our capacity of smiling, breathing, and being peace that we can make peace.

Thich Nhat Hanh, 'Suffering is Not Enough' in *Being Peace* (Berkeley: Parallax Press, 1996), pp. 3–9.

Gary Snyder

Gary Snyder (1930–   ) was born in San Francisco and raised on a farm outside Seattle. He attended Reed College in Oregon, where he studied literature and anthropology. Inspired by D. T. Suzuki's *Essays in Zen Buddhism*, he taught himself to meditate and devoted himself to the practice of Zen meditation while working as a fire lookout in Washington state. In 1952 he enrolled in the Department of Oriental Languages at the University of California at Berkeley to study Chinese and Japanese. He met Allen Ginsberg and Jack Kerouac in San Francisco and participated in the famous Six Gallery reading in 1955, where Ginsberg first recited 'Howl'. The poets gathered there were to become known as the Beats. They read together R. H. Blyth's four-volume translation of Japanese haiku, but much of the Zen flavour of their work came from Snyder, portrayed as Japhy Rider by Kerouac in *The Dharma Bums* (see the chapter on Kerouac, above). Snyder visited Japan in 1956, travelling there again in 1958 to spend seven years practising Zen meditation at Daitokuji monastery. Returning to San Francisco in 1966, he participated in the first 'Be-In' in Golden Gate Park and became involved in the anti-war movement. His work and his poetry have remained committed both to the exploration of Buddhist, especially Zen, practice and to the protection of the environment. He continues to work actively at the local level, serving on the California Arts Council from 1974–80. He currently lives on a mountain farm in the northern Sierra Nevada range in California, where he founded the Ring of Bone zendo (meditation centre). He teaches at the University of California, Davis, where he helped found the 'Nature and Culture' curriculum.

The extracts below, from his 1974 work *Turtle Island*, illustrate the importance of Buddhism for Snyder, both in his poetry and in his social activism.

AVOCADO

The Dharma is like an Avocado!
Some parts so ripe you can't believe it,
But it's good.
And other places hard and green
Without much flavor,
Pleasing those who like their eggs well-cooked.

And the skin is thin,
The great big round seed
In the middle,
Is your own Original Nature –
Pure and smooth,
Almost nobody ever splits it open
Or ever tries to see
If it will grow.

Hard and slippery,
It looks like
You should plant it – but then
it shoots out thru the
          fingers –
gets away.

'ENERGY IS ETERNAL DELIGHT'

A young woman at Sir George Williams University in Montreal asked me, 'What do you fear most?' I found myself answering 'that the diversity and richness of the gene pool will be destroyed –' and most people there understood what was meant.

The treasure of life is the richness of stored information in the diverse genes of all living beings. If the human race, following on some set of catastrophes, were to survive at the expense of many plant and animal species, it would be no victory. Diversity provides life with the capacity for a multitude of adaptations and responses to long-range changes on the planet. The possibility remains that at some future time another evolutionary line might carry the development of consciousness to clearer levels than our family of upright primates.

The United States, Europe, the Soviet Union, and Japan have a habit. They are addicted to heavy energy use, great gulps and injections of fossil fuel. As fossil-fuel reserves go down, they will take dangerous gambles with the future health of the biosphere (through nuclear power) to keep up their habit.

For several centuries Western civilization has had a priapic drive for material accumulation, continual extensions of political and economic power, termed 'progress'. In the Judaeo-Christian worldview men are seen as working out their ultimate destinies (paradise? perdition?) with planet earth as the stage for the drama – trees and animals mere props, nature a vast supply depot. Fed by fossil fuel, this religio-economic view has become a cancer: uncontrollable growth. It may finally choke itself, and drag much else down with it.

The longing for growth is not wrong. The nub of the problem now is how to flip over, as in jujitsu, the magnificent growth-energy of modern civilization into a nonacquisitive search for deeper knowledge of self and nature. Self-nature. Mother nature. If people come to realize that there are many nonmaterial, nondestructive paths of growth – of the highest and most fascinating order – it would help dampen the common fear that a steady state economy would mean deadly stagnation.

I spent a few years, some time back, in and around a training place. It was a school for monks of the Rinzai branch of Zen Buddhism, in Japan. The whole aim of the community was personal and universal liberation. In this quest for spiritual freedom every man marched strictly to the same drum in matters of hours of work and meditation. In the teacher's room one was pushed across sticky barriers into vast new spaces. The training was traditional and had been handed down for centuries – but the insights are forever fresh and new. The beauty, refinement and truly civilized quality of that life has no match in modern America. It is supported by hand labor in small fields, gathering brushwood to heat the bath, well-water and barrels of homemade pickles. The unspoken motto is 'Grow With Less.' In the training place I lost my remaining doubts about China.

The Buddhists teach respect for all life, and for wild systems. Man's life is totally dependent on an interpenetrating network of wild systems. Eugene Odum, in his useful paper 'The Strategy of Ecosystem Development', points out how the United States has the characteristics of a young ecosystem. Some American Indian cultures have 'mature' characteristics: protection as against production, stability as against growth, quality as against quantity. In Pueblo societies a kind of ultimate democracy is practiced. Plants and animals are also people, and, through certain rituals and dances, are given a place and a voice in the political discussions of the humans. They are 'represented.' 'Power to all the people' must be the slogan.

On Hopi and Navajo land, at Black Mesa, the whole issue is revolving at this moment. The cancer is eating away at the breast of Mother Earth in the form of strip-mining. This to provide electricity for Los Angeles. The defense of Black Mesa is being sustained by traditional Indians, young Indian militants, and longhairs. Black Mesa speaks to us through an ancient, complex web of myth. She is sacred territory. To hear her voice is to give up the European word 'America' and accept the new-old name for the continent, 'Turtle Island.'

The return to marginal farmland on the part of longhairs is not some nostalgic replay of the nineteenth century. Here is a generation of white people finally ready to learn from the Elders. How to live on the continent as though our children, and on down, for many ages, will still be here (not on the moon). Loving and protecting this soil, these trees, these wolves. Natives of Turtle Island.

A scaled-down, balanced technology is possible, if cut loose from the cancer of exploitation-heavy-industry-perpetual growth. Those who have already sensed these necessities and have begun, whether in the country or the city, to 'grow with less,' are the only counterculture that counts. Electricity for Los Angeles is not energy. As Blake said: 'Energy Is Eternal Delight.'

Gary Snyder, *Turtle Island* (New York: New Directions Books, 1974), pp. 61, 103–5.

Sulak Sivaraksa

Sulak Sivaraksa (1933–   ) was born in Bangkok, the son of a merchant. He received his university education in Britain, with a law degree from Middle Temple, London. He returned to Thailand in 1961 where he held teaching positions at two universities. In 1963 he founded the *Social Science Review*, a widely read journal that played a crucial role in the student movement that led to the brief demise of the military dictatorship in 1973. He has founded a number of organizations devoted to social welfare in Thailand and has lectured widely both in Thailand and abroad as an activist for peace and human rights. Sivaraksa has been a strong critic of Western consumerism and has looked to Buddhism as an indigenous inspiration for social justice. While lecturing abroad in 1976, he was advised not to return to Thailand after the bloody coup of that year and remained abroad for eighteen months. In 1984 he was arrested under the charge of defaming the monarchy, but was released after an international campaign on his behalf and the intervention of the king. He was charged with the same crime in 1991 after a speech in which he criticized the military government, but was acquitted in 1995. He continues to work to develop alternatives to consumerism and new approaches to education.

As a lay Buddhist activist, Sivaraksa has interpreted classical Buddhist doctrines such as the four truths and no self as a framework for the transformation both of the person and of society. He regards the original disciples of the Buddha as an ideal community, while the Buddhist emperor Ashoka and the Thai king (and former Buddhist monk) Mongkut (who reigned 1851–68) provide models for kingship. He also reveres the meditation practice of the great Thai forest monks of the twentieth century. Sivaraksa distinguishes between 'buddhism', which he regards as the essence of the Buddha's teachings, marked by mindful awareness but free from worship and ritual, and 'Buddhism' that has been tainted with various cultural forms, especially those of the current Thai state. In his view, suffering, the first of the four truths, results from the exploitation that occurs when short-sighted and self-interested economic and political goals are placed above the continued welfare of the community. He offers similar interpretations of a wide range of Buddhist doctrines, seeing in each a call for social action: the precept against sexual misconduct should be used to protect the rights of women; the precept against the use of intoxicants should preclude government support of alcohol and tobacco companies.

His challenge to Buddhists is evident in the lecture presented below, delivered to a meeting of Buddhist leaders from the World Fellowship of Buddhists (WFB) in Thailand in 1976.

TASKS FOR MODERN BUDDHISTS

If I am allowed to be honest, Mr Chairman, I must say that I am very disappointed with the performance of this panel discussion. When I was invited to take part in it, I thought it was great. The WFB must have now grown to maturity, since it dares to allow an outspoken person like me to be among its distinguished delegates. Perhaps it would now like to hear constructive criticism and would do something down to earth, instead of being on a lofty cloud, passing beautiful resolutions without seeing whether they are implemented. It might now perhaps be tired of listening to eulogistical messages with empty contents.

I came down especially from Chiang Mai to attend this meeting and to find out that the same old clichés are still being said 'We Buddhists are the best people in the world. We are full of tolerance. Our teaching is very scientific. Our way is the only way' etc. What do delegates do at home? Do they fight against poverty and social injustice? Do they stand for freedom or do they go along with any autocratic regime? What is the Buddhist way versus modern materialism — be it capitalism, neo-colonialism in the form of multinational firms, or Communism? Once they come to attend such Buddhist organizations as this, do they have the chance to visit poverty-stricken areas, to visit some places where

Buddhist methods are being applied to cure social as well as spiritual illness? Or do delegates only stay in big hotels, see beautiful development projects, visit gigantic Buddhist establishments, and be invited to dinner at Government House? The Prime Minister in fact came to this grand opening. Indeed it is the Thai Government's financial assistance that made the WFB meeting and organization possible. Hence you have to be polite to the Government, to say nice things about it, and yet you say that as a religious institution you are non-political. In fact, by so doing are you not political already? Or does non-politics only mean that we can do anything, provided that that action is not contrary to the wishes of the Government and the Establishment?

The irony is that most governments in the region, nay in the world, do not represent the people, despite democratic systems and all that. So religious people who try to be close to any government are bound to be political one way or the other.

What is wrong with politics, may I ask? It is only wrong – when dealing with politics, economics, or indeed with any profession – if we who claim to be practising Buddhists are not aware of what we are doing. Without sati – mindfulness – we could easily become tools of politicians, businessmen or those tycoons who control the mass media and hence create social norms and values. By giving us so called religious people a little, we are easily bought and we close our eyes to the wickedness and oppression that these people do to other human beings, animals and nature in general. These people tend to stick to forms but not to the substance of Buddhasāsanā. We like them when they perform Buddhist ceremonies, we do not like the young because they rebel against the traditional mode of behaviour, although in many instances the young are much more sincere and try hard to solve social as well as spiritual problems.

The practice of mindfulness – if we do practise it at all – means that loving-kindness (mettā) and compassion (karunā) must be real. We must be willing to share the suffering of our fellow beings – be they human, animal or natural. The practice of meditation does not only mean to close one's eyes to the world problems and say 'we are all right Jack.'

In traditional Asian society, it is possible for people to withdraw from the world, to go to the forest, to contemplate deeply into one's nature and the law of the universe in order to find enlightenment. Indeed those of us who are men and women of the world must try to preserve this tradition and this atmosphere, so that this practice will still be possible in the years to come. For without an enlightened community, Buddhism would be a much poorer way of life. Without the spring of pure water, the stream will indeed be soon dry.

So, fighting against environmental destruction (twenty-five percent of our forestry in this country has been destroyed during the last decade alone), against social injustice (since a small handful of rich people who associate themselves very closely with the politicians destroy our natural environment and create as well as widen the social, political and economic gaps between people) must be the task of modern Buddhists. We can only do so by understanding social reality (vijjā) and by applying loving-kindness and compassion to solving the problems. Hence we cannot agree with the Communists or any violent means. Yet from what happens in Laos, Cambodia and Vietnam – all of which were supposed to be Buddhist lands once – we must learn the lessons and watch the situation mindfully. It is no use making any propaganda efforts against the new regime in those countries. We ought to learn from the failure of our Buddhist brethren there, extend our equanimity (uppekkhā) to them and try to do our best so that we could strive to bring about social revolution and political reform peacefully and justly – in the Buddhist manner. [. . .]

If Buddhists do not take action, Buddhism in our lands, especially those lands which happen to be adjacent to Communist countries, will suffer a similar kind of treatment. Capitalism exploits religion one way, Communism another. We must fight against both.

One action which we Buddhists could do, i.e. if we are aware of the problems, is to appeal to our Government to follow the policy that will make it possible for the people to avoid a war like those in Vietnam, Cambodia and Laos. Such a policy is to take measure to abolish all forms of social injustice. People with goodwill, especially the young, once disappointed because of the government's policy, can turn easily to support violent revolution.

Now if a non-violent way for social justice is prescribed with the support of Buddhist organizations like the Sangha, the WFB, the

Buddhist Associations, and Young Buddhist Federations, people will have an alternative to choose and the movement will quickly take shape. Yet these organizations so far, in this country at least, seem to be inactive. They say they do not want to play politics, while in fact they support the *status quo* all the time. Thus the rich become richer and the poor poorer. Polarization must in fact be abolished and reconciliation put in its place.

Is it too much for us Buddhists to appeal for:

1. The return to the traditional culture and spiritual values, for the elimination of those foreign elements which can cause discord and hatred among the people and can destroy the beauty of our traditions and customs.

2. An educational system that provides equal opportunities to every citizen, rich and poor, city dwellers and country people.

3. An economic policy that does not create gaps between people. There should be a policy which prevents the minority becoming richer and richer, while taking away the chances for a decent living from the majority. The Government should refrain from importing luxurious items for the sake of the consumption of the rich minority, forbid the transferring of money by the rich to deposit in foreign banks outside the country – not to mention the rich buying property abroad!

4. The re-organization of the armed forces, to educate soldiers to become friends of the villagers, not to oppress and terrorize them. The ignorance and ill-behaviour of the soldiers can lead to more opposition that is violent from among the population.

5. The reform of life in the countryside. Efforts should be made to help farmers, small merchants and others to exercise their professions and organize themselves in order to produce better and to sell their products, and to encourage and protect people who are working to help in the work of rural development.

6. Attention to miserable conditions in the slum areas. Land should be distributed to those in the slums who would like to go and settle in the rural areas in order to have a better life. Food and transportation should be provided to those who wish to participate in such a programme.

7. A neutral and independent policy towards the conflicting powers

to maintain a truly independent stand, non-aligned, trying to avoid involvement in any international conflicts in order to preserve peace.

8. A sensible and intelligent policy towards the armed opposition movement. Violent confrontation should be avoided. Sincere and direct contact with the leaders of the movement should be made immediately. Try to listen to every point of criticism and prove to the people by action that points being made by them can be realized in more peaceful ways in cooperation with them.

Let me ask once again, whether such an appeal could be launched. If we cannot say this and cannot act accordingly, can we still call ourselves Buddhists? How can we be followers of the Compassionate One, while we let our Buddhist way go astray, by playing safe, i.e. by not doing anything for fear of upsetting the established social order, which becomes more and more polarized. Such is indeed a cowardly way of living. It does not contribute towards the preservation of the Sāsana, especially in a critical period like this.

Our Bhikkhus and rich lay supporters, on the whole, are not aware of what is happening in the country, of the existing social unrest and injustice. They only believe in propaganda and accusation through the gossips and the mass media. Even a person like me is often accused of being a Communist! They must engage themselves in the work to help the poor people with education and social reform, while not neglecting their duties to learn and practise Buddhism.

To me this is an essential task for modern Buddhists. If we do not take this seriously at this very moment, there will not be much chance to preserve Buddhism as a noble way of life in the near future.

Sulak Sivaraksa, 'Tasks for Modern Buddhists' in *A Buddhist Vision for Renewing Society: Collected Articles by a Concerned Thai Intellectual* (Bangkok: Thai InterReligious Commission for Development, 1994; first published 1981), pp. 122–9.

The Dalai Lama

A central tenet of Mahayana Buddhism is that buddhas and bodhisattvas appear in the world of rebirth in order to serve the suffering. They do not always appear in their more familiar guises, but employ skilful means to assume whatever form is most appropriate for the time and the circumstances. Tibetan Buddhism is unique among Buddhist traditions in having developed this doctrine into the institution of the incarnate lama. All Buddhist traditions recount the story of how the Buddha, prior to his final rebirth as Prince Siddhartha, surveyed the world to choose the proper place for his final incarnation. Tibet developed systems according to which the present incarnations of recently deceased masters could be identified shortly after the birth of the child. Beginning perhaps in the eleventh century, this institution of the incarnate lama became a primary mechanism for passing the power and property, both real and symbolic, of a distinguished monk or lama from one generation to the next. There were eventually several thousand incarnate lamas in Tibet. The best known of these is, of course, the Dalai Lama.

The first Dalai Lama was identified in the fifteenth century. However, the term 'dalai', a Mongolian word meaning 'ocean', was not used until the sixteenth century, when a Tibetan lama named Sonam Gyatso ('Merit Ocean') was called Dalai Lama by a Mongol khan. The fifth Dalai Lama assumed political control of Tibet in 1642, with the help of his Mongol patrons, and since then the Dalai Lama has been the Tibetan head of state (during the minority of the Dalai Lama, the nation was ruled by a regent). Since the time of the fifth, the Dalai Lama has also been considered the human incarnation of the bodhisattva of compassion, Avalokiteshvara, regarded as the protector of the Tibetan people.

The current and fourteenth Dalai Lama was born in 1935. China invaded Tibet in 1950 and the Dalai Lama fled to India following an uprising against the Chinese occupation in 1959. He has lived in exile ever since, gaining increasing popularity as a Buddhist teacher while working ceaselessly for the freedom of Tibet. In 1989 he was awarded the Nobel Peace Prize for his efforts. The address he gave at the ceremony is presented below. Although he rarely mentions the term 'Buddhism', his words are imbued with classical Buddhist teachings of compassion and responsibility for the welfare of others. He begins from the common Buddhist belief that all beings are motivated to find happiness and to avoid suffering, and that all beings are equally deserving of finding happiness and avoiding suffering. Compassion, defined as the wish that others be free from suffering, therefore, is not only the distinguishing feature of the bodhisattva. Rather, the Dalai Lama views compassion as a universal human responsibility, regardless of one's religious beliefs, or lack of beliefs. Compassion is a quality with which all humans are endowed, yet it must be distinguished from attachment (a negative emotion in Buddhist thought) and developed to form the basis of human interaction and human society, serving as the foundation for policies of non-violence. He closes his remarks with a discussion of his hopes for a resolution of the Tibetan crisis, envisioning Tibet as a 'zone of peace' between India and China.

THE NOBEL EVENING ADDRESS
Oslo, Norway

Brothers and Sisters:

It is a great honor to come to this place and to share some of my thoughts with you. Although I have written a speech, it has already been circulated. You know, some of my friends told me it is better to speak in Tibetan and have it translated into English; some say it is better to read my English statement; and some say it is better to speak directly with my broken English. I don't know. Yesterday, I tried my best to be formal but today I feel more free, so I will speak informally. In any case, the main points of my speech are on paper for you to see.

I think it advisable to summarize some of the points that I will consider. I usually discuss three main topics. Firstly, as a human being, as a citizen of the world, every human being has a responsibility for the planet. Secondly, as a Buddhist monk, I have a special connection with the spiritual world. I try to contribute something in that field. Thirdly, as a Tibetan I have a responsibility to the fate of the Tibetan nation. On behalf of these unfortunate people, I will speak briefly about their concerns.

So now, firstly, what is the purpose of life for a human being? I believe that happiness is the purpose of life. Whether or not there is a purpose to the existence of the universe or galaxies, I don't know. In any case, the fact is that we are here on this planet with other human beings. Then, since every human being wants happiness and does not want suffering, it is clear that this desire does not come from training, or from some ideology. It is something natural. Therefore, I consider that the attainment of happiness, peace, and joy is the purpose of life. Therefore, it is very important to investigate what are happiness and satisfaction and what are their causes.

I think that there is a mental factor as well as a physical factor. Both are very important. If we compare these two things, the mental factor is more important, superior to the physical factor. This we can know through our daily life. Since the mental factor is more important, we have to give serious thought to inner qualities.

Then, I believe compassion and love are necessary in order for us to obtain happiness or tranquility. These mental factors are key. I think they are the best source. What is compassion? From the Buddhist viewpoint there are different varieties of compassion. The basic meaning of compassion is not just a feeling of closeness, or just a feeling of pity. Rather, I think that with genuine compassion we not only feel the pains and suffering of others but we also have a feeling of determination to overcome that suffering. One aspect of compassion is some kind of determination and responsibility. Therefore, compassion brings us tranquility and also inner strength. Inner strength is the ultimate source of success.

When we face some problem, a lot depends on the personal attitude towards that problem or tragedy. In some cases, when one faces the difficulty, one loses one's hope and becomes discouraged and then ends up depressed. On the other hand, if one has a certain mental attitude, then tragedy and suffering bring one more energy, more determination.

Usually, I tell our generation we are born during the darkest period in our long history. There is a big challenge. It is very unfortunate. But if there is a challenge then there is an opportunity to face it, an opportunity to demonstrate our will and our determination. So from that viewpoint I think that our generation is fortunate. These things depend on inner qualities, inner strength. Compassion is very gentle, very peaceful, and soft in nature, not harsh. You cannot destroy it easily as it is very powerful. Therefore, compassion is very important and useful.

Then, again, if we look at human nature, love and compassion are the foundation of human existence. According to some scientists, the foetus has feeling in the mother's womb and is affected by the mother's mental state. Then the few weeks after birth are crucial for the enlarging of the brain of the child. During that period, the mother's physical touch is the greatest factor for the healthy development of the brain. This shows that the physical needs some affection to develop properly.

When we are born, our first action is sucking milk from the mother. Of course, the child may not know about compassion and love, but the natural feeling is one of the closeness toward the object that gives milk. If the mother is angry or has ill feeling, the milk may not come fully. This shows that from our first day as human beings the effect of compassion is crucial.

If unpleasant things happen in our daily life, we immediately pay attention to them but do not notice other pleasant things. We experience these as normal or usual. This shows that compassion and affection are part of human nature.

Compassion or love has different levels; some are more mixed than others with desire or attachment. For example, parents' attitudes toward their children contain a mixture of desire and attachment with compassion. The love and compassion between husband and wife – especially at the beginning of marriage when they don't know the deep nature of each other – are on a superficial level. As soon as the attitude of one partner changes, the attitude of the other becomes opposite to what it was. That kind of love and compassion is more of the nature of attachment. Attachment means some kind of feeling of closeness projected by oneself. In reality, the other side may be very negative, but due to one's own mental attachment and projection, it appears as something nice. Furthermore, attachment causes one to exaggerate a small good quality and make it appear 100% beautiful or 100% positive. As soon as the mental attitudes change, that picture completely changes. Therefore, that kind of love and compassion is, rather, attachment.

Another kind of love and compassion is not based on something appearing beautiful or nice, but based on the fact that the other person, just like oneself, wants happiness and does not want suffering and indeed has every right to be happy and to overcome suffering. On such a basis, we feel a sense of responsibility, a sense of closeness towards that being. That is true compassion. This is because the compassion is based on reason, not just on emotional feeling. As a consequence, it does not matter what the other's attitude is, whether negative or positive. What matters is that it is a human being, a sentient being that has the experience of pain and pleasure. There is no reason not to feel compassion so long as it is a sentient being.

The kinds of compassion at the first level are mixed, interrelated. Some people have the view that some individuals have a very negative, cruel attitude towards others. These kinds of individuals appear to have no compassion in their minds. But I feel that these people do have the seed of compassion. The reason for this is that even these people very much appreciate it when someone else shows them affection. A capacity to appreciate other people's affection means that in their deep mind there is the seed of compassion.

Compassion and love are not man-made. Ideology is man-made, but these things are produced by nature. It is important to recognize natural qualities, especially when we face a problem and fail to find a solution. For example, I feel that the Chinese leaders face a problem which is in part due to their own ideology, their own system. But when they try to solve that problem through their own ideology then they fail to tackle that problem. In religious business, sometimes even due to religion, we create a problem. If we try to solve that problem using religious methods, it is quite certain that we will not succeed. So I feel that when we face those kind of problems, it is important to return to our basic human quality. Then I think we will find that solutions come easier. Therefore, I usually say that the best way to solve human problems is with human understanding.

It is very important to recognize the basic nature of humanity and the value of human qualities. Whether one is educated or uneducated, rich or poor, or belongs to this nation or that nation, this religion or that religion, this ideology or that ideology, is secondary and doesn't matter. When we return to this basis, all people are the same. Then we can truly say the words *brother, sister*; then they are not just nice words – they have some meaning. That kind of motivation automatically builds the practice of kindness. This gives us inner strength.

What is my purpose in life, what is my responsibility? Whether I like it or not, I am on this planet, and it is far better to do something for humanity. So you see that compassion is the seed or basis. If we take care to foster compassion, we will see that it brings the other good human qualities. The topic of compassion is not at all religious business; it is very important to know that it is human business, that it is a question of human survival, that it is not a question of human luxury. I might say that religion is a kind of luxury. If you have religion, that is good. But it is clear that even without religion we can manage. However, without these basic human qualities we cannot survive. It is a question of our own peace and mental stability.

Next, let us talk about the human being as a social animal. Even if we do not like other people, we have to live together. Natural law is such that even bees and other animals have to live together in cooperation. I am attracted to bees because I like honey – it is really delicious. Their product is something that we cannot produce, very beautiful, isn't it? I exploit them too much, I think. Even these insects have certain responsibilities, they work together very nicely. They have no constitution, they have no law, no police, nothing, but they work together effectively. This is because of nature. Similarly, each part of a flower is not arranged by humans but by nature. The force of nature is something remarkable. We human beings, we have constitutions, we have law, we have a police force, we have religion, we have many things. But in actual practice, I think that we are behind those small insects.

Sometimes civilization brings good progress, but we become too involved with this progress and neglect or forget about our basic nature. Every development in human society should take place on the basis of the foundation of the human nature. If we lost that basic foundation, there is no point in such developments taking place.

In cooperation, working together, the key thing is the sense of responsibility. But this cannot be developed by force as has been attempted in eastern Europe and in China. There a tremendous effort has to be made to develop in the mind of every individual human being a sense of responsibility, a concern for the common interest rather than the individual interest. They aim their education, their ideology, their efforts to brainwash, at this. But their means are abstract, and the sense of responsibility cannot develop. The genuine sense of responsibility will develop only through compassion and altruism.

The modern economy has no national boundaries. When we talk about ecology, the environment, when we are concerned about the ozone layer, one individual, one society, one country cannot solve these problems. We must work together. Humanity needs more genuine cooperation. The foundation for the development of good relations with one another is altruism, compassion, and forgiveness. For small arguments to remain limited, in the human circle the best method is forgiveness. Altruism and forgiveness are the basis for bringing humanity together. Then no conflict, no matter how serious, will go beyond the bounds of what is truly human.

I will tell you something. I love friends, I want more friends. I love smiles. That is a fact. How to develop smiles? There are a variety of smiles. Some smiles are sarcastic. Some smiles are artificial – diplomatic smiles. These smiles do not produce satisfaction, but rather fear or suspicion. But a genuine smile gives us hope, freshness. If we want a genuine smile, then first we produce the basis for a smile to come. On every level of human life, compassion is the key thing.

Now, on the question of violence and non-violence. There are many different levels of violence and non-violence. On the basis of external action, it is difficult to distinguish whether an action is violent or non-violent. Basically, it depends on the motivation behind the action. If the motivation is negative, even though the external appearance may be very smooth and gentle, in a deeper sense the action is very violent. On the contrary, harsh actions and words done with a sincere, positive motivation are essentially non-violent. In other words, violence is a destructive power. Non-violence is constructive.

When the days become longer and there is more sunshine, the grass becomes fresh and, consequently, we feel very happy. On the other hand, in autumn, one leaf falls down and another leaf falls down. These beautiful plants become as if dead and we do not feel very happy. Why? I think it is because deep down our human nature likes construction, and does not like destruction. Naturally, every action which is destructive is against human nature. Constructiveness is the human way. Therefore, I think that in terms of basic human feeling, violence is not good. Non-violence is the only way.

Practically speaking, through violence we may achieve something, but at the expense of someone else's welfare. That way although we may solve one problem, we simultaneously seed a new problem. The best way to solve problems is through human understanding, mutual respect. On one side make some concessions; on the other side take serious consideration about the problem. There may not be complete satisfaction, but something happens. At least future danger is avoided. Non-violence is very safe.

Before my first visit to Europe in 1973, I had felt the importance of compassion, altruism. On many occasions I expressed the importance of the sense of universal responsibility. Sometimes during this period, some people felt that the Dalai Lama's idea was a bit unrealistic. Unfortunately, in the Western world Gandhian non-violence is seen as passive resistance more suitable to the East. The Westerners are very active, demanding immediate results, even in the course of daily life. But today the actual situation teaches non-violence to people. The movement for freedom is non-violent. These recent events reconfirm to me that non-violence is much closer to human nature.

Again, if there are sound reasons or bases for the points you demand, then there is no need to use violence. On the other hand, when there is no sound reason that concessions should be made to you but mainly your own desire, then reason cannot work and you have to rely on force. Thus, using force is not a sign of strength but rather a sign of weakness. Even in daily human contact, if we talk seriously, using reasons, there is no need to feel anger. We can argue the points. When we fail to prove with reason, then anger comes. When reason ends, then anger begins. Therefore, anger is a sign of weakness.

In this, the second part of my talk, I speak as a Buddhist monk. As a result of more contact with people from other traditions, as time passes I have firmed my conviction that all religions can work together despite fundamental differences in philosophy. Every religion aims at serving humanity. Therefore, it is possible for the various religions to work together to serve humanity and contribute to world peace. So, during these last few years, at every opportunity I try to develop closer relations with other religions.

Buddhism does not accept a theory of god, or a Creator. According to Buddhism, one's own actions are the creator, ultimately. Some people say that, from a certain angle, Buddhism is not a religion but rather a science of mind. Religion has much involvement with faith. Sometimes it seems that there is quite a distance between a way of thinking based on faith and one entirely based on experiment, remaining sceptical. Unless you find something through investigation, you do not want to accept it as fact. From one viewpoint, Buddhism is a religion, from another viewpoint Buddhism is a science of mind and not a religion. Buddhism can be a bridge between these two sides. Therefore, with this conviction I try to have closer ties with scientists, mainly in the fields of cosmology, psychology, neurobiology, physics. In these fields there are insights to share, and to a certain extent we can work together.

Thirdly, I will speak on the Tibetan problem. One of the crucial, serious situations is the Chinese population transfer into Tibet. If the present situation continues for another ten or fifteen years, the Tibetans will be an insignificant minority in their own land, a situation similar to that in inner Mongolia. There the native population is around three million and the Chinese population is around ten million. In East Turkestan, the Chinese population is increasing daily. In Tibet, the native population is six million, whereas the Chinese population is already around seven and one-half million. This is really a serious matter.

In order to develop a closer understanding and harmony between the Chinese and Tibetan – the Chinese call it the unity of the motherland – the first thing necessary to provide the basis for the development of mutual respect is demilitarization, first to limit the number of Chinese soldiers and eventually to remove them altogether. This is crucial. Also, for the purposes of peace in that region, peace and genuine friendship between India and China, the two most populated nations, it is very essential to reduce military forces on both sides of the Himalayan range. For this reason, one point that I have made is that eventually Tibet should be a zone of ahimsa, a zone of non-violence.

Already there are clear indications of nuclear dumping in Tibet and of factories where nuclear weapons are produced. This is a serious matter. Also, there is deforestation, which is very dangerous for the environment. Respect for human rights is also necessary. These are the points I expressed in my Five-Point Peace Plan. These are crucial matters.

We are passing through a most difficult period. I am very encouraged by your warm expression and by the Nobel Peace Prize. I thank you from the depth of my heart.

Tenzin Gyatso, the Dalai Lama, 'The Nobel Evening Address' in *The Dalai Lama, A Policy of Kindness: An Anthology of Writings by and about the Dalai Lama* (Ithaca, NY: Snow Lion Publications, 1990), pp. 119–28.

Cheng Yen

Cheng Yen (1937–   ) was born in Taiwan, the daughter of a middle-class family. When she was sixteen years old, her mother suffered a serious illness. Her daughter prayed to the bodhisattva of compassion, Kuan Yin, vowing to become a lay Buddhist for twelve years if her mother recovered. Her prayer was answered. After the death of her father, Cheng Yen left home to become a Buddhist nun, but could not receive ordination because she did not have her mother's permission. She eventually received vows from the famous monk Yinshun in 1963. Although she underwent the traditional training of a Buddhist nun, she was inspired to work on behalf of the poor, something relatively unusual in the Buddhist tradition. Two events inspired her commitment to the poor. The first was the sight of blood in a hospital that was shed by an aboriginal woman who had suffered a miscarriage and did not have sufficient funds to pay for treatment. The second was what she perceived as a challenge from Catholic nuns on a mission in Taiwan, who claimed that Buddhism was concerned only with personal liberation and not with social ills. In 1966 she founded the Buddhist Compassion Relief Foundation, with a group of five nuns and thirty housewives. The nuns sewed children's shoes and women contributed small sums (collectively around US$30 per month in the early years) in order to provide medical expenses for the poor. Her initial goal was to recruit five hundred members, who together have one thousand eyes and one thousand hands, like the bodhisattva of compassion, Kuan Yin. Today it is the largest charity in Taiwan, with four million members and branches in fourteen countries, devoted to four missions: charity, medicine, education and culture. It provides over US$20 million per year in charity for projects around the world, including famine relief in Africa and the building of hospitals, colleges and research centres.

In the first essay below, she explains the need to translate compassion into action on behalf of the poor and the sick, making her argument within the context of the classical Buddhist practice of 'right effort', one of the constituents of the eightfold path. The second extract is a public address made after the devastating Taiwan earthquake of 1999.

THE FOUR PROPER AREAS FOR DILIGENT EFFORTS (SAMYAK-PRADHANA)

1. Put an End to Existing Evil (Samvara-pradhana)

Before we learn Buddhism, most of us have wandering minds which lead us to evil thoughts. As soon as we start cultivating our Buddha nature, we need to work diligently to develop appropriate attitudes and methods within ourselves. Our attitudes are of utmost importance; evil thoughts should be eradicated completely as soon as their ugly faces come to mind.

In our daily lives, we cannot get away from all manner of people, places and things. We need to deal with these daily encounters with a steady heart that treats even extraordinary events as if they were commonplace and that loves everyone as equals. Human beings interact with each other through both verbal and body language. In this manner, our words and our attitudes communicate our thoughts. The standard we want to set for ourselves is to be gentle and kind in our words and to always embody a congenial and generous attitude. Of course, we often meet people who speak to us rudely and treat us with little or no respect. Nevertheless, we still need to maintain our own self-dignity and not lower our behavioral standards under any circumstances.

Our goal is not to ask others to change themselves; likewise, our goal is not to inventory their weaknesses. It is wrong to take the words other people let slip out unintentionally and use them to build self-justified resentment and hatred inside ourselves. It is also not worth-while to feel hurt or angry when others speak rudely to us, because they may just have bad habits of communicating and may not really mean any harm whatsoever. There are also people who look cold and uncaring on the surface, and yet have loving hearts buried inside. We need to avoid stereotyping and judging others by their outward appearances.

It is important to be constantly mindful of our own attitudes and behaviors. Among the ever-changing people, places and things in our daily lives, we need to focus our minds on our own cultivation instead of on ego-based emotions of self-interest, such as resentment, hatred, affection and anger. If we find ourselves feeling resentful, we must eradicate the resentment as quickly as possible. No negligence or laziness can be allowed in this constant process of self-monitoring and correction. This, then, is what is meant by putting an end to existing evil.

2. Prevent Evil from Arising (Prahana-pradhana)

It is most desirable to always deal with others with a steady heart, one that consistently treats everyone else as we treat ourselves. If we have not yet found ourselves harboring evil thoughts against others, it is important to keep this pure state of mind. Some people treat their acquaintances with kindness and courtesy and get along famously as long as they don't know each other too well. When they become closer and more familiar with each other, they start abandoning gestures of courtesy because they no longer feel the need for them. Soon, conflicts of words and deeds start to arise, and resentment begins to breed. This is why some say, 'All hatred begins with love.'

This is the reason that we need to maintain our initial attitudes of respect and compromise toward others, no matter how intimately we come to know them. Such is the essence of preventing evil from arising: keeping a loving thought of equality toward all people and maintaining a steady mind which is not excited by extraordinary events. Do not give the seeds of impure and mean-spirited thoughts even the slightest chance to sprout in our minds.

3. Bring Good into Existence (Bhavana-pradhana)

For those of you who have started to learn Buddhism but have not yet thought about doing good deeds, you need to take special care to nurture good thoughts such as compassion.

Once a Tzu Chi commissioner brought along a Tzu Chi member from Taipei to visit our headquarters. This visiting member said to me, 'Master, I am very moved by our wonderful Tzu Chi Foundations. We ask people to donate money for good deeds and to fund relief missions. I have found all of these activities extremely meaningful, and I am trying to do as much as I can myself. I would like to join the activities of the Tzu Chi commissioners to raise funds for good causes. But there is one thing that I sincerely ask Master to excuse me from: please do not send me to comfort the sick.'

I asked him, 'Why do you make this request?'

'I am very loving,' he replied, 'but I am afraid to spend time with sick people because I fear that they will infect me. Besides, I have heard that commissioners must chant the holy name of Amitabha Buddha for the dead at their bedsides, and I am also very frightened of dead people. Therefore, I ask Master to please accept my request not to participate in these activities.'

This member has a loving heart, but he has not developed the ultimate good thought of great compassion for all living beings as if we all were one being. If he were able to treat other patients as if they were his own close relatives, he would automatically understand how to handle himself with these patients. If he could feel with his heart that the dying are actually one with himself, just like close relatives, would he still insist on not getting too close to the dead?

Although many people are loving, they have not yet cultivated loving hearts that treat everyone as themselves, the great compassion for all as one. We need to immediately encourage these people to cultivate good thoughts of great compassion and love for all. Many Tzu Chi commissioners used to be afraid of the sick and the dead. After they joined the Tzu Chi Foundation, they were encouraged by the behavior of other commissioners and their own behavior gradually changed. They would follow others in visiting patients, and would even support and care for these patients with their own hands. They not only accompanied others to chant the holy name of Amitabha Buddha for the dead, they even began changing the clothes of the dead. All of these examples demonstrate that, with proper cultivation and training, it is natural for people to spontaneously develop loving thoughts of equality and unity.

That is why we talk about bringing good deeds into existence to nurture and grow good thoughts as soon as possible. Life is ever-changing. When, therefore, is there a better time to build good karma and cultivate good thoughts than now? The time for urging others to cultivate loving thoughts, to realize the true path of life and develop the highest consciousness, is also now.

4. Develop Existing Good Deeds Already Done (Anurakkshana-pradhana)

If other people already have loving hearts, we still need to fervently encourage them to keep these loving hearts forever. We will not settle for loving thoughts and good hearts that only last temporarily. To make the journey of bodhisattvahood, we urge people to keep a constant, diligent heart. This is the meaning of developing existing good deeds already done. Not only are we practicing the ten meritorious acts, but we can actually move up to the level of practicing bodhisattvahood by diligently cultivating ourselves.

'The Four Proper Areas for Diligent Efforts (Samyak-pradhana)', condensed and translated by E. E. Ho and W. L. Rathje, *Tzu Chi Quarterly Magazine* (Buddhist Tzu Chi Foundation, Taiwan), no. 2, vol. 3 (Summer 1996).

NOT LESS RESPONSIBILITY, BUT MORE STRENGTH

I always have three wishes at the beginning of every year:
I ask not for good health, but for an alert, discerning mind;
I ask not that everything will go my way, but that I may have
    perseverance and courage;
I ask not for less responsibility, but for increased strength.

Ladies and gentlemen, Amitabha!

The earthquake of September 21 was the greatest disaster in Taiwan in the last hundred years. We had the opportunity to witness it at the end of the century, so we should take it as a good perception of life.

It is not only the year 1999 that has disturbed me. Actually, I have always felt uneasy every year in the past thirty-odd years, because I understood what the Buddha said about the impermanence of life and the fragility of the land. Therefore, I made a vow to purify people's minds. The minds of most people are confused. If I can illuminate the heart of one person, we will have one more light. If I can purify the mind of one more person, there will be less bad karma.

Recently in Taiwan many people have been talking about 'reformation of the mind.' In my opinion, the mind does not need reformation; instead it needs purification. Everyone is born with a mind of light, but the mind has been defiled and needs to be cleaned. It is just like a light bulb that has been covered with a piece of black cloth. We only have to remove that cloth to let the light shine.

The minds of ordinary people are covered by cloth woven with greed, anger and delusion, and they are unable to show their light. If every mind is purified, the world will be clean and radiant. And that is what I have been trying hard to do for the past thirty-odd years – purify people's minds.

If we look at society now, we notice that more and more people are creating bad karma. People used to be industrious, thrifty and conservative. They might not have created blessings, but they hardly created any bad karma. But people now use any means to gratify themselves. To reach that objective, they even fight and injure each other.

When people create bad karma together, the land will fight back. Therefore, natural disasters happen. On the other hand, people can also make good karma together. That is why I hope to reduce the bad karma and increase the good.

We have a long way to go to realize our goals of helping the poor and educating the rich, but I always try to encourage myself by remembering that thirty years ago I had only thirty followers. Now, after all these years of hard work, tens of thousands of commissioners, teachers and Tzu Cheng Faith Corps members are working together with me. This really encourages and stimulates me.

Everyone Has $300 Billion

The Buddha discovered the truth of the universe and of life, and he imparted to us his pure, bright wisdom. We accept his teachings and act on them. He gave us our wisdom life, so his followers are also called 'the Buddha's students.' We must pass his teachings on to other people and thus extend his wisdom life.

There is a story in the Agama Sutra.

A king came out from his palace one day and took a walk in the city to see how his people were getting on. All he saw were magnificent buildings and plenty of merchandise in the market. He thought, 'My kingdom is very rich and my people lead a good, affluent life.'

In order to find out further how many rich people there were and how much wealth they had, he approached the richest person one day and asked him how much property he had. This person said, 'I have $400 billion worth of property inside and outside.'

The king said, 'I own the whole country and my property is only $400 billion. How can you also own $400 billion? And what do you mean by "inside and outside"?'

'Your Majesty, my outside property is worth $100 billion. To own such valuable property, I am very grateful to you because I can trade freely on your land. Next I have to be grateful to my fellow countrymen.

Because of them, I have earned all this visible property. Then I am grateful to my dependents and servants because they have been working hard for me. So my visible property of $100 billion comes from my trade, the people, and the country.'

'What about the other $300 billion?' asked the king.

'The additional $300 billion is inside and invisible. As I have the Buddha in my heart, his majesty, compassion and wisdom enrich my heart. That is worth $100 billion. I have the Buddha's teachings in my words and I always say good words. That is worth the second $100 billion. Besides, every day I do good deeds. That is worth another $100 billion. So the "inside property" is worth $300 billion. Together with the $100 billion "outside property", the total is $400 billion.'

This story tells us that keeping the Buddha in our hearts, speaking his teachings and doing good deeds are wealth that will never be exhausted.

Keeping the Buddha in our hearts is exactly what I mean when I say, 'Take the Buddha's mind as your own mind.' The Buddha's mind is a compassionate mind, and great love is its outward expression. Always speaking gently and kindly means you speak the Buddha's teachings. If you say good words, you can dignify yourselves. Just having the Buddha in your heart and uttering the Buddha's teachings are not enough. The most important thing is to put what you have learned into practice. If you till the field of blessings, you will reap the blessings.

Love Fills Us with Confidence

In Tzu Chi's Project Hope, we have so far committed ourselves to re-build forty-three schools, both primary schools and middle schools, in quake-ravaged areas in central Taiwan. We are not afraid of taking on such a heavy responsibility. We are only concerned whether we have enough strength. However, if we can combine everyone's strength, I am sure we can reach our goal.

I make three wishes at the beginning of each new year:

1. I ask not for good health, but for an alert, discerning mind;

2. I ask not that everything will go my way, but that I may have perseverance and courage;

3. I ask not for less responsibility, but for increased strength.

Tzu Chi is not rich, but it is full of determination and commitment. Where does the money for reconstruction come from? It comes from everybody's pockets. I hope you will not be afraid of the heavy responsibility. Let the seeds of kindness grow in everyone. The power of love can heal all wounds. The more love we give, the more power of blessing we will obtain. The land will be in peace and the climate will become stable.

Time flies and our life is short. Please make good use of your abilities. When we are dealing with people and events, we must make sure that we not only learn something, but that we take one step further toward enlightenment. Please bear the Buddha in mind, put his teachings in your words, and show love in your actions. All these are 'invisible property' which will never run out.

May all of you cultivate blessings and wisdom.

'Not Less Responsibility, But More Strength', translated by Norman Yuan, *Tzu Chi Quarterly Magazine* (Buddhist Tzu Chi Foundation, Taiwan), no. 1, vol. 7 (Spring 2000).

Fritjof Capra

Fritjof Capra (1939–   ) was born in Vienna and received his doctorate from the University of Vienna in 1966, where he wrote his thesis on the gravitational collapse of neutron stars. He has held academic positions in Paris, Stanford University and Imperial College in London.

In 1975 he published a work that would become a classic of the New Age, *The Tao of Physics*, in which he set forth parallels between Asian Eastern wisdom and modern scientific knowledge. Although speaking often of Buddhism, and especially Zen, Capra offered an eclectic vision of a more general 'Eastern mysticism' that combined elements of Buddhism, Hinduism and Taoism. Capra is a physicist by training and not a scholar of Asian thought and was therefore limited in the sources available to him. He thus made particular use of the works of modern Buddhists such as D. T. Suzuki, Lama Govinda and Philip Kapleau in an attempt to demonstrate one of the central tenets of modern Buddhism: the compatibility of Buddhism and science.

In the passage below, he discusses how the insights of both Eastern mysticism and modern physics are beyond language, leading both Zen masters and theoretical physicists to resort to the use of paradox.

BEYOND LANGUAGE

The contradiction so puzzling to the ordinary way of thinking comes from the fact that we have to use language to communicate our inner experience which in its very nature transcends linguistics.   D. T. Suzuki

The problems of language here are really serious. We wish to speak in some way about the structure of the atoms . . . But we cannot speak about atoms in ordinary language.   W. Heisenberg

The notion that all scientific models and theories are approximate and that their verbal interpretations always suffer from the inaccuracy of our language was already commonly accepted by scientists at the beginning of this century, when a new and completely unexpected development took place. The study of the world of atoms forced physicists to realize that our common language is not only inaccurate, but totally inadequate to describe the atomic and subatomic reality. Quantum theory and relativity theory, the two bases of modern physics, have made it clear that this reality transcends classical logic and that we cannot talk about it in ordinary language. Thus Heisenberg writes:

The most difficult problem . . . concerning the use of the language arises in quantum theory. Here we have at first no simple guide for correlating the mathematical symbols with concepts of ordinary language; and the only thing we know from the start is the fact that our common concepts cannot be applied to the structure of the atoms.*

From a philosophical point of view, this has certainly been the most interesting development in modern physics, and here lies one of the roots of its relation to Eastern philosophy. In the schools of Western philosophy, logic and reasoning have always been the main tools used to formulate philosophical ideas and this is true, according to Bertrand Russell, even of religious philosophies. In Eastern mysticism, on the other hand, it has always been realized that reality transcends ordinary language, and the sages of the East were not afraid to go beyond logic and common concepts. This is the main reason, I think, why their models of reality constitute a more appropriate philosophical background to modern physics than the models of Western philosophy.

The problem of language encountered by the Eastern mystic is exactly the same as the problem the modern physicist faces. In the two pas-

* W. Heisenberg, *Physics and Philosophy*, p. 177.

sages quoted at the beginning of this chapter, D. T. Suzuki speaks about Buddhism* and Werner Heisenberg speaks about atomic physics,† and yet the two passages are almost identical. Both the physicist and the mystic want to communicate their knowledge, and when they do so with words their statements are paradoxical and full of logical contradictions. These paradoxes are characteristic of all mysticism, from Heraclitus to Don Juan, and since the beginning of this century they are also characteristic of physics.

In atomic physics, many of the paradoxical situations are connected with the dual nature of light or – more generally – of electromagnetic radiation. On the one hand, it is clear that this radiation must consist of waves because it produces the well-known interference phenomena associated with waves: when there are two sources of light, the intensity of the light to be found at some other place will not necessarily be just the sum of that which comes from the two sources, but may be more or less. This can easily be explained by the interference of the waves emanating from the two sources: in those places where two crests coincide we shall have more light than the sum of the two; where a crest and a trough coincide we shall have less. The precise amount of interference can easily be calculated. Interference phenomena of this kind can be observed whenever one deals with electromagnetic radiation, and force us to conclude that this radiation consists of waves.

On the other hand, electromagnetic radiation also produces the so-called photoelectric effect: when ultraviolet light is shone on the surface of some metals it can 'kick out' electrons from the surface of the metal, and therefore it must consist of moving particles. A similar situation occurs in the 'scattering' experiments of X-rays. These experiments can only be interpreted correctly if they are described as collisions of 'light particles' with electrons. And yet, they show the interference patterns characteristic of waves. The question which puzzled physicists so much in the early stages of atomic theory was how electromagnetic radiation could simultaneously consist of particles (i.e. of entities confined to a very small volume) and of waves, which are spread out over

* D. T. Suzuki, *On Indian Mahayana Buddhism*, p. 239.
† W. Heisenberg, op. cit., pp. 178–9.

a large area of space. Neither language nor imagination could deal with this kind of reality very well.

Eastern mysticism has developed several different ways of dealing with the paradoxical aspects of reality. Whereas they are bypassed in Hinduism through the use of mythical language, Buddhism and Taoism tend to emphasize the paradoxes rather than conceal them. The main Taoist scripture, Lao Tzu's *Tao Tê Ching*, is written in an extremely puzzling, seemingly illogical style. It is full of intriguing contradictions and its compact, powerful, and extremely poetic language is meant to arrest the reader's mind and throw it off its familiar tracks of logical reasoning.

Chinese and Japanese Buddhists have adopted this Taoist technique of communicating the mystical experience by simply exposing its paradoxical character. When the Zen master Daito saw the Emperor Godaigo, who was a student of Zen, the master said:

We were parted many thousand of *kalpas* ago, yet we have not been separated even for a moment. We are facing each other all day long, yet we have never met.*

Zen Buddhists have a particular knack for making a virtue out of the inconsistencies arising from verbal communication, and with the *koan* system they have developed a unique way of transmitting their teachings completely non-verbally. *Koans* are carefully devised nonsensical riddles which are meant to make the student of Zen realize the limitations of logic and reasoning in the most dramatic way. The irrational wording and paradoxical content of these riddles makes it impossible to solve them by thinking. They are designed precisely to stop the thought process and thus to make the student ready for the non-verbal experience of reality. The contemporary Zen master Yasutani introduced a Western student to one of the most famous *koans* with the following words:

One of the best *koans*, because the simplest, is *Mu*. This is its background: a monk came to Joshu, a renowned Zen master in China hundreds of years ago,

---

* In D. T. Suzuki, *The Essence of Buddhism*, p. 26.

and asked: 'Has a dog Buddha-nature or not?' Joshu retorted, *'Mu!'* Literally, the expression means 'no' or 'not', but the significance of Joshu's answer does not lie in this. *Mu* is the expression of the living, functioning, dynamic Buddha-nature. What you must do is discover the spirit or essence of this *Mu*, not through intellectual analysis but by search into your innermost being. Then you must demonstrate before me, concretely and vividly, that you understand *Mu* as living truth, without recourse to conceptions, theories, or abstract explanations. Remember, you can't understand *Mu* through ordinary cognition, you must grasp it directly with your whole being.*

To a beginner, the Zen master will normally present either this *Mu-koan* or one of the following two:

'What was your original face – the one you had before your parents gave birth to you?'

'You can make the sound of two hands clapping. Now what is the sound of one hand?'

All these *koans* have more or less unique solutions which a competent master recognizes immediately. Once the solution is found, the *koan* ceases to be paradoxical and becomes a profoundly meaningful statement made from the state of consciousness which it has helped to awaken.

In the Rinzai school, the student has to solve a long series of *koans*, each of them dealing with a particular aspect of Zen. This is the only way this school transmits its teachings. It does not use any positive statements, but leaves it entirely to the student to grasp the truth through the *koans*.

Here we find a striking parallel to the paradoxical situations which confronted physicists at the beginning of atomic physics. As in Zen, the truth was hidden in paradoxes that could not be solved by logical reasoning, but had to be understood in the terms of a new awareness; the awareness of the atomic reality. The teacher here was, of course,

---

* In Philip Kapleau, *Three Pillars of Zen*, p. 135.

nature, who, like the Zen master, does not provide any statements. She just provides the riddles.

The solving of a *koan* demands a supreme effort of concentration and involvement from the student. In books about Zen we read that the *koan* grips the student's heart and mind and creates a true mental impasse, a state of sustained tension in which the whole world becomes an enormous mass of doubt and questioning. The founders of quantum theory experienced exactly the same situation, described here most vividly by Heisenberg:

I remember discussions with Bohr which went through many hours till very late at night and ended almost in despair; and when at the end of the discussion I went alone for a walk in the neighbouring park I repeated to myself again and again the question: Can nature possibly be so absurd as it seems to us in these atomic experiments?*

Whenever the essential nature of things is analysed by the intellect, it must seem absurd or paradoxical. This has always been recognized by the mystics, but has become a problem in science only very recently. For centuries, scientists were searching for the 'fundamental laws of nature' underlying the great variety of natural phenomena. These phenomena belonged to the scientists' macroscopic environment and thus to the realm of their sensory experience. Since the images and intellectual concepts of their language were abstracted from this very experience, they were sufficient and adequate to describe the natural phenomena.

Questions about the essential nature of things were answered in classical physics by the Newtonian mechanistic model of the universe which, much in the same way as the Democritean model in ancient Greece, reduced all phenomena to the motions and interactions of hard indestructible atoms. The properties of these atoms were abstracted from the macroscopic notion of billiard balls, and thus from sensory experience. Whether this notion could actually be applied to the world

* W. Heisenberg, op. cit., p. 42.

of atoms was not questioned. Indeed, it could not be investigated experimentally.

In the twentieth century, however, physicists were able to tackle the question about the ultimate nature of matter experimentally. With the help of a most sophisticated technology they were able to probe deeper and deeper into nature, uncovering one layer of matter after the other in search for its ultimate 'building blocks'. Thus the existence of atoms was verified, then their constituents were discovered – the nuclei and electrons – and finally the components of the nucleus – the protons and neutrons – and many other subatomic particles.

The delicate and complicated instruments of modern experimental physics penetrate deep into the submicroscopic world, into realms of nature far removed from our macroscopic environment, and make this world accessible to our senses. However, they can do so only through a chain of processes ending, for example, in the audible click of a Geiger counter, or in a dark spot on a photographic plate. What we see, or hear, are never the investigated phenomena themselves but always their consequences. The atomic and subatomic world itself lies beyond our sensory perception.

It is, then, with the help of modern instrumentation that we are able to 'observe' the properties of atoms and their constituents in an indirect way, and thus to 'experience' the subatomic world to some extent. This experience, however, is not an ordinary one, comparable to that of our daily environment. The knowledge about matter at this level is no longer derived from direct sensory experience, and therefore our ordinary language, which takes its images from the world of the senses, is no longer adequate to describe the observed phenomena. As we penetrate deeper and deeper into nature, we have to abandon more and more of the images and concepts of ordinary language.

On this journey to the world of the infinitely small, the most important step, from a philosophical point of view, was the first one: the step into the world of atoms. Probing inside the atom and investigating its structure, existence transcended the limits of our sensory imagination. From this point on, it could no longer rely with absolute certainty on logic and common sense. Atomic physics provided the scientists with the first glimpses of the essential nature of things. Like the mystics, physicists were now dealing with a nonsensory experience of reality and, like the mystics, they had to face the paradoxical aspects of this experience. From then on therefore, the models and images of modern physics became akin to those of Eastern philosophy.

Fritjof Capra, *The Tao of Physics* (Boston, Mass.: Shambhala, 1991), pp. 45–51.

Chögyam Trungpa

Chögyam Trungpa (1939–87) was born in Tibet and identified as an infant as the eleventh incarnation of the Trungpa lama, a lineage of important teachers in the Kagyu sect of Tibetan Buddhism. He was ordained as a monk and received instruction from some of the leading lamas of Tibetan Buddhism until he was twenty years of age. After the Tibetan uprising against the occupying forces of the Chinese army in March 1959, he escaped across the Himalayas to India on horseback and on foot, accompanied by a group of monks. In 1963 he travelled to England to study at Oxford under a Spaulding Fellowship. In 1967 he moved to Scotland, where he founded a Tibetan meditation centre called Samye Ling. While there he suffered permanent injury in a serious automobile accident and decided thereafter to give up his monastic vows and continue as a lay teacher of Buddhism. In 1969 he moved to the United States, where he established a meditation centre in Vermont, called Tail of the Tiger.

Chögyam Trungpa's extensive training in Tibetan Buddhism and his facility in English combined to make him the first Tibetan lama to reach a wide audience through his many books, beginning with *Meditation in Action* in 1969. During the 1970s he founded the Naropa Institute in Boulder, Colorado, a centre devoted to the study of Buddhism, psychology and the arts, as well as a network of centres around the world, called Dharmadhatus. He also invited several important Tibetan lamas to the United States during this period. Near the end of his short life, Trungpa Rinpoche (as he was known) established a system of teachings called Shambhala Training, which combined Buddhist teachings with other forms of Asian culture, especially the traditional arts of Japan.

Trungpa Rinpoche's fluency in the cultural idioms of the West is evident in the passage below, a chapter from his popular 1973 work *Cutting Through*

Spiritual Materialism, in which he explained how to respond to some of the difficulties encountered by Westerners when they embark on an Asian spiritual path.

THE HARD WAY

Inasmuch as no one is going to save us, to the extent that no one is going magically to enlighten us, the path we are discussing is called the 'hard way.' This path does not conform to our expectation that involvement with the Buddhist teaching will be gentle, peaceful, pleasant, compassionate. It is the hard way, a simple meeting of two minds: if you open your mind, if you are willing to meet, then the teacher opens his mind as well. It is not a question of magic; the condition of openness is a mutual creation.

Generally, when we speak of freedom or liberation or spiritual understanding, we think that to attain these things we need do nothing at all, that someone else will take care of us. 'You are all right, don't worry, don't cry, you're going to be all right. I'll take care of you.' We tend to think that all we have to do is make a commitment to the organization, pay our initiation fee, sign the register and then follow the instructions given us. 'I am firmly convinced that your organization is valid, it answers all my questions. You may program me in any way. If you want to put me into difficult situations, do so. I leave everything to you.' This attitude supplies the comfort of having to do nothing but follow orders. Everything is left to the other person, to instruct you and relieve you of your shortcomings. But to our surprise things do not work that way. The idea that we do not have to do anything on our own is extremely wishful thinking.

It takes tremendous effort to work one's way through the difficulties of the path and actually get into the situations of life thoroughly and properly. So the whole point of the hard way seems to be that some individual effort must be made by the student to acknowledge himself, to go through the process of unmasking. One must be willing to stand alone, which is difficult.

This is not to say that the point of the hard way is that we must be heroic. The attitude of 'heroism' is based upon the assumption that we are bad, impure, that we are not worthy, are not ready for spiritual understanding. We must reform ourselves, be different from what we are. For instance, if we are middle class Americans, we must give up our jobs or drop out of college, move out of our suburban homes, let our hair grow, perhaps try drugs. If we are hippies, we must give up drugs, cut our hair short, throw away our torn jeans. We think that we are special, heroic, that we are turning away from temptation. We become vegetarians and we become this and that. There are so many things to become. We think our path is spiritual because it is literally against the flow of what we used to be, but it is merely the way of false heroism, and the only one who is heroic in this way is ego.

We can carry this sort of false heroism to great extremes, getting ourselves into completely austere situations. If the teaching with which we are engaged recommends standing on our heads for twenty-four hours a day, we do it. We purify ourselves, perform austerities, and we feel extremely cleansed, reformed, virtuous. Perhaps there seems to be nothing wrong with it at the time.

We might attempt to imitate certain spiritual paths, such as the American Indian path or the Hindu path or the Japanese Zen Buddhist path. We might abandon our suits and collars and ties, our belts and trousers and shoes in an attempt to follow their example. Or we may decide to go to northern India in order to join the Tibetans. We might wear Tibetan clothing and adopt Tibetan customs. This will seem to be the 'hard way,' because there will always be obstacles and temptations to distract us from our purpose.

Sitting in a Hindu ashram, we have not eaten chocolate for six or seven months, so we dream of chocolate, or other dishes that we like. Perhaps we are nostalgic on Christmas or New Year's Day. But still we think we have found the path of discipline. We have struggled through the difficulties of this path and have become quite competent, masters of discipline of some sort. We expect the magic and wisdom of our training and practice to bring us into the right state of mind. Sometimes we think we have achieved our goal. Perhaps we are completely 'high' or absorbed for a period of six or seven months. Later our ecstasy disappears. And so it goes, on and on, on and off. How are we going to deal with this situation? We may be able to stay 'high' or blissful for a very long time, but then we have to come back or come down or return to normal.

I am not saying that foreign or disciplinary traditions are not applicable to the spiritual path. Rather, I am saying that we have the notion that there must be some kind of medicine or magic potion to help us attain the right state of mind. This seems to be coming at the problem backwards. We hope that by manipulating matter, the physical world, we can achieve wisdom and understanding. We may even expect expert scientists to do it for us. They might put us into a hospital, administer the correct drugs and lift us into a high state of consciousness. But I think, unfortunately, that this is impossible, we cannot escape what we are, we carry it with us all the time.

So the point we come back to is that some kind of *real* gift or sacrifice is needed if we are to open ourselves completely. This gift may take any form. But in order for it to be meaningful, it must entail giving up our hope of getting something in return. It does not matter how many titles we have, nor how many suits of exotic clothes we have worn through, nor how many philosophies, commitments, and sacramental ceremonies we have participated in. We must give up our ambition to get something in return for our gift. That is the really hard way.

We may have had a wonderful time touring around Japan. We may have enjoyed Japanese culture, beautiful Zen temples, magnificent works of art. And not only did we find these experiences beautiful, but they said something to us as well. This culture is the creation of a whole lifestyle completely different from that of the Western world, and these creations spoke to us. But to what extent does the exquisiteness of culture and images, the beauty of the external forms really shake us, deal with us? We do not know. We merely want to savor our beautiful memories. We do not want to question our experiences too closely. It is a sensitive area.

Or perhaps a certain guru has initiated us in a very moving, extremely meaningful ceremony. That ceremony was real and direct and beautiful, but how much of the experience are we willing to question?

It is private, too sensitive to question. We would rather hoard and preserve the flavor and beauty of the experience so that, when bad times come, when we are depressed and down, we can bring that memory to mind in order to comfort ourselves, to tell ourselves that we have actually done something worthwhile, that, yes, we are on the path. This does not seem to be the hard way at all.

On the contrary, it would seem that we have been collecting rather than giving. If we reconsider our spiritual shopping, can we remember an occasion when we gave something completely and properly, opened ourselves and gave everything? Have we ever unmasked, stripping out of our suit of armor and our shirt and skin and flesh and veins, right down to the heart? Have we really experienced the process of stripping and opening and giving? That is the fundamental question. We must really surrender, give something, give something up in a very painful way. We must begin to dismantle the basic structure of this ego we have managed to create. The process of dismantling, undoing, opening, giving up, is the real learning process. How much of this ingrown toenail situation have we decided to give up? Most likely, we have not managed to give up anything at all. We have only collected, built, adding layer upon layer. So the prospect of the hard way is very threatening.

The problem is that we tend to seek an easy and painless answer. But this kind of solution does not apply to the spiritual path, which many of us should not have begun at all. Once we commit ourselves to the spiritual path, it is very painful and we are in for it. We have committed ourselves to the pain of exposing ourselves, of taking off our clothes, our skin, nerves, heart, brains, until we are exposed to the universe. Nothing will be left. It will be terrible, excruciating, but that is the way it is.

Somehow we find ourselves in the company of a strange doctor. He is going to operate on us, but he is not going to use an anaesthetic because he really wants to communicate with our illness. He is not going to allow us to put on our facade of spirituality, psychological sophistication, false psychological illness or any other disguise. We wish we had never met him. We wish we understood how to anaesthetize ourselves. But now we are in for it. There is no way out. Not because he is so powerful. We could tell him goodbye in a minute and leave. But we have exposed so much to this physician and, if we have to do it all over again, it will be very painful. We do not want to have to do it again. So now we have to go all the way.

Being with this doctor is extremely uncomfortable for us because we are continually trying to con him, although we know that he sees through our games. This operation is his only way to communicate with us, so we must accept it; we must open ourselves to the hard way, to this operation. The more we ask questions – 'What are you going to do to me?' – the more embarrassed we become, because we know what we are. It is an extremely narrow path with no escape, a painful path. We must surrender ourselves completely and communicate with this physician. Moreover, we must unmask our expectations of magic on the part of the guru, that with his magical powers he can initiate us in certain extraordinary and painless ways. We have to give up looking for a painless operation, give up hope that he will use an anaesthetic or sedative so that when we wake up everything will be perfect. We must be willing to communicate in a completely open and direct way with our spiritual friend and with our life, without any hidden corners. It is difficult and painful, the hard way.

Q.   *Is exposing yourself something that just happens, or is there a way of doing it, a way of opening?*
A.   I think that if you are already committed to the process of exposing yourself, then the less you try to open the more the process of opening becomes obvious. I would say it is an automatic action rather than something that you have to do. At the beginning when we discussed surrendering, I said that once you have exposed everything to your spiritual friend, then you do not have to do anything at all. It is a matter of just accepting what is, which we tend to do in any case. We often find ourselves in situations completely naked, wishing we had clothes to cover ourselves. These embarrassing situations always come to us in life.

Q.   *Must we have a spiritual friend before we can expose ourselves, or can we just open ourselves to the situations of life?*

A.   I think you need someone to watch you do it, because then it will seem more real to you. It is easy to undress in a room with no one else around, but we find it difficult to undress ourselves in a room full of people.

Q.   *So it is really exposing ourselves to ourselves?*
A.   Yes. But we do not see it that way. We have a strong consciousness of the audience because we have so much awareness of ourselves.

Q.   *I do not see why performing austerities and mastering discipline is not the 'real' hard way.*
A.   You can deceive yourself, thinking you are going through the hard way, when actually you are not. It is like being in an heroic play. The 'soft way' is very much involved with the experience of heroism, while the hard way is much more personal. Having gone through the way of heroism, you still have the hard way to go through, which is a very shocking thing to discover.

Q.   *Is it necessary to go through the heroic way first and is it necessary to persevere in the heroic way in order to continue on the truly hard way?*
A.   I don't think so. This is what I am trying to point out. If you involve yourself with the heroic way, you add layers or skins to your personality because you think you have achieved something. Later, to your surprise, you discover that something else is needed. One must *remove* the layers, the skins.

Q.   *You speak of the necessity to experience excruciating pain. Can an understanding of the unmasking process make it unnecessary to go through the pain?*
A.   That is a very tricky proposition. Understanding does not mean that you actually do it; you just understand it. We can understand the physiological process of how someone is tortured and how they experience pain, but the actual experience would be altogether different. The philosophical or intellectual understanding of pain is not enough. You must actually feel something properly. The only way to get to the heart of the matter is to actually experience it for yourself, but you do not have

to create painful situations. These situations will occur with the help of a spiritual friend who is a doctor with a sharp knife.

Q.   *If you are in the process of surrendering and your spiritual friend at that point seems to point his scalpel at you and take away your anaesthesia, then that is an extremely terrifying situation. Your spiritual friend seems to be very angry and disgusted and you want to run. Would you explain this?*
A.   That is just the point. It is a matter of an operation without the use of anesthetics. You have to be willing to do it. If you run away, it is like a man who needs an appendectomy running out of the operating room; his appendix might burst.

Q.   *But this is at a very early stage in your relationship with your spiritual friend; you have barely been with him for five minutes. Suddenly the roof falls in and he just leaves you to deal with it. Perhaps he is saying, 'I am not going on this trip with you. Five minutes have passed. Surrender it, give it all up, deal with it yourself, and when you have cut it all loose, then I will talk to you.' That is how I have experienced it.*
A.   You see, it does not matter whether you are a beginning or advanced student. It is a question of how much a person has been with himself. If he has been with himself, then he must know himself. It is like an ordinary illness. Suppose you are travelling from one country to another and you feel ill and decide to see a doctor. He can barely speak your language, but he can feel your body and see what is wrong with you, and he decides to take you immediately to the hospital and operate. It depends upon how far the disease has developed. The intensity of the operation depends on the maturity of the illness in your body. You might explode completely. If you have appendicitis and the doctor waits too long, perhaps in order to become friends with you, then your appendix is going to explode. You would not say that was a very good way of practicing medicine.

Q.   *Why does someone take that first step on the path? What leads him to it? Is it an accident, is it fate, karma, what is it?*
A.   If you expose yourself completely, then you are already on the path. If you give yourself halfway, then you are only part way on the

path. It is going to bounce back on you. If you give less information to your doctor, then you are going to recover much more slowly because you have not told him your whole case history. The more you tell your doctor, the sooner he will be able to cure you.

Q.   *If the truly hard way is to expose myself, then should I allow myself to be exposed to what I judge to be evil, knowing I might get hurt?*
A.   Opening is not a matter of martyring oneself to every threat that comes along. You do not have to stand in front of an oncoming train to open yourself to it. That would be the way of heroism, the false hard way.

Whenever we confront something we regard as 'evil,' it poses as a threat to the self-preservation of ego. We are so busy preserving our existence in the face of this threat that we cannot see the thing clearly at all. To open we have to cut through our desire to preserve our own existence. Then we can see and deal with the situation clearly, as it is.

Q.   *This is not a one-shot deal, is it? I mean you can open yourself in one context, and yet when you find yourself in some other situation suddenly you take hold of a mask and put it over your face, even though you really do not want to do it. It would seem that achieving complete openness is a difficult thing.*
A.   The whole point is that struggle is irrelevant to opening. Once you have stepped on the path, if you give up the struggle itself, that takes care of the whole problem. Then there is no longer any question of wanting or not wanting to be involved with life-situations. The ape instinct of ego dissolves because it is based upon secondhand information rather than upon direct experience of what is. Struggle is ego. Once you give up struggle, then there is no one left to conquer struggle; it just disappears. So you see, it is not a matter of achieving a victory over struggle.

Q.   *When you feel angry, should you just express that anger in order to open?*
A.   When we speak of opening and surrendering as, for instance, in the case of anger, it does not mean we should actually go out and hit someone on the spot. That seems to be more a way of feeding ego rather than a way of exposing your anger properly, seeing its real living quality.

This applies to exposing yourself in general. It is a matter of seeing the basic quality of the situation, as it is, rather than trying to do something with it. Of course if one is completely open to the situation without any preconceptions, then one would know which action is right and which is unskillful. If a particular course of action would be clumsy and unskilled, then you would not take that fork in the road; you would take the road of skillful and creative action. You are not really involved with judgment as such, but you choose the creative way.

Q. *Is collecting things and defending disguises an escapable stage?*
A. We collect things and later it is painful to give them away. It is similar to having stitches in our skin after an operation. It is frightening to have them taken out, we are apprehensive, we have become accustomed to a foreign element in our system.

Q. *Do you think it is possible to begin to see what is, to see yourself as you are without a teacher?*
Q. I do not think it is possible at all. You have to have a spiritual friend in order to surrender and completely open yourself.

Q. *Is it absolutely necessary that the spiritual friend be a living human being?*
A. Yes. Any other 'being' with whom you might think yourself communicating would be imaginary.

Q. *Would the teachings of Christ in themselves be a spiritual friend?*
A. I would not say so. That is an imaginary situation. It is the same with any teachings; they do not have to be the teachings of Christ necessarily. The problem is that we can interpret them ourselves. That is the whole point: written teachings are always open to the interpretation of ego.

Q. *When you speak of opening and exposing yourself, it reminds me a great deal of certain schools of psychotherapy. What do you think is the function of the sort of things people do in psychotherapy?*
A. In most forms of psychotherapy the problem is that, if you regard the process as 'therapeutic,' then you do not really mean it but it is the

therapeutic thing to do. In other words, your therapy is a hobby. Moreover, you see your therapeutic situation as being defined by your case history. Because something went wrong in your relationship with your father and mother, you have this unhealthy tendency to . . . Once you begin to deal with a person's whole case history, trying to make it relevant to the present, the person begins to feel that he has no escape, that his situation is hopeless, because he cannot undo his past. He feels trapped by his past with no way out. This kind of treatment is extremely unskilled. It is destructive because it hinders involvement with the creative aspect of what is happening now, what is here, right now. But on the other hand, if psychotherapy is presented with the emphasis on living in the present moment, working with present problems, not just as regards verbal expression and thoughts alone, but in terms of experiencing the actuality of emotions and feelings, then I think that would be a very balanced style. Unfortunately there are many kinds of psychotherapy and many psychotherapists involved with trying to prove themselves and their own theories rather than working with what is. In fact they find it very frightening to work with what is.

We must simplify rather than complicate the problem with theories of any kind. The situation of nowness, this very moment, contains whole case histories and future determinations. Everything is right here, so we do not have to go any further than this to prove who we were or are or might be. As soon as we try to unravel the past, then we are involved with ambition and struggle in the present, not being able to accept the present moment as it is. It is very cowardly. Moreover, it is unhealthy to regard our therapist or guru as our savior. We must work on ourselves. There is really no other alternative. The spiritual friend might accentuate our pain in certain circumstances. That is part of the physician–patient relationship. The idea is not to regard the spiritual path as something very luxurious and pleasurable but to see it as just facing the facts of life.

Chögyam Trungpa, 'The Hard Way' in *Cutting Through Spiritual Materialism* (Berkeley: Shambhala, 1973), pp. 77–89.

Glossary

This glossary includes some of the more important Buddhist terms that occur in the preceding chapters. Because diacritical marks are often absent or are applied irregularly in the various selections in the main text, they have been omitted here. Unless otherwise noted, the original language of the terms below is Sanskrit. Cross-references to other entries are given in small capitals.

abhidharma: literally, the 'higher teaching', a category of scriptures that provide systematic analyses of the constituents of the person, the process of perception, the nature of enlightenment and other issues of a scholastic nature.

Amitabha: literally, 'Infinite Light', the buddha who presides over the western PURE LAND of Sukhavati, the Land of Bliss. Amitabha's vow to deliver the faithful to his pure land serves as the foundation of much MAHAYANA practice, especially in East Asia.

anatman: literally 'non self', the true nature of the person according to Buddhist thought. The ignorance that is the fundamental cause of suffering is the belief that the person is endowed with a permanent self or atman. Wisdom is the understanding that mind and body are impermanent processes and thus lack such a self.

arhat: literally, 'one who is worthy', one who has followed the path and destroyed all causes for future rebirth, and will enter NIRVANA upon death. Regarded as the ideal in the mainstream traditions, where the Buddha is also described as an arhat, in the MAHAYANA the attainment of an arhat is negatively compared to that of a buddha. Certain arhats were selected by the Buddha to remain in the world until the coming of MAITREYA. These arhats (called *lohans* in Chinese) were objects of particular devotion in East Asian Buddhism.

ashtanga marga: see EIGHTFOLD NOBLE PATH.

atman: see ANATMAN.

Avalokiteshvara: literally, 'the lord who looks down', the BODHISATTVA of compassion, often called upon for salvation in times of danger. A male bodhisattva in India and Tibet, Avalokiteshvara (known as Kuan Yin or Guanyin in Chinese, Kannon in Japanese) assumed a female form in East Asia. The Dalai Lamas of Tibet are considered human embodiments of Avalokiteshvara.

bhikkhu (Pali; Sanskrit: *bhikshu*): a fully ordained Buddhist monk.

bhikkhuni (Pali; Sanskrit: *bhikshuni*): a fully ordained Buddhist nun.

bodhi: generally translated as 'enlightenment' or 'awakening', the goal of Buddhist practice.

bodhisattva: often glossed as 'one who has the intention to achieve enlightenment', a bodhisattva is a person who has compassionately vowed to achieve buddhahood but has not yet done so. All forms of Buddhism set forth the path of the bodhisattva, who works for the welfare of others. In the MAHAYANA, the bodhisattva is presented as the ideal.

buddha nature: see TATHAGATAGARBHA.

buddhasasana: literally, 'the teaching of the Buddha', often translated simply as 'Buddhism'.

cakravartin: often rendered as 'universal monarch', an ideal king who rules according to the teachings of the Buddha. The Indian emperor Ashoka is often described as a cakravartin.

Chan (Chinese): see ZEN.

dependent origination (Sanskrit: *pratityasamutpada*): dependent origination has two meanings in Buddhist thought. The first refers to a twelvefold sequence of causation. The second meaning is a more general notion that everything comes into existence in dependence on something else.

dhamma: see DHARMA.

dharma: (Pali: *dhamma*): although difficult to translate, the term has two general meanings in Buddhism. The first is the teaching or doctrine of the Buddha, both as expounded and as manifested in practice. The second, perhaps rendered as 'phenomenon', refers to the basic constituents of mind and matter.

dharmakaya: literally, 'dharma body', the term used to refer to the transcendent qualities of a buddha. In the MAHAYANA doctrine of the three bodies of the Buddha, the dharmakaya is sometimes presented as the ultimate reality from which the other forms of a buddha derive.

eightfold noble path: more accurately rendered as 'eightfold path of the noble', the path set forth by the Buddha in his first sermon, where he declared that the middle way is the eightfold path. The eight are: correct view, correct attitude, correct speech, correct action, correct livelihood, correct effort, correct mindfulness and correct meditation.

emptiness (Sanskrit: *shunyata*): the absence of substantial nature or intrinsic existence in any phenomenon in the universe. In the Madhyamaka philosophy of Nagarjuna, emptiness is the final nature of reality and the understanding of emptiness is essential for the achievement of enlightenment.

four noble truths: more accurately rendered as 'four truths for the (spiritually) noble', the formulation of the human dilemma and its solution as set forth by the Buddha in his first sermon. They are: the truth of suffering, the truth of origin, the truth of cessation and the truth of the path. Human life is recognized to be qualified by suffering, the cause of that suffering is identified, a state of the cessation of suffering (also known as NIRVANA) is postulated, and a path to that state is prescribed.

Gautama (Pali: Gotama): the clan name of the historical Buddha.

Hinayana: literally, 'Low Vehicle', a pejorative term used by proponents of the MAHAYANA to describe those who do not accept the Mahayana SUTRAS as authentic words of the Buddha. In Mahayana texts, those who follow the Hinayana seek to become ARHATS by following the path of the SHRAVAKA or PRATYEKABUDDHA, rather than following the superior path of the BODHISATTVA to buddhahood. In modern scholarship, Hinayana is also sometimes used in a non-pejorative sense to refer to the many non-Mahayana schools of Indian Buddhism.

jataka: literally, 'birth', a story of one of the Buddha's previous lives as a BODHISATTVA. Among the most popular of Buddhist stories, the tales relate the virtuous deeds of the bodhisattva, often when he was an animal.

kalpa: usually translated as 'aeon' or 'age', the unit of measurement of cosmic time in Buddhist cosmological systems.

kamma: see KARMA.

karma (Pali: *kamma*): literally, 'action', the law of the cause and effect of actions according to which virtuous deeds result in happiness in the future and non-virtuous deeds result in suffering. Karma is accumulated over many lifetimes and fructifies to create present experience.

karuna: often translated as 'compassion', one of the virtues to be cultivated on the Buddhist path.

koan (Japanese): often rendered as 'public case', the Japanese pronunciation of the Chinese legal term *kung-an*, referring to a standard of judgement. A koan is commonly a short statement or exchange drawn from accounts of Chinese CHAN masters. These statements served both as the basis for commentaries by Chan and ZEN teachers and as objects of contemplation.

Kuan Yin: see AVALOKITESHVARA.

lama (Tibetan): a religious teacher. The term is often used to denote an 'incarnate lama'; that is, a teacher who has been identified as the present incarnation of a great teacher of the past.

Mahayana: literally, 'Great Vehicle', a term used by the proponents of SUTRAS that began to appear some four centuries after the death of the Buddha and which were regarded by them as the word of the Buddha. The term has come to mean by extension those forms of Buddhism (today located for the most part in Tibet, China, Korea and Japan) that base their practice on these sutras.

Maitreya: literally, 'Kindness', the next buddha to appear in the world after SHAKYAMUNI. Maitreya is currently a BODHISATTVA residing in a heaven, awaiting the appropriate time to appear.

mandala: literally, 'circle'; in tantric Buddhism a representation (in both two- and three-dimensional forms) of the palace of a buddha. Such representations are particularly important in initiation rites, in which the initiate is said to 'enter the mandala'.

mantra: often translated as 'spell', a syllable or series of syllables (often in some form of Sanskrit), the repetition or recitation of which is said to be efficacious. Mantras are particularly important in tantric Buddhism (see TANTRA), which is sometimes called the Mantrayana or Mantra Vehicle.

Mara: the god of desire who attacked the Buddha prior to his achievement of enlightenment in an effort to prevent him from discovering the path to a state beyond desire.

metta (Pali; Sanskrit: *maitri*): often translated as 'love' or 'kindness', one of the virtues to be cultivated on the Buddhist path.

nirvana (Pali: *nibbana*): literally, 'blowing out', the cessation of suffering and hence the goal of Buddhist practice. The nature of nirvana is widely interpreted in Buddhist literature, with distinctions being made between the vision of nirvana that destroys the seeds of future rebirth and the final nirvana entered upon death. MAHAYANA texts also distinguished between the nirvana of an ARHAT and the enlightenment of a buddha.

perfection (Sanskrit: *paramita*): the deeds performed by a BODHISATTVA on the path to buddhahood, commonly enumerated as six: giving, ethics, patience, effort, concentration and wisdom.

no-self: see ANATMAN.

pancha sila (Pali): see SILA.

perfection of wisdom: see PRAJNAPARAMITA.

prajnaparamita: literally, 'perfection of wisdom', the understanding of reality required to achieve buddhahood, according to many MAHAYANA SUTRAS. The term also describes a genre of Mahayana sutras devoted to the exposition of EMPTINESS and the BODHISATTVA path.

pratyekabuddha: literally, 'individually enlightened one', a disciple of the Buddha devoted to solitary practice who achieves the state of an ARHAT without relying on the teachings of a buddha in his last lifetime. According to MAHAYANA exegetes, the path of the pratyekabuddha along with the path of the SHRAVAKA constitute the HINAYANA.

pure land: also referred to as a 'buddha field', the domain that a buddha creates as an ideal setting for the practice of the DHARMA. Functioning in the MAHAYANA as a form of paradise, rebirth in a pure land, especially the pure land of AMITABHA, is the focus of various practices, especially in East Asia.

refuge: see THREE JEWELS.

rinpoche (Tibetan): literally, 'precious one', a term of respect for a religious teacher in Tibetan Buddhism, used especially for an 'incarnate lama'; that is, a teacher who has been identified as the present incarnation of a great teacher of the past.

Saha world: in Buddhist cosmology, the name of the world (or universe) that we inhabit, the place where suffering is endured.

Shakyamuni: literally, 'Sage of the Shakya Clan', an epithet of the historical Buddha.

samadhi: a state of deep concentration developed through meditation practice. One of the three trainings (along with ethics and wisdom), samadhi, especially a specific level known as serenity (*shamatha*) is regarded as a prerequisite for liberating wisdom.

samsara: also spelled sometimes 'sangsara', literally, 'wandering', the beginningless cycle of birth, death and rebirth, composed of the realms of gods, demigods, humans, animals, ghosts and hell beings. The ultimate goal of Buddhism is liberation from samsara.

sangha: literally, 'community', a term most commonly used to refer to the order of Buddhist monks and nuns, it can be used more generally for any community of Buddhists, including fully ordained monks, fully ordained nuns, male novices, female novices, laymen and laywomen.

sasana: see BUDDHASASANA.

sati (Pali; Sanskrit: *smrti*): often translated as 'mindfulness', a prerequisite for the development of concentration and wisdom.

satori (Japanese): the Japanese translation of BODHI or 'enlightenment', especially as understood in the ZEN tradition.

shastra: an Indian Buddhist treatise, in some cases a commentary on a SUTRA.

shravaka: literally, 'listener', a general term for a disciple of the Buddha, interpreted in the MAHAYANA to designate those who follow the path in order to become an ARHAT. According to Mahayana exegetes, the path of the PRATYEKABUDDHA along with the path of the shravaka constitute the HINAYANA.

Siddhartha (Pali: Siddhattha): the given name of the historical Buddha, meaning 'he who achieves his goal'.

sila (Pali; Sanskrit: *shila*): often translated as 'ethics' or 'morality', that part of Buddhist practice concerned with refraining from non-virtuous deeds of body and speech. Buddhist laypeople often take five precepts, called the 'pancha sila', vowing to refrain from killing humans, stealing, engaging in sexual misconduct, lying and using intoxicants.

stupa: a reliquary containing the remains or possessions of the Buddha or a Buddhist saint. Initially taking the form of a hemisphere in India, stupas developed into a variety of architectural forms across Asia, including the pagoda in East Asia. Stupas have served as important places of pilgrimage throughout the history of Buddhism.

sutra (Pali: *sutta*): literally, 'aphorism', a discourse traditionally regarded as having been spoken by the Buddha or spoken with his sanction.

sutta: see SUTRA.

tantra: literally, 'continuum', tantra in its most general sense means a manual or handbook. In Buddhism it refers to a text that contains esoteric teachings, often ascribed to the Buddha. The teachings of these texts have been referred to in English as 'tantrism'. The adjectival form is 'tantric'. A practitioner of tantra is called a tantrika.

tathagata: literally, 'one who has thus come' or 'one who has thus gone', an epithet of a buddha.

tathagatagarbha: literally, 'embryo' or 'essence of the tathagata', it is the buddha nature which, according to some schools of MAHAYANA Buddhism, exists in all sentient beings.

Theravada (Pali): literally, 'School of the Elders', a branch of the Indian Sthaviravada that was established in Sri Lanka in the third century BCE. In the eleventh century CE the Theravada became the dominant form of Buddhism in Sri Lanka and Southeast Asia. As the last remaining school of the many Indian non-MAHAYANA schools, 'Theravada' is often mistakenly regarded as a synonym of HINAYANA.

three jewels (Sanskrit: *triratna*): the Buddha, the DHARMA and the SANGHA, to whom a Buddhist goes for refuge from the sufferings of SAMSARA. 'Going for refuge' (and reciting the formula 'I go for refuge to the Buddha. I go for refuge to the dharma. I go for refuge to the sangha') is the fundamental practice of Buddhism.

tripitaka (Pali: *tipitaka*): literally, 'three baskets', one of the traditional schemes for organizing Buddhist discourses into three: SUTRA, VINAYA and ABHIDHARMA.

upekkha (Pali; Sanskrit: *upeksha*): often translated as 'equanimity', one of the virtues to be cultivated on the Buddhist path.

Vajrayana: literally, 'Diamond Vehicle' or 'Thunderbolt Vehicle', a term used to designate esoteric or tantric Buddhism (see TANTRA), traditionally regarded as a form of the MAHAYANA capable of leading to buddhahood more quickly than the conventional BODHISATTVA path.

Vijnanavada: see YOGACARA.

vihara: a Buddhist monastery.

vinaya: literally, 'taming', the code of monastic conduct.

yana: 'vehicle' to enlightenment; see HINAYANA and MAHAYANA.

Yogacara: literally, 'practitioners of yoga', a philosophical school originating in India and associated with the fifth-century monk Asanga. Among its many tenets, it is best known for the doctrine of 'mind-only', which describes the world as a projection of consciousness. Also known as Vijnanavada.

zazen (Japanese): seated meditation, usually used to refer to ZEN meditation.

Zen (Japanese): the 'meditation' school of East Asian Buddhism (known as Chan in China and Son in Korea) which traces its lineage back to the Indian master Bodhidharma (who is said to have come to China in the late fifth century) and finally back to the Buddha himself.

Acknowledgments

Every effort has been made to contact all copyright holders. The publishers shall be happy to make good in future editions any errors or omissions brought to their attention.

I gratefully acknowledge permission to reprint the following copyrighted material:

Selections from *Zen Mind, Beginner's Mind* by Shunryu Suzuki. Used by permission of Weatherhill Publications.

'Practising the Seventh Stage of Buddha's Noble Path', from *A Buddhist Bible,* edited by Dwight Goddard, copyright © 1938, renewed copyright © 1966 by E. P. Dutton. Used by permission of Dutton, a division of Penguin Putnam, Inc.

Extract from *Studies in Zen* by D. T. Suzuki published by Rider. Used by permission of The Random House Group Limited.

Extract from *The Priceless Jewel* reprinted with the permission of Sangharakshita and Windhorse Publications from the paper 'The Bodhisattva: Evolution and Self-Transcendence' read at the Wrekin Trust Mystics and Scientists Conference in 1983 and subsequently published in *The Priceless Jewel*, Windhorse Publications, 1993.

Selections from *Turtle Island* by Gary Snyder, copyright © 1974 by Gary Snyder. Reprinted by permission of New Directions Publishing Corporation.

Extract from *The Dharma Bums* by Jack Kerouac. Reprinted by permission of Sterling Lord Literistic, Inc. Copyright © 1986 by Jack Kerouac.

Extract from *The Tibetan Book of the Dead* by W. Y. Evans-Wentz, copyright © 1960 by W. Y. Evans-Wentz. Used by permission of Oxford University Press, Inc.

Acknowledgments

Selections from *Tzu Chi Quarterly Magazine*. Used by permission of the Buddhist Tzu Chi Foundation, Taiwan.

Extract from *Being Peace* (1987) by Thich Nhat Hanh. Reprinted with permission of Parallax Press, Berkeley, California.

Extract from *A Policy of Kindness: An Anthology of Writings by and about the Dalai Lama*, compiled and edited by Sidney Piburn, 1990. Used by permission of Snow Lion Publications, Ithaca, New York.

Extract from *The Retreat Diaries* by William Burroughs, copyright © 1976 by William S. Burroughs. Used by permission of The Wylie Agency, Inc.

Extract from *The Three Pillars of Zen* by Philip Kapleau, copyright © 1965, 1989 by Philip Kapleau. Copyright © 1980 by The Zen Center, Inc. Used by permission of Doubleday, a division of Random House, Inc.

Poems by Allen Ginsberg. Reproduced by permission of Penguin UK.

Finally, I would like to thank Onna Solomon and Andrew Quintman for all of their assistance in putting this book together.